D0811804

Children's Learning in a Digital World

Children's Learning in a Digital World

Edited by
Teena Willoughby and Eileen Wood

Blackwell
Publishing

© 2008 by Blackwell Publishing Ltd

BLACKWELL PUBLISHING
350 Main Street, Malden, MA 02148–5020, USA
9600 Garsington Road, Oxford OX4 2DQ, UK
550 Swanston Street, Carlton, Victoria 3053, Australia

The right of Teena Willoughby and Eileen Wood to be identified as the authors of the editorial material in this work has been asserted in accordance with the UK Copyright, Designs, and Patents Act 1988.

All rights reserved. No part of this publication may be reproduced, stored in a retrieval system, or transmitted, in any form or by any means, electronic, mechanical, photocopying, recording or otherwise, except as permitted by the UK Copyright, Designs, and Patents Act 1988, without the prior permission of the publisher.

Designations used by companies to distinguish their products are often claimed as trademarks. All brand names and product names used in this book are trade names, service marks, trademarks, or registered trademarks of their respective owners. The publisher is not associated with any product or vendor mentioned in this book.

This publication is designed to provide accurate and authoritative information in regard to the subject matter covered. It is sold on the understanding that the publisher is not engaged in rendering professional services. If professional advice or other expert assistance is required, the services of a competent professional should be sought.

First published 2008 by Blackwell Publishing Ltd

1   2008

Library of Congress Cataloging-in-Publication Data

Chldren's learning in a digital world / edited by Teena Willoughby and Eileen Wood
p.   cm.
Includes bibliographical references and index.
ISBN 978-1-4051-6207-4 (hardcover: alk. paper)
1. Computer-assisted instruction.   2. Educational technology.   3. Internet in education.
I. Willoughby, Teena, 1955–   II. Wood, Eileen, 1960–
LB1028.5.C5153   2008
371.33′4—dc22
2007027472

A catalogue record for this title is available from the British Library.

Set in 10.5/12.5 pt Minion
by The Running Head Limited, Cambridge, www.therunninghead.com

For further information on
Blackwell Publishing, visit our website at:
www.blackwellpublishing.com

We dedicate this book to all the people who share our love of "toys," media and otherwise: Mark and Karen, and Rod, Alexander, and Lochlain

Acknowledgments

We would like to thank those who provided the impetus and support for this book. The book follows from a conference held at Brock University, St. Catharines, Ontario, in August 2005. Support for the conference was provided by the Owl Children's Trust, the Brock Research Institute for Youth Studies (BRIYS), and the Canadian Language and Literacy Research Network (CLLRNet).

Réseau canadien de recherche sur le langage et l'alphabétisation

CANADIAN LANGUAGE & LITERACY RESEARCH NETWORK

Partager la science. Éveiller les esprits.   sharing the science. opening minds.

Contents

Contents

List of Figures and Tables

Figures

Tables

Contributors

Philip C. Abrami is a Professor, Director, and Research Chair at the Centre for the Study of Learning and Performance, Concordia University, Montreal, Canada. The Centre develops evidence-based tools for learning and teaching including interactive multimedia for developing reading skills and self-regulated learning. Abrami has authored numerous books, chapters, and journal articles on topics ranging from the social psychology of education to educational technology and systematic reviews of research.

Craig A. Anderson is a Distinguished Professor of Psychology at Iowa State University. His recently published book titled *Violent Video Game Effects on Children and Youth*, with coauthors Doug Gentile and Katherine Buckley, includes the first longitudinal study of violent videogame effects (Oxford University Press, 2007). Dr. Anderson's current research focuses on effects of prosocial and antisocial videogames on helping and hurting.

Malinda Desjarlais received an MA and is currently completing her doctoral degree, both in Psychology at Brock University, St. Catharines, Ontario. Her research interests include the cognitive and social impacts associated with using the Internet, particularly for adolescents and young adults.

Andrea A. diSessa is a Professor of Education at the University of California, Berkeley, and a member of the National Academy of Education. He is the principal investigator of the Boxer Computer Environment Project, an integrated system that allows non-experts to perform a broad range of tasks, including programming. He is the coauthor of *Turtle Geometry: The Computer as a Medium for Exploring Mathematics* (MIT Press, 1981) and author of *Changing Minds: Computers, Learning, and Literacy* (MIT Press, 2001).

James Paul Gee is the Mary Lou Fulton Presidential Professor of Literacy Studies at Arizona State University. He is the author, among other books, of *What Video Games Have to Teach Us about Learning and Literacy* (Palgrave Macmillan, 2003); *Situated Language and Learning: A Critique of Traditional*

Schooling (Routledge, 2004); and *Good Video Games and Good Learning: Collected Essays on Video Games, Learning, and Literacy* (Peter Lang, 2007).

Michael T. Giang is currently a doctoral student in the Psychological Studies in Education program at the UCLA Graduate School of Education & Information Studies. He has also received an MA in General Experimental Psychology from California State University, Northridge. His research interests include peer harassment, acculturation, ethnic identity, and the Internet as a context and tool for identity development.

Mark D. Griffiths is Professor of Gambling Studies at Nottingham Trent University, United Kingdom. He is internationally known for his work on gambling and gaming addictions and has published over 180 refereed research papers, several books, 35 book chapters and over 550 other articles. He has won seven national and international awards for his work including the John Rosecrance Prize (1994), the CELEJ Prize (1998), and the Joseph Lister Prize (2004).

Geoffrey Hipps has a background in early childhood and elementary education and was a teacher at the elementary level for many years. After receiving his MA in Educational Technology from Concordia University, Montreal, Canada, he went to work for the CSLP where he became coordinator of development and research, instructional designer and content developer of the ABRACADABRA project. Geoffrey is currently a Language Arts consultant at the Sir Wilfrid Laurier School Board in the Laval region of Quebec.

Bowen Hui received an MSc in Computer Science in 2003 and currently is a doctoral student in the Department of Computer Science at the University of Toronto. Her research interests include the creation of computational models of human behavior, as well as behavioral decision making and second language acquisition.

Henry Jenkins is the Co-Director of the MIT Comparative Media Studies Program and the author or editor of twelve books on various aspects of media and popular culture, including most recently *Convergence Culture: Where Old and New Media Collide* (New York University Press, 2006) and *Fans, Bloggers, and Gamers: Exploring Participatory Culture* (New York University Press, 2006). He is principal investigator for Project nml (http://www.projectnml.org) and blogs about media literacy, among many other topics, at http://henryjenkins.org.

Yasmin B. Kafai is an Associate Professor at the UCLA Graduate School of Education and Information Studies. She received her doctorate from Harvard University in 1993 while working at the MIT Media Laboratory. Her research focuses on children's learning as designers and players of games and virtual worlds. She is the lead editor of the forthcoming *Beyond Barbie and Mortal Kombat: New Perspectives on Gender and Computer Games* (MIT Press).

Monica Lopez is an Instructional Designer at the Center for the Study of Learning and Performance (CSLP). She has an MA in Educational Technology from Concordia University, Montreal, Canada, and has over 10 years of professional experience in the educational sector. While at the CSLP she has been involved in two research projects to enhance the Success for All Foundation's early literacy curriculum with the introduction of technology.

Richard E. Mayer is Professor of Psychology at the University of California, Santa Barbara. He is Vice President of the American Educational Research Association, past-President of the Division of Educational Psychology of the American Psychological Association, and a recipient of the E. L. Thorndike Award for career achievement in educational psychology. He is the author or editor of 20 books and more than 250 articles and chapters, including *Multimedia Learning* (CUP, 2001), *The Cambridge Handbook of Multimedia Learning* (CUP, 2005), *e-Learning and the Science of Instruction: Second Edition* (with R. Clark, Jossey-Bass, 2007) and *Learning and Instruction: Second Edition* (Prentice-Hall, 2008).

Julie Lynn Mueller is completing her doctoral degree in Social and Developmental Psychology at Wilfrid Laurier University, Waterloo, Ontario, Canada. She has past experience as an elementary school educator and researcher.

John C. Nesbit is an Associate Professor in the Faculty of Education at Simon Fraser University, British Columbia, Canada. He studies how students self-regulate learning and argumentation using visual representations and software tools. Nesbit has published over 30 journal articles and book chapters on topics such as learning from concept maps, evaluation of learning resources, links between achievement goals and study strategies, and methods for analyzing learning event data.

Laurence Peters teaches in the Graduate School at the University of Maryland University College and consults widely through his company Edusolutions123. He is the co-editor of *Scaling Up Success: Lessons from Technology Based Educational Improvement* (Jossey-Bass, 2005) and the co-author of a book, *From Digital Divide to Digital Opportunity* (Rowman and Littlefield, 2003). He is currently writing a book on the role of technology in integrating global perspectives.

Robert Savage is an Associate Professor at McGill University, Montreal, Canada. He obtained his degrees from Oxford and Cambridge universities and his PhD from the University of London in 1998. He has published over 40 research articles in international journals on children's early reading and spelling strategies in normal development. He has recently published research on school-based assessment and preventative early intervention projects for reading and spelling problems.

Edward L. Swing received a BA in Psychology from the College of St. Scholastica, Duluth, Minnesota, in 2005 and is currently pursuing a PhD in Social Psychology at Iowa State University. He is working with Dr. Craig Anderson, studying positive and negative videogame effects as well as other aggression-related research topics.

C. Anne Wade is Manager and Information Specialist at the Centre for the Study of Learning and Performance, Concordia University, Montreal, Canada. She has worked at the CSLP for 18 years, taught a course on Information Literacy for many years, served as the Coordinator of the e-portfolio project since its inception and works extensively with school boards and other partner organizations.

Teena Willoughby is a Professor of Developmental Psychology in the Departments of Child and Youth Studies and Psychology at Brock University, St. Catharines, Ontario, Canada. Her research interests include examining the cognitive and social impact of media/technology on lifestyle choices and learning. In addition, she is interested in adolescent resilience, particularly with regard to academic underachievement and risk behaviors. Willoughby is Director of the Brock Research Institute for Youth Studies, Associate Director of the Lifespan Development Research Centre, and a Chancellor's Research Chair at Brock University.

Philip H. Winne is Professor of Education and Canada Research Chair at Simon Fraser University, British Columbia, Canada. He researches metacognition and self-regulated learning, specifically, how students monitor study tactics and how they use those evaluations to adapt old tactics and invent new ones. Winne has published more than 120 scholarly works. An Associate Editor of the *British Journal of Educational Psychology*, he co-edited the *Handbook of Educational Psychology* (2nd ed.) and the field-leading journal *Educational Psychologist* (2001–2005).

Eileen Wood is a Professor in Developmental Psychology at Wilfrid Laurier University, Ontario, Canada. Her research focuses on cognitive development and, in particular, how learners acquire and retain information. Most recently, her research examines teacher and learner issues when computers are integrated in the classroom. She also studies social implications resulting from technology within and beyond the classroom setting. She has published over 50 research papers and 3 textbooks (one which is now in its fifth edition, and one in a second edition).

Foreword: Seven Criteria for Investigating Children's Learning in a Digital World

Richard E. Mayer

Computer-based games and simulations have the potential to improve how children learn. This is the intriguing premise underlying *Children's Learning in a Digital World*, edited by Teena Willoughby and Eileen Wood. The book's chapters—written by leading experts in the field—contain examples of interventions and ways of thinking intended to improve learning through the use of computer-based software. If you are interested in exploring the possibilities of children's learning in a digital world, this book is for you. In addition, if you are interested in research-based principles for how to design and use pedagogically sound games and simulations, you will find that the chapters in this book point you in the right direction by suggesting further much-needed research.

In this foreword I offer seven criteria for how to take a scientific approach to the issue of children's learning in a digital world: (1) take a learner-centered approach rather than a technology-centered approach, (2) focus on promoting cognitive activity rather than behavioral activity, (3) focus on clear learning outcomes rather than nebulous goals, (4) support evidence-based practice rather than speculation-based practice, (5) provide research evidence that is methodologically sound rather than unsound, (6) provide research that is theoretically grounded rather than ideological, and (7) provide research that is educationally relevant rather than irrelevant. As you read the chapters in this volume, I suggest that you evaluate them on each of these seven criteria. Although no chapter is likely to rate high on all criteria, you will find that each of these criteria is addressed in various places in this volume.

Take a Learner-Centered Approach Rather Than a Technology-Centered Approach

The first criterion is that investigations of children's learning in a digital world should take a learner-centered approach rather than a technology-centered approach (Mayer, 2001, 2005). In a learner-centered approach, the focus is on how the human mind works, and how technology is an aid to human cognition. The primary research issue concerns how to adapt an existing technology to support the natural process of student learning. In contrast, the technology-centered approach focuses on the characteristics of a cutting-edge technology with the primary concern being how to expose learners to that technology. The main problem with the technology-centered approach is that the learner must adapt to the technology rather than be served by the technology, creating an instructional situation that often fails (Cuban, 1986).

The advantage of a learner-centered approach is it allows us to understand how aspects of games and simulations are related to the learner's cognitive processing during learning, and ultimately to specific learning outcomes. For example, in chapter 7 by Nesbit and Winne, the authors begin by describing the cognitive processes underlying self-regulated learning and seek to develop technology—which they call *gStudy*—that helps students become more aware about how and when to use the appropriate processes. In chapter 11, Mueller, Wood, and Willoughby examine how "to use computers as a cognitive tool in knowledge construction." Finally, authors take a learner-centered approach by trying to consider the learner's level of violence (chapter 3 by Swing and Anderson) and the learner's potential for videogame addiction (chapter 4 by Griffiths) in the design of instructional games.

Focus on Promoting Cognitive Activity Rather Than Behavioral Activity

The second criterion is that investigations of children's learning in a digital world should focus on promoting cognitive activity in the learner rather than behavioral activity (Mayer, 2001, 2005). A major reason for using games and simulations is that they cause learners to be more active, but not all forms of activity are equally productive. By focusing on cognitive activity, proponents of games and simulations point to changes in specific cognitive processes during learning. The advantage of this focus is that it allows us to better understand how aspects of computer software or games can affect what is learned. For example, in chapter 10, Desjarlais,

Willoughby, and Wood document that there is a great deal of student activity on the Internet, but note that "prevalence of Internet use, however, does not necessarily mean that it is an effective learning tool" (p. 249). In contrast, by focusing on behavioral activity, proponents of educational games and simulations point to the learners' increased levels of behavioral activity, such as how much they talk with each other or how many buttons they press. The problem with this focus is that learning is not caused by doing things, but rather by building cognitive representations. The goal of instruction is not to promote hands-on activity per se, but rather to promote learning—which depends on the learner's cognitive activity.

Focus on Clear Learning Outcomes Rather Than Nebulous Goals

The third criterion is that investigations of children's learning in a digital world should focus on clear learning outcomes rather than on nebulous goals (Anderson et al., 2001). In focusing on clear learning outcomes, authors tell us about the educational goal of the game and provide a way of measuring what is learned. The advantage of having a clear way to measure what is learned is that it provides a way to determine the effectiveness of the instructional technology (Pellegrino, Chudowsky, & Glaser, 2001). Certainly, when authors present a new educational technology, it is always fair to ask, "What do children learn?" For example, in chapter 6, Abrami, Savage, Wade, Hipps, and Lopez describe an evaluation of reading software that focuses on specific learning outcomes such as word identification (being able to read words aloud) and work attack (being able to read pseudo-words aloud).

In contrast, in focusing on nebulous goals, authors may say that their games are educational without specifying the target learning outcomes the games are intended to promote. Similarly, authors may claim that their games are emotionally engaging, exciting, entertaining, and just plain fun, without specifying exactly what students are supposed to learn from them. Without clear ways of specifying what is learned, it is not possible to determine whether a game has been successful.

Support Evidence-Based Practice Rather Than Speculation-Based Practice

The next criterion is that investigations of children's learning in a digital world should support evidence-based practice rather than speculation-based practice (Shavelson & Towne, 2002). There are many recommendations for how to design and use games in education, but where do those recommendations come from? In taking an evidence-based approach to educational practice, recommendations for how to design and use educational technology are consistent with the existing research base. When an author reviews relevant research before drawing a conclusion, states a recommendation as a to-be-tested hypothesis, or pinpoints the limitations of a recommendation based on available data, these are clues that the author supports evidence-based practice. In contrast, in taking a speculation-based approach to practice, the recommendations come from the opinions and experiences of the authors. Examples include when an author shuns valid data, relies mainly on testimonials, makes bold claims without supporting evidence, starts sentences by saying "I believe," or refers mainly to the opinions of experts. In short, educators should use more than opinions and speculations in determining what works for children's learning in a digital world. For example, in chapter 6 by Abrami et al., the authors acknowledge that "a core principle of all our research and development is evidence-based practice" (p. 132).

Provide Research that Is Methodologically Sound Rather Than Unsound

The next criterion is that investigations of children's learning in a digital world should be grounded in methodologically sound research. Discussions concerning the standards for educational research have attracted much attention among educational researchers (Shavelson & Towne, 2002). The consensus is that there is not one methodology that is best for all research situations and that there is room in the field for experimental studies and observational studies as well as for quantitative data and qualitative data. Yet, the defining feature of methodological soundness is that the data that are collected are useful in addressing the hypotheses under consideration. In short, a sound methodology is one that is capable of generating data that can be used to answer the question under consideration. Overall, when an author is interested in drawing a causal conclusion, an experiment with quantitative measures is in order. Chapter 6 by Abrami et al. provides an impressive example of this latter methodology by summarizing randomized clinical trials of *Alphie's Alley*—a set of computer-based activities aimed at improving children's reading—in which the software is shown to improve reading skills by as much as an effect size of d = .45. In chapter 9, diSessa says "I look toward specific empirical accountability (p. 220)."

Provide Research that Is Grounded in Theory Rather Than Ideology

The next criterion is that investigations of children's learning in a digital world should be grounded in theory rather than ideology (Shavelson & Towne, 2002). Authors who take a theoretically grounded approach offer a clear and testable mechanism for how learning works. They describe a cause-and-effect chain in which aspects of the instructional environment affect internal processing in the learner, which in turn affects what is learned. The hallmark of a theory-grounded approach is that the author is able to derive testable predictions that can be compared against actual data. This type of approach allows our field to progress, as research results allow us to create more useful theories of how to help students learn (Bransford, Brown, & Cocking, 1999). In contrast, in taking an ideological approach to children's learning, authors refer to various "isms" as the basis for their work. The problem with this approach is that ideological stances often are too vague to be tested in research investigations, and therefore do not meet the standards of science (Shavelson & Towne, 2002).

Learning is a change in a person's knowledge due to their experience. The goal of instruction is to foster learning in people by exposing them to productive experiences. Computer-based technologies have the potential for creating learning experiences but that potential will not be fulfilled without a clear understanding how to promote student learning. What is needed is a theory of the cognitive processes underlying learning along with a research base examining which features of computer-based games promote which kinds of learning processes. In chapter 2, Gee attempts to build a theory of technology-supported learning by analyzing the implicit learning theories of successful game designers. Though untested, Gee's analysis suggests an intriguing research agenda.

Provide Research that Is Educationally Relevant Rather Than Irrelevant

The final criterion is that investigations of children's learning in a digital world should be based on educationally relevant research rather than educationally irrelevant research (Shavelson & Towne, 2002). Mayer (2003) has shown that the history of research on learning contains periods when most research was not educationally relevant, by focusing on arbitrary tasks (such as learning lists of nonsense syllables) and non-authentic environments (such as hungry rats running down mazes). Instead, today, there is a large and growing research base on how people learn academic tasks in authentic settings (Bransford, Brown, & Cocking, 1999; Mayer, 2003). The authors of the book you are holding clearly seek to focus on educationally relevant issues. In addition, some authors expand the conception of educational relevance beyond formal school settings to include informal learning settings (such as accessing the web from home computers). As an example of this latter group, in chapter 8, Kafai and Giang describe an on-line educational game called Whyville that attracts about 14,000 users per day.

Conclusion

"Videogames have the potential to be powerful educational tools" (p. 72). This quote from Swing and Anderson (chapter 3) epitomizes the optimism of this book. Indeed, this book contains a glimpse into the possibilities of children's learning in the digital world including Jenkins' description of the New Literacies Project in chapter 1, or Peters' descriptions of the Computer Clubhouse project in chapter 5, or Kafai and Giang's descriptions of the Whyville science education website in chapter 8. Currently, the field is in its infancy. There are obstacles to overcome for the field to attain its full potential. For example, in chapter 11, Mueller, Wood, and Willoughby provide convincing evidence that the "potential of computer technology is not being realized" (p. 273). Peters, in chapter 5, makes the same point: "Educational games offer an extremely promising way to bridge formal and informal learning, but so far the promise has not met the reality" (p. 112).

In conclusion, as you assess each chapter against these seven criteria, you likely will be reminded of how much needs to be done. The chapters in this book provide many provocative ideas, describe some potentially exciting educational software, and point to some examples of "what works." Yet, investigating children's learning in a digital world is a largely incomplete task—there is much that can and will be done and this book highlights some key areas to be developed. A fitting end of this foreword is to quote the book's editors (from the introduction to Part I): "we need well-designed studies that can provide more evidence for the suggestions we have generated in this book" (p. 13).

References

Anderson, L. W., Krathwohl, D. R., Airasian, P. W., Cruikshank, K. A., Mayer, R. E., Pintrich, P. R., et al. (2001). *A taxonomy for learning, teaching, and assessing.* New York: Longman.

Bransford, J. D., Brown, A. L., & Cocking, R. R. (1999). *How people learn.* Washington, DC: National Academy Press.

Cuban, L. (1986). *Teachers and machines: The classroom use of technology since 1920.* New York: Teachers College Press.

Mayer, R. E. (2001). *Multimedia learning.* New York: Cambridge University Press.

Mayer, R. E. (2003). *Learning and instruction.* Upper Saddle River, NJ: Prentice Hall.

Mayer, R. E. (2005). Introduction to multimedia learning. In R. E. Mayer (Ed.), *Cambridge handbook of multimedia learning* (pp. 1–16). New York: Cambridge University Press.

Pelligrino, J., Chudowsky, J. N., & Glaser, R. (2001). *Knowing what students know: The science and design of educational assessment.* Washington, DC: National Academy Press.

Shavelson, R. J., & Towne, L. (2002). *Scientific research in education.* Washington, DC: National Academy Press.

Part I
Informal Learning with Technologies: Opportunities and Challenges

Introduction

Teena Willoughby and Eileen Wood

Children learn in both formal and informal learning contexts. When we think about learning, we often think about formal classroom contexts where children are provided with explicit instruction from trained professionals. Less often, we think about the many informal learning situations that children encounter in their everyday lives. For example, children learn from their peers, parents, and the media, both explicitly and through observation. In addition, children learn from exploration. These informal and formal contexts provide a forum for rich and comprehensive learning opportunities. The presence of technologies in both formal and informal contexts makes them a particularly salient learning tool. This book highlights learning in both formal and informal contexts, specifically with respect to computer technologies (e.g., Internet, videogames, software applications). The chapters in this first section of the book identify critical issues related to informal learning contexts. Information about formal learning contexts follows in the second section of the book.

Informal learning with technologies is an increasingly important cognitive and socialization agent for contemporary youth (Arnett, 1995). Informal learning most often takes place outside of the classroom, with limited direction from teachers or parents. It is often thought of as being a leisure activity, such as playing computer games or using the Internet for communication purposes. Many children and adolescents today have access to these technologies outside of the classroom. In fact, given the dramatic technological advancements in the last few years, youth today can chat online with peers across the world as well as have access to sophisticated simulation and role-playing games that can be combined with online multiplayer features.

Even more importantly, young people have the ability to be game designers and active participants in the technology. Understanding the impact of informal technology use is, for the most part, still in its infancy. There have been clear indications, however, that informal learning with technologies provides both opportunities and challenges for children and adolescents. This section of the book outlines these opportunities and challenges.

The chapter by Jenkins (chapter 1) is a particularly striking consideration of the social and cultural impact that technologies can provide. Drawing upon current examples, Jenkins demonstrates the power of technology for crossing cultures, where individuals around the world can communicate and share together common interests that may have previously been restricted to smaller cultural groups. Similarly, his work points to the tremendous potential for developing new cultures as a function of the medium itself, where youth are "participants" rather than "consumers." Combining the technologies available through computers with the communication system available through the Internet, new "social worlds" can be developed and exist in a way not possible before. Using these technologies, then, may shape the social fabric of our society.

The chapter by Jim Gee (chapter 2) provides a provocative argument that good computer games simulate the way the human mind works. Therefore computer games provide an excellent opportunity to study children's learning. Further, he outlines 13 principles that game designers often imbed in their games which support well-documented learning principles. These principles may be the key to why computer games are so successful. Importantly, Gee discusses ways these principles are often not included in formal learning contexts.

Not all the research on children's informal learning with technologies has reported positive findings, however. For example, repeated playing of violent computer games has been related to increased aggressive and delinquent behavior, and Edward Swing and Craig Anderson outline some of that research in chapter 3. They also summarize why violent videogames may be worse than violent television shows and films. Good videogames follow general learning principles that make them great teaching tools. The down side is that not all of that learning is positive, but Swing and Anderson suggest some ways that we can reduce the harmful effects.

Concerns also have been raised about excessive technology use. The chapter by Mark Griffiths (chapter 4) provides some compelling discussion on whether excessive computer gaming should be characterized as an addiction. He also suggests that excessive technology use is rare but that males tend to be the most excessive users of computer games. Griffiths notes as well that clear gender differences have been found in the type of games that are played. Boys are more likely than girls to play aggressive games, while girls are more likely than boys to play puzzlers and platform games. Griffiths notes the lack of supported explanations for these differences, and outlines the need for further research.

For example, what might be *causes* and what might be *effects* of these differences in game playing is still unknown. In addition, these gender differences obscure the fact that within-group differences are also significant. In other words, there are many girls who play computer games and boys who do not play computer games. It is only on average, or across the groups of boys and girls, that we find gender differences in computer gaming. It also is important to note, however, that girls are more likely than boys to embrace the use of technologies for information gathering and for communication purposes, although both males and females report that their most prevalent activities when using the Internet are engaging in online chat discussions and email (Willoughby, 2007).

In addition, it is clear that both boys' and girls' passion for technologies is tied more to typical informal learning contexts, such as peer communication and gaming, than it is to formal learning contexts. The gap between technology use in formal (e.g., classroom) and informal (e.g., home) settings remains large. The chapter by Laurence Peters (chapter 5) provides a review of this important challenge. He presents a critical consideration of the power of technologies in informal learning contexts and the importance that having and using technologies effectively could have for education. The openness of learners to the potential of computer technologies is an opportunity that schools can use to their advantage. Promoting and supporting opportunities for technology use is important for educators who need to work within existing social "cultures" within the school, but they must also be open to new and emerging cultures that are opening up as a function of technology.

At the same time, we need well-designed studies that can provide more evidence for the suggestions we have generated in this section. Only then can we create new learning opportunities for children and adolescents, regardless of the context or format. In fact, the chapter authors in this section of the book provide clear examples of how we can do that, with a focus on both the opportunities and challenges that youth face when using technologies in informal learning contexts. A better understanding of these processes can offer insights into how we can create better learning opportunities in formal learning contexts such as the classroom.

References

Arnett, J. J. (1995). Adolescents' uses of the media for self-socialization. *Journal of Youth and Adolescence. Special Issue: Adolescents' uses of the media*, 24 (5), 519–533.

Willoughby, T. (2007). *A short-term longitudinal study of Internet and computer game use by adolexcent boys and girls: Prevalence, frequency of use, and psychosocial predictors*. Manuscript submitted for publication.

Chapter 1

Media Literacy—Who Needs It?

Henry Jenkins

In my book, *Convergence Culture* (Jenkins, 2006a), I offer a description of our present moment of media change and try to identify trends which are redefining the relationship between media producers and consumers. This essay outlines some of the implications of those changes for the media literacy movement.

Two seemingly contradictory trends are shaping the current media landscape: On the one hand, new media technologies have lowered production and distribution costs, expanded the range of available delivery channels, and enabled consumers to archive, annotate, appropriate, and re-circulate media content. At the same time, there has been an alarming concentration of the ownership of mainstream commercial media, with a small handful of multinational media conglomerates dominating all sectors of the entertainment industry. No one seems capable of describing both sets of changes at the same time let alone show how they impact each other. Some fear that media is out of control, others that it is too controlled. Some see a world without gatekeepers, others a world where gatekeepers have unprecedented power. At the intersection between these two forces lies convergence culture. Convergence culture is what comes after the digital revolution.

In the world of media convergence, every important story gets told, every brand gets sold, and every consumer gets courted across multiple media platforms. *Convergence Culture* (Jenkins, 2006a) rejects what it calls the "Black Box Fallacy"—the idea that convergence should be understood primarily in terms of the merging of technological functions within media devices. Rather, my book sees convergence as a cultural process. Convergence alters the relationship between existing technologies, industries, markets, genres, and audiences. Media companies are learning how to accelerate the flow of media content across delivery channels to expand revenue opportunities, broaden markets, and reinforce viewer commitments. Consumers are learning how to use these different media technologies to bring the flow of media more fully under their control and to interact with other consumers.

In this new media landscape, children are participants—not spectators, not even consumers in the traditional sense of the term. They are actively shaping media content—a process which offers them new opportunities for emotional growth and intellectual development but which also poses new kinds of ethical responsibilities. Let's be clear that participation refers to something different from interactivity: Interactivity is a property of technologies; participation refers to what the culture does with these new media resources. The iPod is a technology which enables new kinds of interactions with recorded sound (and video); podcasting is a new form of participation which has grown up around this technology. As we develop a better understanding of the affordances of new media technologies, new kinds of participatory cultures grow up around them.

My own work is motivated by a belief in the potential benefits of these new participatory cultures in terms of diversifying media content, fostering a more empowered public, and making media companies more responsive to their consumers. Many of the key political struggles in the 21st century may center on our right to participate (which can be abstracted from the first amendment rights to speech, press, assembly, petition, and religion). In *Convergence Culture* (Jenkins, 2006a), I argue that by participating in popular culture, consumers—young and old—acquire skills in collaboration and knowledge sharing which may be fundamental to the future of democratic citizenship. Yet even if you are still driven by a desire to protect children from exposure to media violence or commercial interests, then you need to understand the shift in the way media operates. Even if you want to focus on television rather than new media, the emergence of participatory media is fundamentally altering the ways people relate to broadcast media. None of us can pretend to have all of the answers: the changes are still occurring, and so far they have moved in unpredictable directions. If educators do not study the changing media landscape, they are in no position to help students navigate its twisty pathways.

This essay describes some of the ways that youth are experiencing these changes in their relationship to popular culture. I will focus on notions of role play, pop cosmopolitanism, complexity, and knowledge sharing which are central to any understanding of the pedagogical potentials of contemporary popular culture; I will suggest ways that these experiences challenge the underlying assumptions shaping our current media literacy curriculum. The chapter will end with a first stab at naming and illustrating some of the core skills which educators will need to be fostering in the coming decade.

Education for the digital revolution has stressed tools above all else: The challenge was to wire the classroom and prepare kids for the demands of the new technologies. Little effort was made to give kids a context for thinking about these changes or to help them think about the new responsibilities and challenges they faced as participants in the digital culture. Convergence culture is no longer purely digital—as wave after wave of portable technologies have reshaped the flow of media within our culture. We can no longer afford to simply focus on the technologies and ignore the cultural changes which are occurring around and through them. And we really cannot afford to remain so fixated on television and mass media that we ignore the emergence of participatory culture altogether.

I am one of the principal investigators for the New Media Literacies Project, launched in spring 2006 by the MacArthur Foundation. The Project's central focus is to identify skills, knowledge, and competencies young people need to become meaningful participants—skills which will be central to learning, citizenship, community, and cultural expression. We hope to identify and promote a range of different interventions through schools, afterschool programs, public institutions, and commercial culture itself designed to promote these new-media literacies. We are just beginning our work by trying to spark a public dialogue about the future of media education.

Many educators and policy makers may ask: Media literacy—who needs it? First and foremost, adults need media literacy education. Our education schools offer little guidance for teachers in how to talk with their students about the significant media changes taking place all around them. Most of the groups offering advice to parents focus on restricting access if not prohibiting media outright and thus do little to help moms and dads understand what it would take to construct a meaningful relationship to media. Our legal authorities are striking out blindly, trying to regulate media changes they do not yet fully understand. Our children are immersed in this emerging culture while adults too often remain on the outside looking in. Marc Prensky (2001) writes about the widening gap between "digital natives" and "digital immigrants," suggesting that these two generational cohorts are never going to experience digital media in the same way because of such fundamental differences in backgrounds and experiences. Adults, he says, compute with an accent. But, make no mistake, kids need media literacy education, too. We will see some vivid examples throughout this essay of informal learning communities where kids develop core cultural competencies through their participation in popular culture. Yet these skills are unevenly distributed across the population and even the most media-literate kids are often not asking hard questions about the ways media reshape our perceptions of the world. We owe it to all of these constituencies to be up to date in our understanding of the media landscape and forward-thinking in our conception of what constitutes media literacy.

In Yoyogi Park

Our story starts in Yoyogi Park on a bright Sunday afternoon one spring. Yoyogi Park is a center for youth culture in Tokyo—near Akiharbara, which used to be the electronics sector but is increasingly known as the Otaku (or fan) district, and Harajuku, where fashionable young girls go to buy clothes. In my short time in Japan, I had already discovered the way cultural practices—forms of consumption for the most part—mapped onto spatial locations, much the way the geography of the World Wide Web structures the interactions between various American subcultures and fan communities. Every group seemed to have their own district, their own homeland, within contemporary Tokyo. The second thing that had struck me is the public nature of these passions and fascinations—the need to act out one's fantasy, the desire to form affiliations with others who shared one's tastes. Yoyogi Park is where all of this comes together. In this realm, to consume is to participate and to participate is to assume some kind of new identity.[1]

As you approach Yoyogi Park from the Harajuku train station, the first thing you see are the Cosplay Kids. These are young girls (and a few young boys) who have come to Yoyogi dressed as characters from anime, manga, or Jpop. They have come to see and be seen. Often, if you go into the manga shops, you can find brightly colored fliers urging fans of a particular cartoon series to rendezvous in the park on a certain date often with very specific directions about what to wear. Yet because there are so many different fan communities, one can see many different identities being performed on this somewhat narrow piece of concrete—spies with shiny new weapons, space adventurers and demonic figures, people in Goth or renaissance courtly garb, the furries who are fascinated with anthropomorphic animals, Nanas who most often wear Victorian nurse and nanny uniforms, and so forth. Many of them spend a good deal of time posing for pictures being taken not simply by tourists but also by their fellow fans; these pictures are being recorded by cell phone, camcorder, or digital cameras, and many of them are soon to be distributed via the web. The costumes and makeup are elaborate, richly detailed, and for the most part, home crafted. The kids take great pride in their costumes though they may own multiple costumes reflecting multiple cultural identities.

For many Americans visiting Tokyo for the first time, all of this is apt to seem alien or typically Japanese. But I knew about this cosplay before I arrived, in part because of an interview my graduate student, Vanessa Bertozzi, had done with a 17-year-old American girl named Chloe Metcalf. One of a number of teenagers we contacted as part of the Young Artist project, Chloe was active in the American cosplay community. Here's some of what she told Vanessa:

I have been really interested in Japanese culture since I was in sixth grade. When I was in the seventh grade, I started studying Japanese on my own. When I got into high school, I started taking Japanese courses at Smith College. I got into costuming through anime which is actually how I got interested in Japanese. And I taught myself how to sew . . . I'm a stage hog. I like to get attention and recognition. I love acting and theater. The biggest payoff of cosplay is to go to the conventions where there are other people who know who you are dressed as and can appreciate your effort. At the first convention I ever went to, I must have had fifty people take my picture and at least ten of them came up and hugged me. It's almost like whoever you dress up as, you become that person for a day . . . People put the pictures up on their websites after the con. So after a con, you can search for pictures of yourself and if you are lucky, you will find five or ten. (Bertozzi & Jenkins, in press)

A number of things interest me about Chloe. First is the degree to which she transforms fantasies born of media consumption into various kinds of performance. In this context, I see performance, impersonation, enactment as important kinds of media literacy skills which are often neglected in our recent focus on visual or digital literacy. A growing body of literature shows that children acquire basic literacies and competencies through learning to manipulate core cultural materials (Dyson, 1997; Wolfe & Heath, 1992). As they do so, they negotiate a space between self and other which helps them to work through issues of personal identity and cultural membership. These ways of playing with texts become more and more sophisticated as children mature, with adolescence becoming a central site for identity play and self-invention. For Chloe, assuming the role of a Jpop character becomes a way of expressing her mastery over favorite texts—fusing her identity with that of a fictional character. Role play is a persistent interest among contemporary youth, whether we are looking at the cosplay of young anime fans, the role-play that takes place around *Yu-Gi-Oh!* or *Magic* or *Hero* clips, the fusion with a digital avatar through computer gaming or fantasy role-playing, or the construction of alternative personas in subcultural communities like the Goths. Kids have told me that role-play allows them to become the person they want to be rather than simply satisfying adult demands or accepting the often unwelcome identities projected upon them at school.[2]

The identity Chloe constructs doesn't simply involve breaking with the parochialism of her local culture, it also requires the creation of strong emotional bonds with cultures from other parts of the world, cultures that are not easily accessible in a marketplace which historically has been highly protective of its local culture industries. When she told Vanessa that a particular Jpop group was "her favorite group in the whole wide world," one has the sense that she is actually talking on a global scale, especially when she adds that the group is little known outside of its genre or beyond the Asian context. She has sought out more and more information about forms of Asian popular culture. And in the process, she has begun to re-imagine her relations to the world—seeing herself as tied in important ways to the kinds of Japanese youth culture I had encountered in Yoyogi Park.

This search for more information expresses itself across a range of media— the videos or DVDs she watches of Japanese-produced anime, the recordings of Jpop music on MP3 or on CD, the information she finds on the Internet as well as information she shares with her fellow fans about her own activities, the physical costumes she generates as well as all of the photographs that get taken of her costumes, the magazines and comics she reads to learn more about Japanese popular culture, her face to face contacts with fellow fans. An elaborate underground economy exists to support the circulation of these materials, including grassroots efforts to translate and dub illegally imported anime so that it can be made accessible to a broader public.

These activities around popular culture in turn translate into other kinds of learning, including much that would warm the hearts of educators. As a middle school student Chloe began to study Japanese language and culture first on her own and later at a local college. This is a story one hears again and again from language instructors—how kids like Chloe are moving from interest in Asian popular culture towards seeking out classes in Asian cultures and languages. Here we run up against old anxieties about marketing and cultural imperialism which have animated earlier stages of the American media literacy movement. Some would argue that Chloe is not so much learning or experimenting as being possessed by cultural materials not of her own making. Others would argue that she is simply a victim of the economic expansion of Japanese media companies into the American marketplace. Yet it would be a mistake to see Chloe and the other American cosplayers as simply duplicating cultural experiences imported into the US or buying into media franchises. Rather, they are as much involved in transformation as consumption, in localization as globalization.

We can see this more clearly if we walk another few yards into Yoyogi Park. Here you see a very different kind of cultural phenomenon—a pack of fifty or more Japanese rockabilly fans dancing to recordings of Elvis, wearing black leather jackets and exaggerated greaser haircuts, and performing flamboyant and energetic dance moves which mix traditional rock and roll with break-dancing. They call themselves the *rokku n roraa* (rock 'n' rollers) and by all reports they have been coming to the park every weekend for several decades to pay tribute to the King. At first glance it is easy to see their passionate response to American popular culture but one needs to look more closely to see the ways that those influences have been reabsorbed back into more distinctly Japanese cultural practices. For one thing, this is a highly hierarchical culture with many rituals designed to ensure discipline within the rank and file as well as respect for the most esteemed members. In this case, the leader of the pack is the only one allowed to wear a red jacket—an insignia of rank modeled after the red jacket which James Dean wore in *Rebel Without a Cause*. In their cultural mythology, the only person more powerful than Elvis is Jimmy Dean. Much as the *rokku n roraa* translate American culture into Japanese culture, Chloe and her friends pull the Japanese practice of cosplay back into the social dynamics of 21st century suburban America. Even as they seek to connect with other cultures, they read them through the lens of their own culture.

For another thing, there is the gender segregation of the group. If cosplay is mostly but not exclusively female, the *rokku n roraa* are overwhelmingly but not exclusively male. I keep finding myself wondering what it meant for the two female members of the pack to dress in Elvis drag and dance with all of these muscular guys in the park. How might the fantasies provided by American popular culture allow them to escape constraints on gender performance in their own country? Or conversely, how are American boys taking advantage of the cross-dressing elements of cosplay to escape repressive constraints on male gender performance in the United States? In both cases, these youths seek a kind of freedom or fluidity of identity denied them in their own country but granted them more readily by engaging in cultural practices from elsewhere.

A long tradition of cultural scholarship has focused on the ways that youth around the world have used American cultural imports to break free from the parochialism of their own societies—even if only temporarily and even if only in the confines of their own imaginations. Much less has been written about the ways American youth escape the parochialism of their own culture through engaging with forms of popular culture imported from Japan, China, India, or Latin America. In a recent essay (Jenkins, 2006b) I described these practices as pop cosmopolitanism. Historically, cosmopolitans sought knowledge and experience which took them beyond the borders of their local community. We associate the term *cosmopolitanism* with various forms of high culture—fine wine, painting, music, dance, theater, the art cinema, gourmet cooking, and so forth. Yet today, popular culture performs this same function for a growing number of young people around the world. Their mastery over these cultural materials help participating youth form emotional bonds, however imaginary, with their counterparts in other countries—not simply with Japan where this culture originates but in many other countries where these materials are also consumed. It provides common cultural currency for exchanges on the Internet which may cut across national borders. This turn towards global identities is all the more striking when you consider the unilateralism currently shaping American foreign policy and the anti-Americanism which is surfacing around the world. Kids may be learning how to become global citizens through their engagement with popular culture at a time when their parent cultures are increasingly shaped by fundamentalism and nationalism.

I came to a new understanding of this pop cosmopolitanism when I stopped for groceries in a chain store in Clayton, Georgia, a small community in the foothills of the Blue Ridge Mountains. As I stood in line, I heard the man in front of me ask in a broad southern accent why the "roly-poly" and very white checkout girl had a Japanese name on her badge. The checkout girl tried to explain to him that this was an identity she assumed through her cosplay and that many of her friends—especially on the Internet—knew her through that name. He was perplexed and demanded to know "how in the world she got interested in that." I could have pointed out the fact that this grocery store didn't sell *Time*, *Newsweek*, or *Entertainment Weekly*— but did carry about a dozen gun magazines and the American edition of the Japanese manga, *Shonen Jump*. She pointed towards the growing popularity of *Pokémon* and *Yu-Gi-Oh!* and the young kid in the grocery cart, little more than a toddler, who pulled out his *Pokémon* cards and started waving them proudly to his father. They left the store and I told the checkout girl that I was an otaku myself. She was shocked both because she had never met an anime fan quite as old as I was and because she didn't know that there were any other fans locally. We talked briefly and I went on my way but I often reflect on that moment as one that illustrates a kind of transition in our culture—each person in the story having a somewhat different relation to the flow of Asian popular culture into the American market— the father finding it inexplicable, his son finding it normal, the girl finding it a source of personal identity, and me finding it a kind of intellectual interest. I also think often of what being connected to anime fandom must have meant to this Appalachian girl—a connection to the world beyond the often narrow confines of this town, a means of knowledge and experience which set her apart both from the adults around her but apparently from many of her classmates. We might well imagine that this experience meant for her some of the same things that imitating Elvis might have meant to the Japanese women I saw in Yoyogi Park.

I have devoted time on my experiences as a tourist visiting Yoyogi Park because I think what I saw there—and what I saw in the north Georgia grocery store—illustrates the complexity of young people's relationship to popular culture. Those relationships cannot be reduced to traditional dualisms of production and consumption. In no meaningful sense are these kids simply consumers of cultural materials produced by others even if they are very much drawn to the content of commercial culture. Rather, I would argue that they are participants—shaping the flow of cultural materials across national borders, tapping into a global information network to support their activities, transforming the media they consume into new forms of cultural expression, moving beyond the constraints placed on them in their local environments to tap a freedom that comes from stepping outside one's own culture and embracing pop cosmopolitanism.

At the same time, it doesn't make sense to talk about this purely in terms of new media or digital culture. The availability of new technologies has enabled some of their activities but kids are also enacting these interests through more traditional forms of cultural practice. Chloe, for example, told us about a friend who had taught himself how to make his own buttons in order to more perfectly recreate the costumes of a Japanese Jpop band. What would it mean to think of these kinds of activities as a kind of media literacy put into practice? To recreate Japanese costumes and customs, they must first study and then master them. They are understanding these cultures from the inside out—drawing on personal reflection to flesh out things they might otherwise have known only through books or media representations. As they mimic these cultural practices, they are drawn towards further research, trying to master the language, trying to understand the much older traditions which gave rise to this popular culture, trying to understand the lives of their friends in other parts of the world. We can see performance and role playing as a catalyst which motivates media literacy on the one hand and informal learning of academic disciplines on the other. Of course, it is worth noting how few American schools offer Japanese as a language or provide any real opportunity for kids to dig this deeply into Asian culture. These informal learning communities, in fact, are teaching kids things that most adults would see as valuable but which they can't learn in schools.

I Don't See Any Dummies Around Here

One of the most persistent criticisms of popular culture, represented in a stream of pop bestsellers with titles like *The Closing of the American Mind* or *Slouching Towards Gomorrah*, is that commercial culture's push to reach every consumer has resulted in a "dumbing down" of our culture. This is what cocktail party intellectuals tell each other as they strut with pride over the fact that they "don't even own a television set." Somehow responding with "I don't even own a book" doesn't carry the same cultural weight. Because these media-phobic people invest little of themselves in the media they consume, they get very little back from the experience. They never really learn how to appreciate the complexity of popular culture and as a result, they can see little beyond the surface. If I never learn to appreciate modern dance, I am thought to be a bumpkin. If I never learn to appreciate contemporary television, I can proclaim myself an intellectual and write books that get reviewed favorably in the literary section of the *New York Times*. Despite our eagerness to think the worst about contemporary popular culture, a growing body of scholarship is finding enormous complexity in various sectors of American popular culture.

The two most important researchers currently discussing complexity in popular culture (present company excluded) are James Paul Gee and Steven Johnson. Since Gee's perspective is represented in this collection already (see chapter 2), I want to take a few paragraphs to discuss the argument Johnson puts forth in his bestselling book, *Everything Bad Is Good for You* (2005). As he summarizes the book on its very first page, "Popular culture has, on average, grown more complex and intellectually challenging over the past thirty years . . . Think of it as a kind of positive brainwashing: The popular media steadily, but almost imperceptibly, making our minds sharper, as we soak in entertainment usually dismissed as so much lowbrow stuff" (p. xiii). As the book proceeds, Johnson describes the kinds of complex challenges posed by "games that force us to probe and telescope-television shows that require the mind to fill in the blanks, or exercise its emotional intelligence. Software that makes us sit forward, not lean back" (p. 136). Johnson offers a good description of the current media landscape, though we might add films with elliptical editing and nonlinear narratives, mainstream comics which play with genre or challenging compositional structures, media franchises which disperse information across multiple media or which mix and match different modes of representation within the same media experience. These new structures, he suggests, offer "the cognitive benefits conventionally ascribed to reading: attention, patience, retention, the parsing of narrative threads" (p. 23).

Johnson's (2005) other big claim is that consuming such culture makes us more intelligent—he goes so far as to say that it is rewiring our brains. I would be a little more conservative in my claims: It might be more accurate to say that it demanding new kinds of literacy and requiring new forms of consumption. Consuming all of these media is certainly changing how we read and write. As Johnson notes, "we deal with text now in shorter bursts, following links across the Web, or sifting through a dozen e-mail messages. The breadth of information is wider in this world, and it is more participatory" (p. 185).

Alarmists call this the death of literacy yet they ignore previous shifts in the ways we read and write—for example, the shift in rhetoric from the great 19th century American writers (Hawthorne, say) and the great writers of the early 20th century (Steinbeck or Hemingway), a move towards a sparser, more robust, less discursive style of writing which reflected the rhythms of the telegraph and the modern city. Rather, it seems more useful to think of these texts as making new demands on their readers and in return, as Johnson (2005) also suggests, readers making more demands on texts. As he explains, "Aiming for the lowest common denominator might make sense if the show's going to be seen only once, but with a guarantee of multiple viewings, you can venture into more challenging, experimental realms and still be rewarded for it" (p. 160). What seemed challenging a decade ago seems simple by today's standard as audience members develop new skills for processing such stories. Again, many of these skills get read negatively in traditional accounts—as a loss of attention span, for example, but we can also read these skills as adaptive to the demands of the modern workplace where the ability to multitask, to make predictions on partial information, to make rapid assessment of the value of new data, to shift perspectives, and to operate within an expanded social network are all required to perform most jobs well.

One can quibble with some of Johnson's formulations—a tendency to choose the richest contemporary examples and the most trivial older examples can stack the deck, a too easy dismissal of issues of content (which either cedes the case if you think contemporary media are morally complex or begs the question if you think the content is simplistic or relativistic), a lack of serious consideration for the production contexts which are giving rise to these new kinds of complexity or the consumption practices which are supporting them. To be fair, Johnson is a journalist who is painting with broad strokes in the hopes of starting a conversation. And that he has more than accomplished.

For my money, Johnson doesn't go far enough in terms of identifying the many different forms of complexity in contemporary popular culture. Here are some more forms of media complexity:

Genre complexity: Genres represent formulas which enable the construction and interpretation of popular narratives. Historically, genre theorists saw each work as working within one and only one genre tradition. Westerns were distinguished from musicals. Increasingly, genre theory has realized that most works operate within more than one genre, shifting between different formulas to create new interests and to broaden their consumer base. The most complex contemporary works depend on the viewer's ability to recognize the interplay between multiple genre traditions within the same work.[3] Consider, for example, DC's Elseworlds comics. Here, the familiar DC superheroes—Batman, Superman, Wonder Woman, and the like—get reworked through different genres or different historical periods. So, for example, *Superman's Metropolis* (Lofficer, Thomas, & McKeever, 1997) reads the hero's origin stories against the background of Fritz Lang's German Expressionist classic; *The Kents* (Ostrander, Truman, & Mandrake, 2000) is a multigenerational saga set in Kansas in the 19th century—a western about Clark Kent's ancestors; and *Red Son* (Millar, 2004) imagines what would have happened if Superman had landed in Russia rather than the United States.

Visual complexity: Many people complain that they don't know how to read comics—it's really pretty simple and mostly involves reading left to right, top to bottom, like any other book. Yet, some visual artists develop much more challenging visual styles. David Mack, for example, has developed a collage-like aesthetic which does not depend on linear processing of panels but rather invites the reader to scan across a page organized with little or no clear hierarchy of information. The same page may mix and match multiple kinds of written texts (some printed, some handwritten), multiple kinds of images (some highly abstract, others highly representational), as well as explore bold plays with color and texture which evoke feelings which operate independently of any story information. There is no right order to read this page but as we accumulate and process all of these different streams of information, the gestalt (and the decipherment process itself) packs a powerful emotional punch. One can certainly connect Mack with a range of high art traditions—including artist books which are interested in the materiality of the book as an artefact—but what is striking is that Mack has done some of his best work at the heart of the commercial comic book industry, working, for example, within Marvel's cash-cow Daredevil franchise.[4]

Narrative complexity: As Johnson suggests, contemporary television series have become more sophisticated in their narrative structures—linking together plotlines involving multiple characters, unfolding story information across long arcs, and depending on viewers to draw on back story which might have been revealed several seasons before. For example, the contemporary hit series, *Lost*, involves more than 18 different recurring characters, many of whom may fade into the background in one episode and emerge as the main character for another. It has involved elaborate and extended flashbacks, tracing how each character came to be on the island, and over time, we are expected to read their present actions against what we learn from the past, and we may learn new details which force us to rethink what we thought we knew about their pasts. Johnson suggests that it is by making sense of such complex sets of characters that we can begin to master skills in navigating the ever-expanding social networks which shape our everyday interactions.

Ethical complexity: At the same time, other devices, such as the confessional in reality television which opens up a gap between what characters do and how they reflect on their own actions, helps us to recognize the negotiation between competing identities which is also part of how we manage social relations in the present epoch. Reality television series, such as *Survi-*

vor or *Amazing Race*, produce a series of ethical dramas which become the focus of audience evaluation and discussion. While what occurs on-screen may often seem amoral, what occurs in the audience can have profound ethical implications. In a world where few of us know our neighbors, reality contestants put themselves forward as the subjects of gossip. Gossip has historically served important social functions, enabling a bonding through the mutual disclosure of secrets and the social negotiation of values. By talking about what we see on television, viewers living in a multicultural society can compare moral evaluations and develop a fuller understanding of how we each see the world.

Paradigmatic complexity: As James Paul Gee (2005) has noted, a child's mastery over the *Pokémon* characters is an intellectual accomplishment of the order of mastering chemistry's periodic table or the pantheon of Greek gods. There are several hundred characters, each of whom has multiple states of being, all of which relate to each other through an elaborate system of antagonisms and alliances. The information one needs to understand the *Pokémon* universe is not contained within any single source (though the phenomenon has produced a healthy share of reference books which promise to tell us everything we need to know). Rather, it has to be gathered together across many different media (television series, films, games, cards, coloring books, comics, and the web). As David Buckingham and Julian Sefton-Green (2004) argue, *Pokémon* isn't something you watch or buy: It is something you do. The dispersion of information about the characters not only motivates more consumption, it also provides a context for social interactions among young fans as they compare notes and pool knowledge.

Cognitive complexity: As writers like Gee (2005) or Kurt Squire (2005) note, contemporary computer games make more and more demands on their players. Squire, for example, has explored what kids might learn about history by playing a game like *Civilization III*. He found that the game allows players to set their own goals and test their own hypotheses, encouraging young learners to ask "what if" questions about, say, why Europeans colonized North America rather than the other way around. By asking these questions, and by manipulating complex sets of variables, the kids were able to test their hypotheses and ground them in a deeper understanding of core historiographic principles—for example, in understanding the role that geography and climate played in shaping the interactions between historic civilizations. In the process of such play, kids acquired a broad range of concepts, such as monarchy or monotheism, which are central to the national social science standards.

Cultural complexity: We have already discussed the complicated ways that kids are borrowing images, sounds, personas, and stories from around the world, mixing and matching them to form their own cultural identities.

Popular filmmakers around the world are similarly combining different cultural traditions to create works which can only be fully appreciated by stepping beyond the limits of your own cultural community: for example, *Bride and Prejudice*, a recent Bollywood film based on the Jane Austen novel, or *Tears of the Black Tiger*, a Thai western which sets a traditional Hollywood story in the context of traditional Thai society. Such films reflect a transitional moment in their countries of origin—a move from national to global modes of production and consumption, a shift from traditional to modern societies. More and more Asian films are being produced for diasporic communities worldwide rather than simply for local consumption, and these films reflect the betwixt and between perspectives of their "desi" consumers.

What these different forms of complexity have in common is that they reward those who have invested themselves and worked hard to achieve a particular depth of understanding of a given work. The underground cartoonist Peter Bagge (2003) drew a comic strip in 2000 which depicted a group of friends exiting a theater showing *The Matrix*.[5] The first two young men are extolling the virtues of the production, while the third one mumbles "I don't get it." Bagge's cartoon captures the sense of inadequacy many viewers felt in response to the *Matrix* movies, walking away with a sense that they must have missed something. Historically, the kinds of films which produced such feelings of inadequacy were art films imported from Europe or independent films circulating outside the commercial cinema. Yet *The Matrix* was a Hollywood blockbuster which embodied the various kinds of complexity I identified above.

How do we make sense of the production and circulation of such complex works? Our comprehension depends on two shifts—one technological, the other cultural. The technological shift can be described as distributed cognition—the idea that we can accomplish more difficult challenges as we learn to offload basic cognitive processes into our technologies (Salomon, 1996). So, for example, I was able to follow far fewer television series and was more liable to miss crucial episodes before I got my Tivo. Similarly, my ability to archive episodes—in my case, primarily by collecting video tapes—can enable me to go back and watch key moments in the series whenever I encounter something that confuses me. Television shows can now enjoy the affordances of books and other printed matter: I can reread them; I can scan through them looking for specific passages; I can share those passages with a friend as the start of a conversation; we can debate our critical interpretations, and so forth. Of course, my archive is only as valuable as the annotations which surround it. The next generation of technological change will make it easier to search and index video so that we can recall key moments when we need them.

More important, however, have been cultural changes in the ways we consume media—what Pierre Levy calls the emergence of collective intelligence. Levy (2000) argues that a new kind of power has emerged in the age of networked computing, one which may eventually prove as important as the nation state or commodity capitalism. He is interested in the ways online communities form to solve certain kinds of problems by pooling information, sharing knowledge, and criticizing and refining prior formulations. In such a world, nobody knows everything, everyone knows something, and what is known by one member becomes accessible to the group as a whole. So, for example, the young *Pokémon* fans, who each know some crucial detail about the various species, constitute a collective intelligence whose knowledge gets extended each time two kids on the playground share something about the franchise with each other. Many of adults work in jobs which require collaboration between various specialists and experts to solve shared problems. Such knowledge sharing can take on more and more sophisticated functions as it moves online and as the range of potential participants broadens geographically and culturally. So, for example, *Matrix* fans have created elaborate concordances which help them keep track of information about the Zion resistance movement. *Survivor* fans have used the Internet to track down information and identify the names of contestants before they are announced by the network; they have used satellite photographs to identify the location of the *Survivor* base camp despite the producer's "no fly over" agreements with local governments. Such knowledge communities change the very nature of media consumption—a shift from the personalized media that was so central to the idea of the digital revolution towards socialized or communalized media that is central to the culture of media convergence.

Right now, we are experimenting with collective intelligence through our recreational lives but it is quickly spilling over into other aspects of our culture. One can see the development of the Wikipedia, for example, where thousands of people worldwide contribute information to create a vast reference library, as the extension of collective intelligence into the educational space. We can see Moveon.org's "Bush in 30 Seconds" contest, where hundreds of amateur filmmakers submitted anti-Bush spots for use during the last presidential campaign, as collective intelligence applied to the political sphere. Or we can see an online publication like Slashdot, where readers collectively assess the value of any given submission and thus determine its visibility, as collective intelligence applied to journalism (Chan, 2002). And we might think about the fostering of brand communities by major corporations as the attempt to court collective intelligence in order to promote consumer loyalty. And the list continues.

By contrast, our schools have done little to move beyond the focus on the autonomous learner, still marking most forms of collaboration as "cheating" at a time when most of us spend most of our time collaborating at work and in our communities. And even many groups promoting 21st century skills still emphasize individualized skills sets. For example, The New Media Consortium recently issued a report which offered this summary of the emerging competencies:

> 21st century literacy is the set of abilities and skills where aural, visual, and digital literacy overlap. These include the ability to understand the power of images and sounds, to recognize and use the power to manipulate and transform digital media, to distribute them pervasively, and to easily adapt them to new forms.

It's a very good start but such a description seems not to recognize that part of what is significant about the new-media literacies is the shift in the ways we interact with each other. The social dimensions of these new literacies crops up here only in terms of the phrase "to distribute them pervasively," which holds onto the sender–receiver model. Even a slight shift away from distribution to "circulation" might introduce the idea that others play an active part in this process. But we really need to push further talking about how meaning emerges collectively and collaboratively in the new media environment and how creativity operates differently in an open-source culture based on sampling, appropriation, transformation, and repurposing. The social production of meaning is more than individual interpretation multiplied; it represents a qualitative difference in the ways we make sense of cultural experience. It thus represents a profound change in how we understand literacy. We need to integrate these new knowledge cultures into our schools—not only through group work but also through long distance collaborations with other educational spaces. Students need to discover what it is like to contribute their own expertise to a process which involves many intelligences, a process which they encounter readily in their participation in fan discussion lists or blogging, for example, and which will be an assumed skill in the future workplace. Our present educational practices stress the autonomous individual over the social network, with most forms of collaboration distrusted as cheating.

So far, we have identified a range of factors pushing us to rethink what we mean by media literacy:

1 the growing centrality of participatory culture—enabled by the rise of new media technologies but having implications which stretch far beyond them.

2 the emergence of "pop cosmopolitanism," a new way of living in the world, which requires greater cultural knowledge.

3 the emergence of new forms of complexity in popular culture which in turn require new skills and competencies.
4 the emergence of new kinds of social viewing practices—or what we are calling here *collective intelligence*—which require new skills in information sharing, assessment, and collaboration, which by and large are not being taught through our schools.

So What Are We Gonna Do About It?

Hmmm. Where do we go from here? Many essays about media literacy start by sounding an alarm, describing all of the negative things that are happening to our children and youth because they spend so much time consuming media and are at the mercy of Madison Avenue. Such essays end with a call for the teacher or parent to come to the rescue. This time, however, I have been describing the powerful skills which young people are developing on their own through the ways they are interacting with, participating within, and sharing their knowledge about popular culture. So, why do they need us? What role does formal media literacy education play in the world I have just described and what forms should it take?

Here's where the alarm bell rings: If we agree that the skills and activities described above are valuable, helping to prepare kids for full participation in our culture, then we have to own up to the fact that these skills are unevenly distributed across our society. So far, much of the discussion of the digital divide has emphasized problems of access, seeing the issue primarily in technical terms—but as I have already suggested, a medium is more than a technology. As activists have sought a variety of means to broaden access to digital media, they have created a hodge-podge of different opportunities for participation. Some have extended access to these resources through the home and others have limited, filtered, regulated access through schools and public libraries. What you can do in your own home with unlimited access to new media technologies is very different than what you can do on a school or library computer, with people waiting in line behind you, and no ability to save your work from one visit to the next. As we have waited for one segment of the population to get wired, those who were early adapters have fully integrated these capabilities into their lifestyles and have made what they do online a central aspect of their cultural identities. Beyond such technical problems, there are a range of cultural factors which diminish the likelihood that different groups will participate. Race, class, gender, language differences amplify these inequalities in opportunities for participation. One reason we see early adopters is that some groups not only feel more confidence in engaging with new technologies but also some groups seem more comfortable going public with their views about culture.

We can learn a great deal about what schools need to do by looking at some of the groups which have experimented with the new skills and competencies we hope to promote—homeschoolers and the disabled community. Here's how my graduate student Vanessa Bertozzi (2005) describes some of her core insights into the homeschooling movement:

> De-institutionalization forms the basis of progressive homeschooling, known by some as "unschooling." This type of homeschooling emphasizes child-directed learning, often interdisciplinary and informal in style. The Place of the home with its security and privacy (interesting to note the political connotations those words have in the current news media) opens up as a flexible Space full of possibilities. Many of these unschoolers follow an Emersonian ideal, steeped in 60s counter-culture and grounded on the pragmatics of self-sufficiency. This philosophy becomes manifest in very practical ways: Not only do unschoolers practice the right to think for themselves, but they also have more free time to pursue their passions. Going further, they have the determination to see their DIY media productions through to completion and the self-confidence to then share their creations with the world. It would be wrong to say that unschoolers are necessarily more creative than their schooled counterparts (though some might claim that as a self-selecting group they do tend to be). However, I believe that there are certain distinguishing characteristics of the unschooling lifestyle that predispose these kids to a more enriching, participatory use of media. These young people are less distracted by homework and "busywork." Their learning environments provide the sort of adaptable setting and time to integrate media literacy in a "naturalistic" way of learning.
>
> The role of community must also be looked at through this lens. Support groups online have made homeschooling easier in an age where unschoolers are a geographically dispersed minority. Social networking allow for greater ease in swapping expertise and organizing field trips, for instance. Distanced learning programs and open source communities (such as MIT's Open Courseware) function really well for self-motivated and passionate self-learners. Subsequently, the communities that surround such sites tend to be dedicated and responsive to community members who need a helping hand. In this way, homeschoolers who seek out such collective intelligence communities can gain access to knowledge that isn't even necessarily divulged through homeschooling communications per se. (Bertozzi, 2005)

At one time, the biggest downside of homeschooling was that it left kids socially isolated, cut off from their peer culture. But in the age of media convergence, these kids are spending more time networking online; they are using the web and the cell phone to "smart mob" field trips, sending out a call for all the homeschoolers to go to a particular museum at a particular time, and thus instantly creating a context for shared learning. They are spending more time on individual projects, including media productions, which they circulate via the web.

Kids with disabilities—especially the blind—are also leading the way towards exploring these new modes of learning. Many of these kids become very adept at navigating through the new media landscape to access the same materials or have the same kinds of experiences as other kids. Media change, as Alicia "Kestrell" Verlager (2005) argues, has been driven by the desire to transform human perception and sensation and has often been led by those who felt frustrated by limits placed on their ability to process the world around them. Leading innovators have either themselves been disabled or have conjured up metaphors of disability as a means of thinking through the challenges of technological development. Disabled consumers also play important roles in testing and evaluating new technological features—such as text recognition or speech recognition software—which will later be adopted more widely across the computer industry. Such consumers develop rich conceptual vocabularies for thinking about media technologies in order to make their needs and demands known to the development community. Far from being left behind by media change, the disabled are pushing ahead of the able-bodied population in their understanding of the media changes taking place around them.

For those of us who care about education, it should be both chilling—and inspiring—to realize that the greatest media literacy may be possessed by those least touched (homeschoolers) or worst served by the current educational system (the disabled). As we turn towards the schools, however, we are seeing two troubling developments. On the one hand, those kids who are most advanced in their mastery over the new-media literacies are often deskilled as they enter the classroom: In order to ensure a uniform experience, these kids are stripped of their technologies and robbed of their best techniques for learning. Such kids cannot wait to get out of school in order to get back to the activity of learning. On the other hand, many kids who have had no exposure to these new kinds of participatory cultures outside school find themselves struggling to keep up with their peers. Schools have an important role to play in ensuring the more equitable distribution of these skills across the population.

The problem, as I have suggested, is that even many of the best current media literacy programs are still focused on media consumption and not participation. For example, I admire Elizabeth Thoman and Tessa Jolls (2005) at the Center for Media Literacy for developing clear-headed, pragmatic, and even-handed resources for media education. Yet consider how they phrase the five key questions which run through their literature:

1 Who created the message?
2 What creative techniques are used to attract my attention?
3 How many different people understand this message differently than me?
4 What lifestyles, values, and points of view are represented in—or omitted from—this message?
5 Why is this message being sent?

There is a lot one can praise about these questions: They understand media as operating within a social and cultural context; they recognize that what we take from a message is different from what the author intended; they focus on interpretation and context as well as motivation; they are not tied up with a language of victimization. Yet, note that each question operates on the assumption that the message was created elsewhere and that we are simply its recipients. We would add new complexity and depth to each of these questions if we rephrased them to emphasize our own active participation in selecting, creating, remaking, critiquing, and circulating media content.

Through the MacArthur New Literacies Project, we have begun to identify a series of basic skills or competencies which reflect what the early adapters are doing in the new media environment. What follows is a partial list of skills which are emerging in and around computer games culture with some suggestions of what they might mean for classroom teachers.

Play refers to a process of exploration and experimentation. Think of games as problem sets. Each step forward involves trying out possible solutions: Some work, some don't, all must get refined through further play. When children play *Sim City*, they explore principles of urban planning; they experiment with different designs; they tweak their designs in response to feedback; and in the process, they develop an understanding of, for example, the relationship of mass transit to population density.

Performance: Games also involve trying on and performing different identities. Game identities are a complex mix of fact and fiction, self and other. Much of the first part of any contemporary game is spent customizing these characters. Children playing history games find themselves drawing both on their own life experiences and on things they have learned in class, much as an actor draws on a broad range of experience and knowledge in preparing for a part. This kind of performance encourages self-reflection and cultural analysis.

Expression refers to the ability to create new content, often inspired by the culture around us. In the new games culture, players are encouraged to design their own characters, make scrapbooks of their game play experience, animate movies using game avatars and share them with other consumers, take the game design tools and make their own additions to commercial games. For example, players of *Star Wars Galaxies*, a massively multiplayer game, have begun staging elaborate musical numbers which require the choreographing and synchronization of hundreds of players hitting the right combination of buttons at the same time in order to produce music videos. The result is bizarre—blue-skinned and snake-haired dancing women getting jiggy with Lawrence Welk Christmas songs—but the challenges of producing them give us new respect for what they have accomplished. More and more kids are learning to express their ideas through digital movies or games. We are also seeing schools and arts centers—from OnRampArts in South Central Los Angeles to the Urban Games Academies held in Atlanta and Baltimore—teaching kids how to make their own games. Thinking about how to translate school curriculum into game content forces students to think about what they can do with the things they are learning and how to determine what content is most important.

Collaboration describes how members of online communities share information, pool knowledge, compare notes, evaluate evidence, and solve large-scale problems. This process is perhaps most spectacularly illustrated by alternative reality games, informational scavenger hunts conducted in both digital and real spaces and involving teams of hundreds of people working together to master a particular set of puzzles. For example, in *I-Love-Bees*, a game designed to promote *Halo 2*, players had to recognize patterns of numbers as global positioning data, figure out that each of those numbers referred to the location of pay phones scattered across all fifty U.S. states, get people to go to those locations at a specific time, and await instructions for the next set of problems (McGonigal, 2005).

Judgment: Through games, young people are learning how to play, perform, express themselves, and collaborate in large-scale communities. Yet, there is another skill often missing—judgment. Researchers using games in the classroom are finding that children are adept at learning new content through games but the game itself remains largely transparent: Few kids ask about the motives or accuracy of the ways games depict the world (Schrier, 2005). Judgment requires not only an awareness of the traditional concerns of media literacy educators (about who is creating what images for what purposes) but also newer questions about ethics, focused on the choices that kids are making as game players and game creators. Up until now, media literacy education has been preoccupied with effects—what media do to kids. A focus on ethics allows one to address many of the same concerns but from the perspective of your own choices and responsibilities—what kids are doing with media.

Each of these skills has implications for how we will live, work, and vote in the future. Each can heighten our consciousness of ourselves and our surrounding culture. Students need to learn a new vocabulary to reflect on these new media experiences and their responsibilities as members of such communities.

The few organizations out there who are promoting the instruction of these new skills and competencies often adopt too narrow a perspective on their value and importance. Too often these skills are understood primarily in terms of their value in enhancing traditional school learning, as if the child's entire life was taking place within the school house. Instead we should recognize participation and collaboration as central to the way our future society will function and thus see these not as schoolroom skills but as lifelong competencies. These are the things that kids need to learn to succeed in the 21st century. They are not simply ways to motivate mastery over the same old stuff that kids have been learning for generation.

That said, we also need to guard against the tendency to throw out the baby with the bathwater. New-media literacy skills must build on traditional literacy skills. One cannot, for example, be part of an online community without being able to read and write. Each emerging medium demands new competencies, but those skills required by earlier media should still remain a central aspect of a good education. We seem to be pulled by polarizing tendencies—to protect traditional literacy by ignoring media change or to ignore traditional literacy as we seize the opportunities represented by new media. That's my concern about the current turn towards "visual literacy" training, which seems to operate on the assumption that communications in the future will be picture-based rather than text-based. Such an approach ignores the complex interactions between words and images that run across human history. And it ignores a range of other kinds of media experience centering around sound or tactility which do not fall comfortably into either category. The educated person of the future will be able to comprehend and express their ideas through the broadest possible range of media.

By the same token, we want to build upon several decades of important groundwork already done in the media literacy movement. That movement has helped to build the infrastructure which we need in order to expand access to these new participatory skills; it has developed many classroom activities which introduce students to core concepts they need to analyze the current media landscape; and perhaps most importantly, it has raised ethical concerns about media which need to be part of any further agenda for change. In short, I come not to bury media literacy but to expand it—opening it up to new perspectives and approaches which more fully respond to the situations young people face in their everyday lives.

In the ideal society, media literacy principles will be taught through every possible venue. In schools, they should be understood not as some added subject which our teachers are obligated to fit somewhere into the already overcrowded schedule. Rather, media literacy should be understood as a paradigm shift, much like multiculturalism or globalization. Media change impacts every aspect of our society. Media literacy has implications for all of the existing school subjects. In each subject, what we teach and how we teach should be reshaped by expectations of what it takes to prepare kids to be full participants within a mediated society. These principles of media literacy should be part of every other educational context—taught through informal clubs and activities, through churches and community organizations, through museums, libraries, and public institutions, and through the media itself. Indeed, in so far as popular culture and educational television has been instrumental across the past several decades in promoting traditional literacy (think *Sesame Street*), then we should demand that future programming should help kids to better understand their rights and responsibilities in the ever-changing media environment.

This is a tall order. We are going to need a large community of people focused on achieving these goals. The MacArthur Project hopes to generate a public conversation about the kinds of media literacy education needed as we move into the 21st century.

Notes

1   For more about this distinctly Japanese mode of cultural production and consumption, see Ito (2005). Ito has since become interested in the ways that American Otaku culture represents "one prototype for emergent forms of literacy." See The New Media Consortium (2005).
2   For more on role play and identity formation, see Geraldine Blustein (2004).
3   For more on these issues, see Henry Jenkins (in progress).
4   Johnson specifically cites *Lost* as an example of complexity in contemporary television during an appearance at the MIT Communications Forum. See http://web.mit.edu/comm-forum/forums/popular_culture.htm.
5   For a fuller discussion of *The Matrix*, see Henry Jenkins (2006a).

References

Bagge, P. (2003). Get it?, http://whatisthematrix.warnerbros.com, reproduced in A. Wachowski & L. Wachowski (Eds.), *The Matrix comics*. New York: Burlyman Entertainment.

Bertozzi, V. (2005, October). Personal correspondence.

Bertozzi, V., & Jenkins, H. (in press). Artistic expression in the age of participatory culture: How and why young people create. In B. Ivey & S. Tepper (Eds.), *Engaging art: The next great transformation of America's cultural life*. New York: Routledge.

Blustein, G. (2004). *Girl-making: A cross-cultural ethnography of growing up.* Oxford, UK: Berghahn Books.

Buckingham, D., & Sefton-Green, J. (2004). Structure, agency, and pedagogy in children's media culture. In J. Tobin (Ed.), *Pikachu's global adventure: The rise and fall of Pokémon* (pp. 12–33). Durham, NC: Duke University Press.

Chan, A. J. (2002). *Collaborative news networks: Distributed editing, collective action, and the construction of online news on Slashdot.* Master's thesis, Comparative Media Studies Program, MIT.

Dyson, A. H. (1997). *Writing superheroes: Contemporary childhood, popular culture, and classroom literacy.* New York: Teachers College Press.

Gee, J. P. (2005). *Language, learning, and gaming: A critique of traditional schooling.* New York: Routledge.

Jenkins, H. (2006a). *Convergence culture: Where old and new media collide.* New York: New York University Press.

Jenkins, H. (2006b). Pop cosmopolitanism: Mapping cultural flows in an age of convergence. In H. Jenkins (Ed.), *Fans, bloggers, and gamers: Essays on participatory culture.* New York: New York University Press.

Jenkins, H. (in progress). Just men in tights: Revising silver age comics in an era of diversification.

Ito, M. (2005). Technologies of the childhood imagination: Yugioh, media mixes and everyday cultural production. In J. Karaganis & N. Jeremijenko (Eds.), *Network/netplay: Structures of participation in digital culture.* Durham, NC: Duke University Press.

Johnson, S. (2005). *Everything bad is good for you: How today's popular culture is actually making us smarter.* New York: Riverhead.

Levy, P. (2000). *Collective intelligence: Mankind's emerging world in cyberspace.* New York: Perseus.

Lofficer, R., Thomas, R., & McKeever, T. (1997). *Superman's Metropolis.* New York: DC.

Mack, D. (2005). *Daredevil: Echo-Vision Quest* (New York: Marvel).

McGonigal, J. (2003). *This is not a game: Immersive aesthetics and collective play.* Retrieved from http://www.seanstewart.org/beast/mcgonigal/notagame/paper.pdf

Millar, M. (2004). *Superman: Red son.* New York: DC.

New Media Consortium. (2005). *Media literacy: A global imperative.* (Stanford, CA: The New Media Consortium). http://www.adobe.com/education/pdf/globalimperative.pdf.

Ostrander, J., Truman, T., & Mandrake, T. (2000). *Superman: The Kents.* New York: DC.

Prensky, M. (2001). Digital natives, digital immigrants, *On the Horizon*, NCB University Press. Retrieved from http://www.marcprensky.com/writing/Prensky%20%20Digital%20Natives,%20Digital%20Immigrants%20-%20Part1.pdf

Salomon, S. (1996). *Distributed cognitions: Psychological and educational considerations.* Cambridge, UK: Cambridge University Press.

Schrier, K. (2005). *Revolutionizing history education: Using augmented reality games to teach histories.* Master's thesis, Comparative Media Studies Program, MIT.

Squire, K. (2005). Civilization III as a world history sandbox. In M. Bittanti (Ed.), *Civilization and its discontents: Virtual history, real fantasies.* Milan: Lugologica Press. Retrieved from http://labweb.education.wisc.edu/room130/PDFs/civ3-education-chapter.doc

Verlager, A. K. (2005, October). Personal communication.

Wolfe, S. A., & Heath, S. B. (1992). *The braid of literature: Children's world of reading.* Cambridge, MA: Harvard University Press.

Chapter 2

Good Videogames, the Human Mind, and Good Learning

James Paul Gee

Introduction

This chapter has two main points to make and, in turn, the chapter falls into two main parts. My first point—a point some will find startling at first—is that good videogames (by which I mean both computer games and games played on platforms like the Xbox, Cube, or PlayStation) represent a technology that illuminates how the human mind works. My second point follows, in part, from this first one. It is that good videogames incorporate good learning principles and have a great deal to teach us about learning in and out of schools, whether or not a videogame is part of this learning.

Videogames and the Mind

Videogames are a relatively new technology replete with important, and not yet fully understood, implications (Gee, 2003). Scholars have historically viewed the human mind through the lens of a technology they thought worked like the mind. Locke and Hume, for example, taking the technology of literacy as their guide, argued that the mind was like a blank slate on which experience wrote ideas. Much later, modern cognitive scientists argued that the mind worked like a digital computer, calculating generalizations and deductions via a logic-like rule system (Newell & Simon, 1972). More recently, some cognitive scientists, inspired by distributed parallel-processing computers and complex adaptive networks, have argued that the mind works by storing records of actual experiences and constructing intricate patterns of connections among them (Clark, 1989; Gee, 1992). So we get different pictures of the mind: mind as a slate waiting to be written on, mind as software, mind as a network of connections.

Human societies get better through history at building technologies that more closely capture some of what the human mind can do and getting these technologies to do mental work publicly. Writing, digital computers, and networks each allow us to externalize some functions of the mind.

Though they are not commonly thought of in these terms, videogames are a new technology in this same line. They are a new tool with which to think about the mind and through which we can externalize some of its functions. Videogames of the sort I am concerned with—games like *Half-Life 2*, *Rise of Nations*, *Full Spectrum Warrior*, *Morrowinds: The Elder Scrolls*, and *World of WarCraft*—are what I would call "action-and-goal-directed preparations for, and simulations of, embodied experience." A mouthful, indeed, but an important one.

To make clear what I mean by the claim that games act like the human mind and are a good place to study and produce human thinking and learning, let me first briefly summarize some recent research in cognitive science, the science that studies how the mind works (Bransford, Brown, & Cocking, 2000). Consider, for instance, the remarks below (in the quotes below, the word "comprehension" means "understanding words, actions, events, or things"):

> . . . comprehension is grounded in perceptual simulations that prepare agents for situated action. (Barsalou, 1999a, p. 77)

> . . . to a particular person, the meaning of an object, event, or sentence is what that person can do with the object, event, or sentence. (Glenberg, 1997, p. 3)

What these remarks mean is this: Human understanding is not primarily a matter of storing general concepts in the head or applying abstract rules to experience. Rather, humans think and understand best when they can imagine (simulate) an experience in such a way that the simulation prepares them for actions they need and want to take in order to accomplish their goals (Barsalou, 1999b; Clark, 1997; Glenberg & Robertson, 1999).

Let's take weddings as an example, though we could just as well have taken war, love, inertia, democracy, or anything. You don't understand the word or the idea of weddings by meditating on some general definition of weddings. Rather, you have had experiences of weddings, in real life and through texts and media. On the basis of these experiences, you can simulate different wedding scenarios in your mind. You construct these simulations differently for different occasions, based on what actions you need to take to accomplish specific goals in specific situations. You can move around as a character in the mental simulation as yourself, imaging your role in the wedding, or you can "play" other characters at the wedding (e.g., the minister), imaging what it is like to be that person.

You build your simulations to understand and make sense of things, but also to help you prepare for action in the world. You can act in the simulation and test out what consequences follow, before you act in the real world. You can role-play another person in the model and try to see what motivates their actions or might follow from them before you respond in the real world. So I am arguing that the mind is a simulator, but one that builds simulations to purposely prepare for specific actions and to achieve specific goals (i.e., they are built around win states).

Videogames turn out to be the perfect metaphor for what this view of the mind amounts to, just as slates and computers were good metaphors for earlier views of the mind. To see this, let me now turn to a characterization of videogames and then I will put my remarks about the mind and games together.

Videogames usually involve a visual and auditory world in which the player manipulates a virtual character (or characters). They often come with editors or other sorts of software with which the player can make changes to the game world or even build a new game world. The player can make a new landscape, a new set of buildings, or new characters. The player can set up the world so that certain sorts of actions are allowed or disallowed. The player is building a new world, but is doing so by using and modifying the original visual images (really the code for them) that came with the game. One simple example of this is the way in which players can build new skateboard parks in a game like *Tony Hawk's Pro Skater*. The player must place ramps, trees, grass, poles, and other things in space in such a way that players can manipulate their virtual characters to skate the park in a fun and challenging way.

Even when players are not modifying games, they play them with goals in mind, the achievement of which counts as their "win state" (and it's the existence of such win states that, in part, distinguishes games from simulations). These goals are set by the player, but, of course, in collaboration with the world the game designers have created (and, at least in more open-ended games, players don't just accept developer's goals, they make real choices of their own). Players must carefully consider the design of the world and consider how it will or will not facilitate specific actions they want to take to accomplish their goals.

One technical way that psychologists have talked about this sort of situation is through the notion of "affordances" (Gibson, 1979). An "affordance" is a feature of the world (real or virtual) that will allow for a certain action to be taken, but only if it is matched by an ability in an actor who has the wherewithal to carry out such an action. For example, in the massive multiplayer game *World of WarCraft* stags can be killed and skinned (for making leather), but only by characters that have learned the skinning skill. So a stag is an affordance for skinning for such a player, but not for one who has no such skill. The large spiders in the game are not an affordance for skinning for any players, since they cannot be skinned at all. Affordances are relationships between the world and actors.

Playing *World of WarCraft*, or any other videogame, is all about such affordances. The player must learn to *see* the game world—designed by the developers, but set in motion in particular directions by the players, and, thus, co-designed by them—in terms of such affordances (Gee, 2005). Broadly speaking, players must think in terms of "What are the features of this world that can enable the actions I am capable of carrying out and that I want to carry out in order to achieve my goals?"

So now, after our brief bit about the mind and about games, let's put the two together. The view of the mind I have sketched, in fact, argues, as far as I am concerned, that the mind works rather like a videogame. For humans, effective thinking is more like running a simulation than it is about forming abstract generalizations cut off from experiential realities. Effective thinking is about perceiving the world such that the human actor sees how the world, at a specific time and place (as it is given, but also modifiable), can afford the opportunity for actions that will lead to a successful accomplishment of the actor's goals. Generalizations are formed—when they are—bottom-up from experience and imagination of experience. Videogames externalize the search for affordances, for a match between character (actor) and world, but this is just the heart and soul of effective human thinking and learning in any situation.

As a game player you learn to see the world of each different game you play in a quite different way. But in each case you see the world in terms of how it will afford the sorts of embodied actions you (and your virtual character, your surrogate body in the game) need to take to accomplish your goals (to win in the short and long run). For example, you see the world in *Full Spectrum Warrior* as routes (for your squad) between cover (e.g., corner to corner, house to house) because this prepares you for the actions you need to take, namely attacking without being vulnerable to attack yourself. You see the world of *Thief* in terms of light and dark, illumination and shadows, because this prepares you for the different actions you need to take in this world, namely hiding, disappearing into the shadows, sneaking, and otherwise moving unseen to your goal.

When we sense such a match, in a virtual world or the real world, between our way of seeing the world, at a particular time and place, and our action goals—and we have the skills to carry these actions out—then we feel great power and satisfaction. Things click, the world looks as if it were made for us. While commercial games often stress a match between worlds and characters like soldiers or thieves, there is no reason why other games could not let players experience such a match between the world and the way a particular type of scientist, for instance, sees and acts on the world (Gee, 2004). Such games would involve facing the sorts of problems and challenges that type of scientist does, and living and playing by the rules that type of scientist uses. Winning would mean just what it does to a scientist: feeling a sense of accomplishment through the production of knowledge to solve deep problems.

I have argued for the importance of videogames as "action-and-goal-directed preparations for, and simulations of, embodied experience." They are the new technological arena—just as were literacy and computers earlier—around which we can study the mind and externalize some of its most important features to improve human thinking and learning. But games have two other features that suit them to be good models for human thinking and learning externalized out in the world. These two additional features are: (a) they distribute intelligence via the creation of smart tools, and (b) they allow for the creation of "cross-functional affiliation," a particularly important form of collaboration in the modern world.

Consider first how good games distribute intelligence (Brown, Collins, & Dugid, 1989). In *Full Spectrum Warrior*, the player uses the buttons on the controller to give orders to two squads of soldiers. The instruction manual that comes with the game makes it clear from the outset that players, in order to play the game successfully, must take on the values, identities, and ways of thinking of a professional soldier: "Everything about your squad," the manual explains, "is the result of careful planning and years of experience on the battlefield. Respect that experience, soldier, since it's what will keep your soldiers alive" (p. 2). In the game, that experience—the skills and knowledge of professional military expertise—is distributed between the virtual soldiers and the real-world player. The soldiers in the player's squads have been trained in movement formations; the role of the player is to select the best position for them on the field. The virtual characters (the soldiers) know part of the task (various movement formations) and the player must come to know another part (when and where to engage in such formations). This kind of distribution holds for every aspect of military knowledge in the game.

By distributing knowledge and skills this way—between the virtual characters (smart tools) and the real-world player—the player is guided and supported by the knowledge built into the virtual soldiers. This offloads some of the cognitive burden from the learner, placing it in smart tools that can do more than the learner is currently capable of doing by him- or herself. It allows the player to begin to act, with some degree of effectiveness, before being really competent—"performance before competence." The player thereby eventually comes to gain competence through trial, error, and feedback, not by wading through a lot of text before being able to engage in activity. Such distribution also allows players to internalize not only the knowledge and skills of a professional (a professional soldier in this case) but also the concomitant values ("doctrine," as the military says) that shape and explain how and why that knowledge is developed and applied in the world. There is no reason why other professions—scientists, doctors, government officials, urban planners (Shaffer, 2004)—could not be modeled and distributed in this fashion as a deep form of value-laden learning (and, in turn, learners could compare and contrast different value systems as they play different games).

Finally, let me turn to the creation of "cross-functional affiliation." Consider a small group partying (hunting and questing) together in a massive multiplayer game like *World of WarCraft*. The group might well be composed of a Hunter, Warrior, Druid, and Priest. Each of these types of characters has quite different skills and plays the game in a different way. Each group member (player) must learn to be good at his or her special skills and also learn to integrate these skills as a team member within the group as a whole. Each team member must also share some common knowledge about the game and game play with all the other members of the group—including some understanding of the specialist skills of other player types—in order to achieve a successful integration. So each member of the group must have specialist knowledge (intensive knowledge) and general common knowledge (extensive knowledge), including knowledge of the other member's functions.

Players—who are interacting with each other, in the game and via a chat system—orient to each other not in terms of their real-world race, class, culture, or gender (these may very well be unknown or if communicated made up as fictions). They must orient to each other, first and foremost, through their identities as game players and players of *World of WarCraft* in particular. They can, in turn, use their real-world race, class, culture, and gender as strategic resources if and when they please, and the group can draw on the differential real-world resources of each player, but in ways that do not force anyone into pre-set racial, gender, cultural, or class categories.

This form of affiliation—what I will call cross-functional affiliation—has been argued to be crucial for the workplace teams in modern "new capitalist" workplaces, as well as in modern forms of social activism (Beck, 1999; Gee, 2004; Gee, Hull, & Lankshear, 1996). People specialize, but integrate and share, organized around a primary affiliation to their common goals and using their cultural and social differences as strategic resources, not as barriers.

Good Videogames and Good Learning

So videogames, though a part of popular culture, are, like literacy and computers, sites where we can study and exercise the human mind in ways that may give us deeper insights into human thinking and learning, as well as new ways to engage learners in deep and engaged learning. And, in fact, one of the biggest contributions the study of good videogames can make is to illuminate ways in which learning works when it works best for human beings. In part because they externalize the way in which the human mind thinks, good videogames often organize learning in deep and effective ways.

Many good computer and videogames, games like *Deus Ex*, *The Elder Scrolls III: Morrowind*, or *Rise of Nations*, are long, complex, and difficult, especially for beginners. As we well know from school, young people are not always eager to do difficult things. When adults are faced with the challenge of getting them to do so, two choices are often available. We can force them, which is the main solution schools use. Or, a temptation when profit is at stake, though not unknown in school either, we can dumb down the product. Neither option is open to the game industry, at least for the moment. They can't force people to play and most avid gamers don't want their games short or easy games. Indeed, game reviews regularly damn easy or short games.

For people interested in learning, this raises an interesting question. How do good game designers manage to get new players to learn their long, complex, and difficult games and not only learn them but pay to do so? It won't do simply to say games are "motivating." That just begs the question of "Why?" Why is a long, complex, and difficult videogame motivating? I believe it is something about how games are designed to trigger learning that makes them so deeply motivating.

So the question is: How do good game designers manage to get new players to learn long, complex, and difficult games? The answer, I believe, is this: The designers of many good games have hit on profoundly good methods of getting people to learn and to enjoy learning. They have had to, since games that were bad at getting themselves learned didn't get played and the companies that made them lost money. Furthermore, it turns out that these learning methods are similar in many respects to cutting-edge principles being discovered in research on human learning (for details, see Gee, 2003, 2004, 2005 and the references therein).

Good game designers are practical theoreticians of learning, since what makes games deep is that players are exercising their learning muscles, though often without knowing it and without having to pay overt attention to the matter. Under the right conditions, learning, like sex, is biologically motivating and pleasurable for humans (and other primates). It is a hook that game designers own to a greater degree—thanks to the interactivity of games—than do movies and books.

But the power of videogames resides not just in their present instantiations but in the promises the technologies by which they are made hold

out for the future. Game designers can make worlds where people can have meaningful new experiences, experiences that their places in life would never allow them to have or even experiences no human being has ever had before. These experiences have the potential to make people smarter and more thoughtful.

Good games already do this and they will do it more and more in the future. *Star Wars: Knights of the Old Republic* immerses the player in issues of identity and responsibility: What responsibility do I bear for what an earlier, now transformed, "me" did? *Deus Ex: Invisible War* asks the player to make choices about the role ability and equality will or won't play in society: If we were all truly equal in ability would that mean we would finally have a true meritocracy? Would we want it? In these games, such thoughtful questions are not abstractions, they are part and parcel of the fun and interaction of playing.

I care about these matters both as a cognitive scientist and as a gamer. I believe that we can make school and workplace learning better if we pay attention to good computer and videogames. This does not necessarily mean using game technologies in school and at work, though that is something I advocate. It means applying the fruitful principles of learning that good game designers have hit on, whether or not we use a game as a carrier of these principles. My book *What Video Games Have to Teach Us About Learning and Literacy* (2003) lists many of these principles. Science educator Andy diSessa's book *Changing Minds: Computers, Learning, and Literacy* (2000) offers many related principles without ever mentioning videogames (see also chapter 9 by diSessa in this book).

There are many good principles of learning built into good computer and videogames. These are all principles that could and should be applied to school learning tomorrow, though this is unlikely given the current trend for skill-and-drill, scripted instruction, and standardized multiple choice testing. The principles are particularly important for so-called "at risk" learners, students who have come to school under-prepared, who have fallen behind, or who have little support for school-based literacy and language skills outside of school.

The principles are neither conservative nor liberal, neither traditionalist, nor progressive. They adopt some of each side, reject some of each, and stake out a different space. If implemented in schools they would necessitate significant changes in the structure and nature of formal schooling as we have long known it, changes that may eventually be inevitable anyway given modern technologies.

I list a baker's dozen below. We can view this list as a checklist: The stronger any game is on more of the features on the list, the better its score for learning. The list is organized into three sections: I Empowered Learners;

II Problem Solving; III Understanding. Under each item on the list I first give a principle relevant to learning, then a comment on games in regard to that principle, as well as some example games that are strong on that principle. I then discuss the educational implications of the principle. Those interested in more ample citations to research that supports these principles and how they apply to learning things like science in school should consult the references in cited in Gee (2003, 2004, 2005). I should point out as well that the first part of this chapter has already discussed some of learning principles that we don't need to discuss further below, since distributed knowledge and cross-functional affiliation are themselves powerful forms of social organization for learning and knowledge building. So is the way in which good videogames teach players to look for and build affordances into their learning environments.

I Empowered Learners

1 Co-design

Principle: Good learning requires that learners feel like active agents (producers) not just passive recipients (consumers).

Games: In a videogame, players make things happen. They don't just consume what the "author" (game designer) has placed before them. Videogames are interactive. The player does something and the game does something back that encourages the player to act again. In good games, players feel that their actions and decisions—and not just the designers' actions and decisions—are co-creating the world they are in and the experiences they are having. What the player does matters and each player, based on his or her own decisions and actions, takes a different trajectory through the game world.

Example: The Elder Scrolls: Morrowind is an extreme example of a game where each decision the player makes changes the game in ways that ensure that each player's game is, in the end, different from any other player's. But at some level this is true of most games. Players take different routes through *Castlevania: Symphony of the Night* and do different things in different ways in *Tony Hawk's Underground*.

Education: Co-design means ownership, buy-in, engaged participation. It is a key part of motivation. It also means learners must come to understand the design of the domain they are learning so that they can make good

choices about how to affect that design. Do student decisions ar
make a difference in the classroom curriculum? Are students
design their own learning? If the answers are no, what gives st
feeling of being agents in their own learning? Forced and enforced group
discussions are about as far as interactivity goes in most classrooms, if it
goes that far. The whole curriculum should be shaped by learners' actions
and react back on the learner in meaningful ways.

2 *Customize*

Principle: Different styles of learning work better for different people.
People cannot be agents of their own learning if they cannot make decisions about how their learning will work. At the same time, they should be
able (and encouraged) to try new styles.

Games: Good games achieve this goal in one (or both) of two ways. In some
games, players are able to customize the game play to fit their learning and
playing styles. In others, the game is designed to allow different styles of
learning and playing to work.

Example: Rise of Nations allows players to customize myriad aspects of the
game play to their own styles, interests, and desires. *Deus Ex* and its sequel
Deus Ex: Invisible War both allow quite different styles of play (and thus
learning, too) to succeed.

Education: Classrooms adopting this principle would allow students to discover their favored learning styles and to try new ones without fear. In the
act of customizing their own learning, students would learn a good deal not
only about how and why they learn, but about learning and thinking themselves. Can students engage in such customization in the classroom? Do
they get to reflect on the nature of their own learning and learning in general? Are there multiple ways to solve problems? Are students encouraged
to try out different learning styles and different problems solutions without
risking a bad grade?

3 *Identity*

Principle: Deep learning requires an extended commitment and such a
commitment is powerfully recruited when people take on a new identity
they value and in which they become heavily invested—whether this be a
child "being a scientist doing science" in a classroom or an adult taking on
a new role at work.

Games: Good games offer players identities that trigger a deep investment on the part of the player. They achieve this goal in one of two ways. Some games offer a character so intriguing that players want to inhabit the character and can readily project their own fantasies, desires, and pleasures onto the character. Other games offer a relatively empty character whose traits the player must determine, but in such a way that the player can create a deep and consequential life history in the game world for the character.

Example: Metal Solid Gear offers a character (Solid Snake) that is so well developed that he is, though largely formed by the game's designers, a magnet for player projections. *Animal Crossing* and *The Elder Scrolls: Morrowind* offer, in different ways, blank-slate characters for whom the player can build a deeply involving life and history. On the other hand, an otherwise good game like *Freedom Fighters* offers us characters that are both too anonymous and not changeable enough by the player to trigger deep investment.

Education: School is often built around the "content fetish," the idea that an academic area like biology or social science is constituted by some definitive list of facts or body of information that can be tested in a standardized way. But academic areas are not first and foremost bodies of facts, they are, rather, first and foremost, the activities and ways of knowing through which such facts are generated, defended, and modified. Such activities and ways of knowing are carried out by people who adopt certain sorts of identities, who adopt certain ways with words, actions, and interactions, as well as certain values, attitudes, and beliefs.

Learners need to know what the "rules of the game" are and who plays it. They need to know how to take on the identity of a certain sort of scientist, if they are doing science, and operate by a certain set of values, attitudes, and actions. Otherwise they have no deep understanding of a domain and will surely never know why anyone would want to learn or even spend a lifetime of learning in that domain in the first place.

Ironically, when learners adopt and practice such an identity and engage in the forms of talk and action connected to it, facts come free—they are learned as part and parcel of being a certain sort of person needing to do certain sorts of things for one's own purposes and goals (Shaffer, 2004). Out of the context of identity and activity, facts are hard to learn and last in the learner's mind a very short time indeed.

4 Manipulation and distributed knowledge

Principle: As I suggested in the first part of this chapter, cognitive research suggests that for humans perception and action are deeply interconnected

(Barsalou, 1999a, b; Clark, 1997; Glenberg, 1997; Glenberg & Robertson, 1999). Thus, fine-grained action at a distance—for example, when a person is manipulating a robot at a distance or watering a garden via a webcam on the Internet—causes humans to feel as if their bodies and minds have stretched into a new space (Clark, 2003). More generally, humans feel expanded and empowered when they can manipulate powerful tools in intricate ways that extend their area of effectiveness.

Games: Computer and videogames inherently involve action at a (albeit virtual) distance. The more and better a player can manipulate a character, the more the player invests in the game world. Good games offer characters that the player can move intricately, effectively, and easily through the world. Beyond characters, good games offer the player intricate, effective, and easy manipulation of the world's objects, objects which become tools for carrying out the player's goals.

Example: Tomb Raider, Tom Clancy's Splinter Cell, and *ICO* allow such fine-grained and interesting manipulation of one's character that they achieve a strong effect of pulling the player into their worlds. *Rise of Nations* allows such effective control of buildings, landscapes, and whole armies as tools that the player feels like god. *Prince of Persia* excels both in terms of character manipulation and everything in its environment serving as effective tools for player action.

One key feature of the virtual characters and objects that game players manipulate is that they are "smart tools." The character the player controls—Lara Croft, for example—knows things the player doesn't, for instance how to climb ropes, leap chasms, and scale walls. The player knows things the character doesn't, like when, where, and why to climb, leap, or scale. The player and the character each have knowledge that must be integrated together to play the game successfully. This is an example of distributed knowledge, knowledge split between two things (here a person and a virtual character) that must be integrated.

A game like *Full Spectrum Warrior* takes this principle much further. In this game, the player controls two squads of four soldiers each. The soldiers know lots and lots of things about professional military practice, for example, how to take various formations under fire and how to engage in various types of group movements in going safely from cover to cover. The player need not know these things. The player must learn other aspects of professional military practice, namely what formations and movements to order, when, where, and why. The real actor in this game is the player and the soldiers blended together through their shared, distributed, and integrated knowledge.

Education: What allows a learner to feel that his or her body and mind have extended into the world being studied or investigated, into the world of biology or physics, for example? Part of what does this is "smart tools," namely tools and technologies that allow the learner to manipulate that world in a fine-grained way. Such tools have their own in-built knowledge and skills that allow the learner much more power over the world being investigated than he or she has unaided by such tools.

Let me give one concrete example of what I am talking about. Galileo discovered the laws of the pendulum because he knew and applied geometry to the problem, not because he played around with pendulums or saw a church chandelier swinging (as myth has it). Yet it is common for liberal educators to ask children innocent of geometry or any other such tool to play around with pendulums and discover for themselves the laws by which they work. This is actually a harder problem than the one Galileo confronted—geometry set possible solutions for him and led him to think about pendulums in certain ways and not others. Of course, today there are a great many technical tools available beyond geometry and algebra (though students usually don't even realize that geometry and algebra are smart tools, different from each other in the way they approach problems and the problems for which they are best suited).

Do students in the classroom share knowledge with smart tools? Do they become powerful actors by learning to integrate their own knowledge with the knowledge built into their tools? The real-world player and the virtual soldiers in *Full Spectrum Warrior* come to share a body of skills and knowledge that is constitutive of a certain type of professional practice. Do students engage in authentic professional practices in the classroom through such sharing? Professional practice is crucial here, because, remember, real learning in science, for example, is constituted by *being a type of scientist doing a type of science* not reciting a fact you don't understand. It is thinking, acting, and valuing like a scientist of a certain sort. It is "playing by the rules" of a certain sort of science.

II Problem Solving

5 *Well-order problems*

Principle: Given human creativity, if learners face problems early on that are too freeform or too complex, they often form creative hypotheses about how to solve these problems, but hypotheses that don't work well for later problems (even for simpler ones, let alone harder ones). They have been "sent down a garden path." The problems learners face early on are crucial and should be well designed to lead them to hypotheses that work well, not just on these problems, but as aspects of the solutions of later, harder, problems as well.

Games: Problems in good games are well ordered. In particular, early problems are designed to lead players to form good guesses about how to proceed when they face harder problems later on in the game. In this sense, earlier parts of a good game are always looking forward to later parts.

Example: Return to Castle Wildenstein and *Fatal Frame 2: Crimson Butterfly,* though radically different games, both do a good job of offering players problems that send them down fruitful paths for what they will face later in the game. They each prepare the player to get better and better at the game and to face more difficult challenges later in the game.

Education: Work on connectionism and distributed parallel processing in cognitive science has shown that the order in which learners confront problems in a problem space is important (Clark, 1989; Elman, 1991a, b). Confronting complex problems too early can lead to creative solutions, but approaches that won't work well for even simpler later problems. "Anything goes"—"just turn learners loose in rich environments"—"no need for teachers"—these are bad theories of learning; they are, in fact, the progressive counterpart of the traditionalists' skill-and-drill.

Learners are novices. Leaving them to float amidst rich experiences with no guidance only triggers human beings' great penchant for finding creative but spurious patterns and generalizations that send learners down garden paths (Gee, 1992, 2001). The fruitful patterns or generalizations in any domain are the ones that are best recognized by those who already know how to look at the domain, know how the complex variables at play in the domain relate and interrelate to each other. And this is precisely what the learner does not yet know. Problems spaces can be designed to enhance the trajectory through which the learner traverses them. This does not mean leading the learner by the hand in a linear way. It means designing the problem space well.

6 Pleasantly frustrating

Principle: Learning works best when new challenges are pleasantly frustrating in the sense of being felt by learners to be at the outer edge of, but within, their "regime of competence." That is, these challenges feel hard but doable. Furthermore, learners feel—and get evidence—that their effort is paying off in the sense that they can see, even when they fail, how and if they are making progress.

Games: Good games adjust challenges and give feedback in such a way that different players feel the game is challenging but doable and that their effort is paying off. Players get feedback that indicates whether they are on the right road for success later on and at the end of the game. When players lose to a boss, perhaps several times, they get feedback about the sort of progress they are making so that at least they know if and how they are moving in the right direction towards success.

Example: Ratchet and Clank: Going Commando, Halo, and *Zone of the Enders: The Second Runner* (which has different difficulty levels) manage to stay at a doable but challenging level for many different sorts of players. They also give good feedback about where the player's edge of competence is and how it is developing, as does *Sonic Adventure 2 Battle. Rise of Nations* allows the player to customize many aspects of the difficulty level and gain feedback of whether things are getting too easy or too hard for the player.

Education: School is often too easy for some kids and too hard for others even when both are in the same classroom. Motivation for humans lies in challenges that feel challenging but doable and in gaining continual feedback that lets them know what progress they are making. Learners should be able to adjust the difficulty level while being encouraged to stay at the outer edge of, but inside, their level of competence. They should gain insight into where this level is and how it is changing over time. Good games don't come in grade levels that players must be "at." They realize that it doesn't matter when the player finishes or how he or she did in comparison to others—all that matters is that the player learns to play the game and comes to master it. Players who take longer and struggle longer at the beginning are sometimes the ones who, in the end, master the final boss most easily.

There are no "special" learners when it comes to videogames. Even an old guy like me can wander the plains of Morrowind long enough to pick up the ropes and master the game. The world doesn't go away, I can enter any time; it gives me constant feedback, but never a final judgment that I am a failure; and the final exam—the final boss—is willing to wait until I am good enough to beat him.

7 *Cycles of expertise*

Principle: Expertise is formed in any area by repeated cycles of learners practicing skills until they are nearly automatic, then having those skills fail in ways that cause the learners to have to think again and learn anew (Bereiter & Scardamalia, 1993). Then they practice this new skill set to an automatic level of mastery only to see it, too, eventually be challenged. In fact, this is the whole point of levels and bosses. Each level exposes the players to new challenges and allows them to get good at solving them. They are then confronted with a boss that makes them use these skills together with new ones they have to learn, and integrate with the old ones, to beat the boss. Then they move on to a new level and the process starts again.

Games: Good games create and support the cycle of expertise, with cycles of extended practice, tests of mastery of that practice, then a new challenge, and then new extended practice. This is, in fact, part of what constitutes good pacing in a game.

Example: Ratchet and Clank: Going Commando, Final Fantasy X, Halo, Viewtiful Joe, and *Pikmin* do a good job of alternating fruitful practice and new challenges such that players sense their own growing sophistication almost as an incremental curve as the game progresses.

Education: The cycle of expertise has been argued to be the very basis of expertise in any area. Experts routinize their skills and then challenge themselves with the new problems. These problems force them to open up their routinized skills to reflection, to learn new things, and then to integrate old and new. In turn this new integrated package of skills, a higher level of mastery, will be routinized through much practice. Games let learners experience expertise, schools usually don't. The cycle of expertise allows learners to learn how to manage their own lifelong learning and to become skilled at learning to learn. It also creates a rhythm and flow between practice and new learning and between mastery and challenge. It creates as well a feeling of accumulating knowledge and skills, rather than standing in the same place all the time or always starting over again at the beginning.

8 Information "on demand" and "just in time"

Principle: Human beings are quite poor at using verbal information (i.e., words) when given lots of it out of context and before that can see how it applies in actual situations. They use verbal information best when it is given "just in time" (when they can put it to use) and "on demand" (when they feel they need it).

Games: Good games give verbal information—for example, the sorts of information that is often in a manual—"just in time" and "on demand" in a game. Players don't need to read a manual to start but can use the manual as a reference after they have played a while; by this time too the game has already made concrete much of the verbal information in the manual through the player's experiences.

Example: System Shock 2 spreads its manual out over the first few levels in little green kiosks that give players—if they want it—brief pieces of information that will soon thereafter be visually instantiated or put to use by the player. *Enter the Matrix* introduces new information into its "on demand" glossary when and as it becomes relevant and useable and marks it clearly as new. The first few levels of *Goblin Commander: Unleash the Hoard* allows the player to enact the information that would be in manual, step by step, and then the game seamlessly moves into more challenging game play.

Education: If there is one thing we know, it is that humans are not good at learning through hearing or reading lots of words out of contexts of application that give these words situated or experiential meanings. Game manuals, just like science textbooks, make little sense if one tries to read them before having played the game. All one gets is lots of words that are confusing, have only quite general or vague meanings, and are quickly forgotten. After playing the game, the manual is lucid and clear because now every word in it now has a meaning related to an action-image, can be situated in different contexts of use for dialogue or action. The player even learns how to readjust (situate, customize) the meanings of game-related words for new game contexts. Now, of course, the player doesn't need to read the manual cover to cover but can use it as reference work to facilitate his or her own goals and needs.

Lectures and textbooks are fine "on demand," used when learners are ready for them, not otherwise. Learners need to play the game a bit before they gets lots of verbal information; they need to be able to get such information "just in time" when and where they need it and can see how it actually applies in action and practice. Since schools rarely do this, we all familiar with the well-known phenomenon that students with A gradess because they can pass multiple choice tests can't apply their knowledge in practice.

9 *Fish tanks*

Principle: In the real world, a fish tank can be a little simplified ecosystem that clearly displays some critical variables and their interactions that are otherwise obscured in the highly complex eco-system in the real world. Using the term metaphorically, fish tanks are good for learning: If we create simplified systems, stressing a few key variables and their interactions, learners who would otherwise be overwhelmed by a complex system (e.g.,

Newton's Laws of Motion operating in the real world) get to see some basic relationships at work and take the first steps towards their eventual mastery of the real system (e.g., they begin to know what to pay attention to).

Games: Fish tanks are stripped-down versions of the game. Good games offer players fish tanks, either as tutorials or as their first level or two. Otherwise it can be difficult for newcomers to understand the game as a whole system, since they often can't see the forest because of the trees.

Example: Rise of Nations' tutorial scenarios (like "Alfred the Great" or "The 100 Years War") are wonderful fish tanks, allowing the player to play scaled-down versions of the game that render key elements and relationships salient.

Education: In traditional education, learners hear words and drill on skills out of any context of use. In progressive education, they are left to their own devices immersed in a sea of complex experience, for example studying pond ecology. When confronted with complex systems, letting the learner see some of the basic variables and how they interact can be a good way into confronting more complex versions of the system later on. This follows from the same ideas that give rise to the well-ordered problems principle above. It allows learners to form good strong fruitful hypotheses at the outset and not go down garden paths by confronting too much complexity at the outset.

The real world is a complex place. Real scientists do not go out unaided to study it. Galileo showed up with geometry, ecologists show up with theories, models, and smart tools. Models are all simplifications of reality and initial models are usually fish tanks, simple systems that display the workings of some major variables. With today's capacity to build simulations, there is no excuse for the lack of fish tanks in schools (there aren't even many real fish tanks in classrooms studying ponds!).

10 *Sandboxes*

Principle: Sandboxes in the real world are safe havens for children which still look and feel like the real world. Using the term metaphorically, sandboxes are good for learning: If learners are put into a situation that feels like the real thing, but with risks and dangers greatly mitigated, they can learn well and still feel a sense of authenticity and accomplishment.

Games: Sandboxes are game play much like the real game, but where things cannot go too wrong too quickly or, perhaps, even at all. Good games offer players, either as tutorials or as their first level or two, sandboxes. You can't expect newcomers to learn if they feel too much pressure, understand too little, and feel like failures.

Example: Rise of Nations' "Quick Start" tutorial is an excellent sandbox. You feel much more of the complexity of the whole game than you do in a fish tank, but risks and consequences are mitigated compared to the "real" game. The first level of *System Shock 2* is a great example of a sandbox—exciting play where, in this case, things can't go wrong at all. In many good games, the first level is a sandbox or close to it.

Education: Here we face one of the worst problems with school: It's too risky and punishing. There is nothing worse than a game that lets you save only after you have gone through a whole long arduous level. You fail at the end and have to repeat everything, rather than being able to return to a save part-way through the level. You end up playing the beginning of the level perfectly over and over again until you master the final bits. The cost of taking risks, trying out new hypotheses, is too high. The player sticks to the tried and true well-trodden road, because failing will mean boring repetition of what he or she already well knows.

Good games don't do this. They create sandboxes in the beginning that make the player feel competent when they are not ("performance before competence") and thereafter they put a moratorium on any failures that will kill joy, risk taking, hypothesizing, and learning. Players do fail, of course; they die and try again, but in a way that makes failure part of the fun and central to the learning.

In school, learners, especially so-called "at risk" learners need what Stan Goto (2003) has called "horizontal learning"—time to "play around," to explore the area they are about to learn, to see what is there and what the lay of the land is, before they are forced up the vertical learning ladder of ever new skills. They need always to see failure as informative and part of the game, not as a final judgment or a device to forestall creativity, risk taking, and hypothesizing.

11 Skills as strategies

Principle: There is a paradox involving skills: People don't like practicing skills out of context over and over again, since they find such skill practice meaningless; but, without lots of skill practice, they cannot really get any good at what they are trying to learn. People learn and practice skills best when they see a set of related skills as a strategy to accomplish goals they want to accomplish.

Games: In good games, players learn and practice skill packages as part and parcel of accomplishing things they need and want to accomplish. They see the skills first and foremost as a strategy for accomplishing a goal and only secondarily as a set of discrete skills.

Example: Games like *Rise of Nations, Goblin Commander: Unleash the Hoard,* and *Pikmin* all do a good job at getting players to learn skills while paying attention to the strategies these skills are used to pull off. *Rise of Nations* even has skill tests that package certain skills that go together, show clearly how they enact a strategy, and allow the player to practice them as a functional set. The training exercises (which are games in themselves) that come with the *Metal Gear Solid* and *Metal Gear Solid: Sons of Liberty* are excellent examples (and are great fish tanks as well).

Education: We know very well that learning is a practice effect for human beings—the conservatives are right about that, we humans need practice and lots of it. But skills are best learned (often in sets) as strategies for carrying out meaningful functions.

Sounding-out letters, together with thinking of word families and looking for sub-patterns in words, works best when seen as functional devices to comprehend and use texts. It's not that one can't get reading tests passed by drilling isolated skills out of context—one certainly can. But what happens is that we then fuel the so-called "fourth-grade slump," the long-known phenomenon in which children seem to do all right learning to read (decode) in the early grades (at least in terms of passing tests), but then cannot handle the complex oral and written language they confront later in the content areas of school, e.g., science, math, social studies, etc. (Chall, Jacobs, & Baldwin, 1990; see the papers in the special issue of the *American Educator* 2003 devoted to what they call the "fourth-grade plunge").

These children aren't learning to "play the game"—and the game in school is ultimately using oral and written language to learn academic areas which all use language far more complicated than our everyday vernacular forms of language. Learners need to know how skills translate into strategies for playing the game.

III Understanding

12 System thinking

Principle: People learn skills, strategies, and ideas best when they see how they fit into an overall larger system to which they give meaning. In fact, any experience is enhanced when we understand how it fits into a larger meaningful whole. Players cannot view games as "eye candy," but must learn to see each game (actually each genre of game) as a distinctive semiotic system affording and discouraging certain sorts of actions and interactions.

Games: Good games help players see and understand how each of the elements in the game fits into the overall system of the game and its genre (type). Players get a feel for the "rules of the game"—that is, what works and what doesn't, how things go or don't go in this type of world.

Example: Games like *Rise of Nations*, *Age of Mythology*, *Pikmin*, *Call of Duty*, and *Mafia* give players a good feel for the overall world and game system they are in. They allow players to develop good intuitions about what works and about how what they are doing at the present moment fits into the trajectory of the game as a whole. Players come to have a good feel for and understanding of the genre of the game they are playing (and in *Pikmin's* case, this is a rather novel and hybrid genre). *Metal Gear Solid* and *Metal Gear Solid: Sons of Liberty* come with training exercises that strip away the pretty graphics to make clear how the player is meant to read the environment to enhance effective action and interaction in the game. If players stare at the pretty fish in the island paradise of *Far Cry*, they'll die in a minute. Players have to think of the environment they are in as a complex system that must be properly understood to plan effective action and anticipate unintended consequences on one's actions.

Education: We live, in today's high-tech, global world, amidt a myriad of complex systems, systems which interact with each other (Kelly, 1994). In such a world, untended consequences spread far and wide. In such a world being unable to see the forest for the trees is potentially disastrous. In school, when students fail to have a feeling for the whole system which they are studying, when they fail to see it as a set of complex interactions and relationships, each fact and isolated element they memorize for their tests is meaningless. Further, there is no way they can use these facts and elements as leverage for action—and we would hardly want them to, given that acting in complex systems with no understanding can lead to disasters. Citizens with such limited understandings are going to be dangers to themselves and others in the future.

13 *Meaning as action image*

Principle: Humans do not usually think through general definitions and logical principles. Rather, they think through experiences they have had and imaginative reconstructions of experience. You don't think and reason about weddings on the basis of generalities, but in terms of the wedding you have been to and heard about and imaginative reconstructions of them. It's your experiences that give weddings and the word *wedding* meaning(s). Furthermore, for humans, words and concepts have their deepest meanings when they are clearly tied to perception and action in the world.

Games: This is, of course, the heart and soul of computer and videogames (though it is amazing how many educational games violate this principle). Even barely adequate games make the meanings of words and concepts clear through experiences the player has and activities the player carries out, not through lectures, talking heads, or generalities. Good games can achieve marvelous effects here, making even philosophical points concretely realized in image and action.

Example: Games like *Star Wars: Knights of the Old Republic, Freedom Fighters, Mafia, Metal of Honor: Allied Assault*, and *Operation Flashpoint: Cold War Crisis* do a very good job at making ideas (e.g., continuity with one's past self), ideologies (e.g., freedom fighters vs. terrorists), identities (e.g., being a soldier), or events (e.g., the Normandy Invasion) concrete and deeply embedded in experience and activity.

Education: This principle is clearly related to the information "just in time" and "on demand" principle above. For human beings the comprehension of texts and the world is "grounded in perceptual simulations that prepare agents for situated action" (Barsalou, 1999a, p. 77). If you can't run any models in your head—and you can't if all you have is verbal, dictionary-like information—you can't really understand what you are reading, hearing, or seeing. That's how humans are built. And note, by the way, that this means there is a kinship between how the human mind works and how videogames work, since videogames are, indeed, perceptual simulations that the player must see as preparation for action or fail.

Conclusion

When we think of games, we think of fun. When we think of learning we think of work. Games show us this is wrong. They trigger deep learning that is itself part and parcel of the fun. It is what makes good games deep.

For those interested in spreading games and game technology into schools, workplaces, and other learning sites, it is striking to meditate on how few of the learning principles I have sketched out here can be found in so-called educational games. "Non-educational" games for young people, such as *Pajama Sam, Animal Crossing, Mario Sunshine,* and *Pikmin,* all use many of the principles fully and well. Not so for many a product used in school or for business or workplace learning. It is often said that what stops games from spreading to educational sites is their cost, where people usually have in mind the wonderful "eye candy" that games have become. But I would suggest that it is the cost to implement the above principles that is the real barrier. And the cost here is not just monetary. It is the cost, as well, of changing people's minds about learning—how and where it is done. It is the cost of changing one of our most change-resistant institutions: schools.

Let me end by making it clear that the above principles are neither "conservative" nor "liberal," "traditional" nor "progressive." The progressives are right in that situated embodied experience is crucial. The traditionalists are right that learners cannot be left to their own devices, they need smart tools, and, most importantly, they need good designers who guide and scaffold their learning (Kelly, 2003). For games, these designers are brilliant games writers like Warren Spector and Will Wright. For schools, these designers are teachers.

References

American Educator. (2003). Spring issue. Retrieved from http://www.aft.org/pubs-reports/american_educator/spring2003/index.html

Barsalou, L. W. (1999a). Language comprehension: Archival memory or preparation for situated action. *Discourse Processes, 28,* 61–80.

Barsalou, L. W. (1999b). Perceptual symbol systems. *Behavioral and Brain Sciences, 22,* 577–660.

Beck, U. (1999). *World risk society.* Oxford, UK: Blackwell.

Bereiter, C., & Scardamalia, M. (1993). *Surpassing ourselves: An inquiry into the nature and implications of expertise.* Chicago: Open Court.

Bransford, J., Brown, A. L., & Cocking, R. R. (2000). *How people learn: Brain, mind, experience, and school: Expanded edition.* Washington, DC: National Academy Press.

Brown, J. S., Collins, A., & Dugid, P. (1989). Situated cognition and the culture of learning. *Educational Researcher, 18,* 32–42.

Chall, J. S., Jacobs, V., & Baldwin, L. (1990). *The reading crisis: Why poor children fall behind.* Cambridge, MA: Harvard University Press.

Clark, A. (1989). *Microcognition: Philosophy, cognitive science, and parallel distributed processing.* Cambridge, MA: MIT Press.

Clark, A. (1997). *Being there: Putting brain, body, and world together again.* Cambridge, MA: MIT Press.

Clark, A. (2003). *Natural-born cyborgs: Why minds and technologies are made to merge.* Oxford, UK: Oxford University Press.

diSessa, A. A. (2000). *Changing minds: Computers, learning, and literacy*. Cambridge, MA: MIT Press.

Elman, J. (1991a). Distributed representations, simple recurrent networks and grammatical structure. *Machine Learning 7*: 195–225.

Elman, J. (1991b). *Incremental learning, or the importance of starting small*. Technical Report 9101, Center for Research in Language, University of California at San Diego.

Gee, J. P. (1992). *The social mind: Language, ideology, and social practice*. New York: Bergin & Garvey.

Gee, J. P. (2001). Progressivism, critique, and socially situated minds. In C. Dudley-Marling & C. Edelsky (Eds.), *The fate of progressive language policies and practices* (pp. 31–58). Urbana, IL: NCTE.

Gee, J. P. (2003). *What video games have to teach us about learning and literacy*. New York: Palgrave/Macmillan.

Gee, J. P. (2004). *Situated language and learning: A critique of traditional schooling*. London: Routledge.

Gee, J. P. (2005). *Why video games are good for your soul: Pleasure and learning*. Melbourne: Common Ground.

Gee, J. P., Hull, G., & Lankshear, C. (1996). *The new work order: Behind the language of the new capitalism*. Boulder, CO: Westview.

Gibson, J. J. (1979). *The ecological approach to visual perception*. Boston: Houghton Mifflin.

Glenberg, A. M. (1997). What is memory for. *Behavioral and Brain Sciences, 20*, 1–55.

Glenberg, A. M., & Robertson, D. A. (1999). Indexical understanding of instructions. *Discourse Processes, 28*, 1–26.

Goto, S. (2003). Basic writing and policy reform: Why we keep talking past each other. *Journal of Basic Writing, 21*, 16–32.

Kelly, A. E. (Ed.). (2003). Theme issue: The role of design in educational research. *Educational Researcher, 32*, 3–37.

Kelly, K. (1994). *Out of control: The new biology of machines, social systems, and the economic world*. Reading, MA: Addison-Wesley.

Newell, A., & Simon, H. A. (1972). *Human problem solving*. Englewood Cliffs, NJ: Prentice-Hall.

Shaffer, D. W. (2004). Pedagogical praxis: The professions as models for post-industrial education. *Teachers College Record, 10*, 1401–1421.

Chapter 3

How and What Do Videogames Teach?

Edward L. Swing and Craig A. Anderson

The pervasiveness of videogames in modern society, especially among children, suggests that it is important to understand how and what these videogames are teaching the individuals who play them. Although playing videogames can produce positive outcomes, such as increased persistence at difficult tasks, there are also potential negative outcomes, such as increased aggression. The General Learning Model illustrates how these positive and negative outcomes are produced, both in the form of immediate short term effects and through cumulative long term effects. In this chapter, we will explore the effects of videogames as explained by the General Learning Model. Some important public policy issues relating to the teaching effects of videogames will also be addressed.

The General Learning Model

The General Learning Model (GLM) is based on both early aggression theories and violent-media research as well as social-cognitive models and developmental approaches to learning. The GLM is general enough to explain many ways in which videogames teach and influence behavior (Buckley & Anderson, 2006). This model is also useful for its ability to integrate the short term and long term learning effects that videogames can produce.

Input variables

A person's behavior is a product of two types of input variables: personal and situational (see Figure 3.1). Person variables include all of the characteristics of a person as they exist before the learning encounter: personality traits, previous experience, behavioral tendencies, beliefs, attitudes, and mood state. These internal variables tend to be consistent over time and

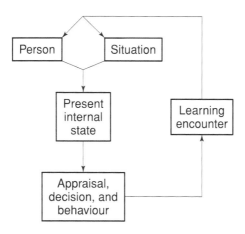

Figure 3.1. The General Learning Model: simplified view.

across situations as a result of people consistently using the same knowledge structures (e.g., scripts, beliefs, and schemata) in shaping their behavior (Anderson & Bushman, 2002; Anderson & Huesmann, 2003; Mischel & Shoda, 1995). Situational variables are the characteristics of the context in which the individual is currently placed ("situated"). This includes media, objects, settings, and other people that make up the learning environment. Although situational variables can and do vary quite a bit over time, they also show some consistency over time, as individuals are often in the same or similar situations repeatedly.

As with learning in general, the ability to learn from videogames is related to many variables, including age, grade level, ability level (this includes learning disabilities and low school performance), income level, and self-esteem (Lieberman, 1998). Some factors that influence learning from videogames are more specific to this form of learning. These variables include individual media-exposure history and the degree to which an individual's comprehension of information is affected by surrounding information (e.g., field-dependence vs. field-independence) (Ghinea & Chen, 2003). Some variables may affect learning through their connection with the specific content that is being learned. For example, learning from violent videogames may be affected by the player's sex, age, experiences with bullying, social problem-solving skills, emotional regulation ability, hostile personality, history of aggressive behavior, level of parental supervision and restriction of videogame play, and aggressive attitudes, beliefs, goals, and scripts (Anderson & Bushman, 2002).

Situational variables also have an impact on an individual's ability to learn from a videogame. The most important situational variables related to learning are probably aspects of the games themselves. For example, variables such as the level of interest and involvement a game creates, game content (violent, nonviolent, educational), and amount of current game exposure (duration per exposure, number of exposures per week, number of weeks) all affect the amount of learning and what is learned. Videogames may also produce different types and amounts of learning depending on whether they focus on drill-and-practice of factual information (e.g., *Reader Rabbit* or *Knowledge Munchers*), or simulations that model reality (e.g., *The Sims* or *MS Flight Simulator*) (Murphy, Penuel, Means, Korbak, Whaley, & Allen, 2002; Squire, 2003). Some situational variables may enhance the learning effect of violent videogames. Aggressive cues (weapons and aggressive words), provocation, frustration, pain, drugs, and other incentives can have such an effect (Anderson & Bushman, 2002).

Person variables and situational variables can combine in additive and interactive ways to increase or inhibit learning. An example of such an interaction between person and situational variables is that children with low self-esteem (a person variable) who play a game in which they control a character that is similar to themselves, and which is challenging but not too difficult (a situational variable), tend to show increased self-esteem (Lieberman, 1998). Many researchers view learning as a process through which a person's predispositions are modified through situational influences, as self-esteem was modified in Lieberman's (1998) study (Huesmann, 1997; Tremblay, 2000). This is similar to the way that social-cognitive models of aggression describe the interaction of person and situational variables in influencing an individual's present internal state. For example, pain and trait hostility interact in influencing aggressive cognitions such that a person who is high in trait hostility will have a disproportionately strong reaction to pain (Anderson, Anderson, Dill, & Deuser, 1998).

Present internal state

Personal and situational input variables exert their influence on behavior through an individual's present internal state. This state is made up of three major components: cognition, affect, and arousal. These components are all interrelated, such that each one exerts influence on the other two, and all of these components play a role in the process of learning.

Cognition. Personal and situational input variables can influence behavior by making thoughts and scripts related to various constructs more accessible. According to script theory, situational variables can bias a person's response to a situation by activating scripts that make certain responses more likely to occur (Huesmann, 1986). The activation of knowledge structures such as behavioral scripts can occur outside of conscious awareness or control

(Schneider & Shiffrin, 1977; Todorov & Bargh, 2002). Although many cognitive processes such as the activation of these scripts are unconscious, others begin as conscious processes but become automatized over time and with repetition.

A variety of cognitive variables, such as attributions, beliefs, thoughts, attitudes, perceptual schemata, expectation schemata, and behavioral scripts are influenced by input variables. For example, Anderson and Bushman (2001) found that playing a violent videogame increased aggressive thoughts. In this case, a situational input variable (the violent content of the videogame) was affecting people's cognitive state. Similar effects can result from personological input variables. An individual who has an aggressive personality would be more likely to demonstrate a hostile attribution bias. The effects of these input variables can also be more positive. Playing a videogame with prosocial elements could increase the accessibility of prosocial thoughts and constructs.

Affect. Mood and emotion provide another route by which input variables can influence behavior. Two of the ways that affect can influence learning and behavior are through mood-congruent cognition and mood-dependent memory. In the case of mood-congruent cognition, individuals are better able to process information that is consistent with their current mood. One good example of this is the tendency for depressed people to recall more more negative information than they do positive information (Berry, 1997). Similarly, aversive stimuli like heat, which can create negative affect, can activate cognitive structures that lead to aggressive cognitions and behavior (Anderson, 1989; Anderson, Anderson, Dorr, DeNeve, & Flanagan, 2000; Berkowitz, 1990). Mood-dependent memory, on the other hand, is the phenomenon in which the retrieval of information is best when a person is in the same mood they were in when they learned that information (regardless of the affect of the information itself). In other words, people tend to pay more attention to information that is consistent with their mood, think about this mood-consistent information longer, and recall this information better when they are in the same mood.

The mere-exposure effect is another way by which affect influences learning and behavior: repeated exposure to an object increases the object's attractiveness. This can occur even when the individual is not aware of their exposure to it (Kunst-Wilson & Zajonc, 1980). This may occur in videogames as players are repeatedly exposed to particular characters and stories. The emotional responses to these recurring elements can keep players engaged in a game and motivated to continue playing (Lieberman, 2006). The mere-exposure effect can occur with a stimulus that is initially either neutral or positive. But in some cases the stimulus initially induces fear or other aversive affect. In these cases it is possible for repeated exposure to produce systematic desensitization; that is, a reduction in the initially aversive emotions. Systematic desensitization is maximized if the initially aversive or feared stimulus is presented in a positive context. In relation to videogames, this means that although the violence contained in a videogame may be initially aversive, repeated exposure within the context of a fun game can reduce negative reactions to the violence (e.g., Carnagey, Anderson, & Bushman, 2006).

Arousal. Most videogames, whether they are designed for education or entertainment, tend to be arousing. The level of arousal produced by a game influences how much learning it can produce. If a videogame does not produce a sufficient amount of arousal, the player may be too bored to pay attention and learn from it. However, too much arousal can actually inhibit the learning of new information (Deshpande & Kawane, 1982; Yerkes & Dodson, 1908). For well learned material, this inhibition in the retrieval and use of information is less likely (Berkowitz, 1990). With less familiar information, arousal is more likely to inhibit the learning and use of the information.

Interrelationships of internal states

Although input variables influence cognition, affect, and arousal, these internal states also can exert substantial influence on each other; cognition and arousal have been shown to influence affect (Schachter & Singer, 1962) and affect can influence cognition and arousal (Bower, 1978). When arousal is too high, the learning of new information may be inhibited. When it is too low, the lack of motivation can also reduce the ability to learn. Furthermore, hostile cognitions or angry affect can determine the scripts and knowledge structures that guide a person's behavior.

Learning encounters

The factors that constitute the present internal state lead to appraisal and decision-making processes that result in some kind of action. This action can be either thoughtful or impulsive, depending on factors such as the valence of the appraisal and the presence of sufficient attentional resources to give the action more careful consideration. In an educational context, an example of such an action is trying to recall the answer to a test question. The entire episode, from input variables to the action that eventually results may be described as a learning encounter (see Figure 3.2). Playing a videogame may be thought of as a series of learning encounters. A single learning encounter within a videogame may last only a few seconds, or it can even last hours.

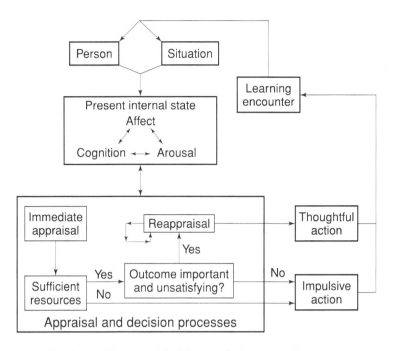

Figure 3.2. The General Learning Model: expanded causes and processes.

According the General Learning Model, learning encounters have both short term and long term effects on an individual. A learning encounter may exert short term effects on an individual through both person variables and situation variables that make up the inputs of subsequent learning encounters. Of more interest is the potential of these episodes to produce long term effects, through repeated episodes of a similar type. Such repeated episodes can result in changes in personality processes, long term affective changes, and changes to a variety of types of knowledge structures (e.g., content information, procedures, beliefs, attitudes, perceptual schemata for both basic and social patterns, behavioral scripts, and expectation schemata). To relate this back to learning from videogames, an example of such a long term change is that repeatedly playing a videogame that includes a specific form of violence (e.g., gang warfare) could lead to the development of behavioral scripts for that type of violence. Similarly, repeated exposure to videogames that simulate the operations of a business (e.g., *Sim Theme Park*) could lead to the development of knowledge structures (including scripts) for such business operations.

Learning encounters can also exert long term effects by influencing the situational variables that make up the input of future episodes. This may

69

happen when changes in knowledge structures affect an individual's relationship with teachers, parents, or peers. The development of different knowledge structures may also produce changes by influencing the types of social and non-social situations an individual is likely to encounter. As an example of how such a change in personality might occur, a series of learning encounters that led a person to expect hostile reactions from their peers could lead the person to seek out or create situations in which aggression and confrontation are more likely. Similarly, improvements in school performance brought about by repeated exposure to educational videogames could lead to improved relationships with teachers and parents, and to seeking out additional situational contexts that have academic possibilities.

bad

good

positive and negative

Videogame Effects

As with any type of media, videogames have the potential to have positive or negative effects on the people who play them. However, videogames are of particular interest because they are very effective teaching tools. Before examining the reasons videogames are effective at teaching, it is worth covering some of the important distinctions concerning videogame effects.

Important distinctions

Short term effects vs. long term effects. When researchers describe short term effects of a videogame, they are referring to effects that are immediate; that is, while playing the game or shortly after playing. Such effects could persist for as long as a half-hour or so after playing, but will tend to diminish rapidly over time. Long term effects may be thought of as delayed effects. These effects tend to accumulate with repeated practice and rehearsal of the videogame content. It is worth noting that while it may often be the case that a videogame will produce similar short term and long term effects, this is not necessarily the case. A videogame could potentially lead to an increase in prosocial behavior as a short term effect, but still increase aggression in the long term. For example, a videogame that increased hostility towards an outgroup might produce such opposite short term and long term effects if the player is playing the videogame in an in-group setting but later has repeated interactions with the outgroup.

Learning vs. performance. Although people often view performance as a necessary indicator that learning has occurred, this approach can be misleading. It is possible to learn skills, beliefs, attitudes, or other knowledge structures even if a person does not have an immediate opportunity to demonstrate such learning outcomes. It makes sense to look for performance as an indication of learning because the performance of a behavior or the use of a knowledge structure obviously indicates learning. However, the absence of such performance does not indicate that no learning has occurred. It may be that the situation in which the learned knowledge structures or behavior is evoked occurs years later, or it may not ever occur at all.

Manifest effects vs. latent effects. With respect to videogames, manifest effects can be described as the effects of the game that are intended, while latent effects are those effects that are unintended. Although a game may be designed for one purpose, it may produce other unintended effects as well. For example, just because a videogame was designed to be entertaining does not mean that it cannot produce an unintended increase in aggression. Also, note that the latent effects of a videogame are not necessarily negative. Videogames can produce positive effects (e.g., improved perceptual-motor skills) even if there was never any intention of producing such an effect.

Effectiveness of videogames as teaching tools

There are several reasons why videogames are very effective teaching tools (Gentile & Gentile, 2005). Some of the major reasons are outlined in Table 3.1. One such reason is the ability of videogames to capture and hold a person's attention. Videogames do this in part through the use of perceptual cues, such as rapid changes in scene or interesting auditory stimuli that naturally capture attention. Videogames can also offer clear objectives, which are especially appealing because these goals can be adapted to the skills and knowledge of the player. Even the pace of learning can be adapted to the abilities of the individual player. The use of naturally attention-grabbing stimuli and adaptable goals can help ensure that a videogame has a person's attention, which increases the potential to learn from it.

Videogames also are effective because of the active role of the player

Table 3.1. Videogames: great teaching tools.

– Can capture and hold attention (e.g., orienting response)
– Offer clear objectives which can be adaptable to prior knowledge and skill
– Match objectives and pace to the abilities of the learner
– Active learning, including feedback and the ability to practice until mastery
– Overlearning
– Include both extrinsic (e.g., points) and intrinsic rewards (e.g., competence)
– Subsequent rewards require knowledge and skills learned at earlier points in the game
– Massed and distributed practice

Adapted from Gentile & Gentile (2005)

in the learning encounters. Players receive rapid feedback on their performance, and can repeatedly practice a skill or carry out a script until it is mastered. In many cases, skills are overlearned, which improves the long term retention of the learning produced by the game. The same skills mastered early in a game are often required later on in the game as well, which contributes to this process of overlearning. It is common in educational situations for information or skills to be taught without this sort of overlearning that occurs in videogames. Unfortunately, this often means that students do not have the sort of chances to apply or rehearse the knowledge in ways that would lead to long term retention. For many videogame players, their playing time constitutes both massed practice (in that they play for long duration in each sitting) and distributed practice (by playing the game frequently), which is also ideal for increasing learning.

The level of attention players give to videogames and the amount of time spent playing are both due in part to the effective systems of rewards that most videogames utilize. These rewards include both extrinsic and intrinsic rewards. Extrinsic rewards tend to be relatively obvious, as these are often an intentional part of the game, such as "points." Extrinsic rewards can also include entertaining visual and sound effects. Intrinsic rewards occur outside of the videogame itself, but are a result of playing it. For example, videogames can give players a sense of accomplishment and competence, or improve their self-esteem (Lieberman, 1998). These rewards are intrinsic to the experience of playing the game itself, rather than being overt in the sense that game points are. Several features, such as adaptability and multiple forms of rewards, are responsible for giving videogames the ability to attract and hold players' attention, and the gameplay allows players to thoroughly learn the knowledge structures presented in the videogame.

Positive videogame effects

Videogames have the potential to be powerful educational tools. These games can teach both specific content and skills that are beneficial, and also exert more general positive effects on those who play them. Schools, the military, and other industries and organizations have already successfully utilized videogames as teaching tools, but there is the potential for much greater benefit to be derived from videogames.

Unintended effects. Playing videogames can have various positive effects on an individual. These effects are, in many cases, unintended by those who design and those who play these videogames. One such general skill that videogames have proven effective in teaching is hand–eye coordination. People who play videogames are better able to pay attention to cues across the visual field and can attend to a greater number of cues, compared to those who do not play videogames (Green & Bavelier, 2003). Although such advantages in coordination may not be important in most real-world contexts, one study recently found that surgeons who had experience in playing videogames were faster at performing laparascopic surgeries and also made fewer mistakes (Rosser, Lynch, Haskamp, Yalif, Gentile, & Giammaria, 2004). Laparascopic surgery is a less invasive method of operation, in which surgical devices are controlled by keypads and joysticks while progress is viewed on a monitor. The finding that videogames experience is related to better performance at specific skills, such as surgical techniques, suggests that deliberate efforts to improve performance in these areas through videogames could prove successful.

Another positive effect that videogames have is increasing children's positive attitudes towards computers and computer use. Given the importance of computers in many occupational fields in the modern world, such attitudes are likely to benefit an individual to the extent that it increases computer familiarity and use. In some videogames, basic aspects of computer programming are incorporated into the game, giving players an opportunity to develop skills which are potentially beneficial in other computer-related contexts.

Videogames can also teach players task persistence, a useful ability in many contexts. It is common in many videogames for players to fail in their initial attempts at a particular task. In fact, many games are designed so that immediate success is nearly impossible, but by developing skills and persisting in their efforts, they gradually perform better at the challenge and are eventually rewarded with success. The fact that success is contingent on repeated efforts rather than natural ability or task difficulty could transfer into other areas of their life, showing the player that difficult tasks can be achieved through persistence.

Intended effects. Many videogames have been created to teach players specific content and skills. There are many computer games that have been designed to teach traditional school content, and such games have proven effective in teaching subjects such as algebra, geometry (Corbett, Koedinger, & Hadley, 2001), biology (Ybarrondo, 1984), photography (Abrams, 1986), and computer programming (Kahn, 1999). For example, the Pennsylvania Department of Migrant Education was able to successfully teach math, reading, English fluency, and critical thinking skills to migrant children through a videogame (Winograd, 2001). Research indicates that educational software programs are effective at improving early reading and math development (Murphy et al., 2002).

The educational effects of videogames have extended beyond traditional educational subjects to include the teaching of various life skills. Videogames have used virtual reality environments to help teach basic life skills such as grocery shopping to students with severe learning disabilities (Standen, & Cromby, 1996). Lieberman (1997) found that a videogame was able to successfully teach diabetic children to practice better health behaviors to take care of their disease. NASA research on attentional abilities of fighter pilots led indirectly to the creation of a videogame designed to teach children diagnosed with Attention-Deficit Hyperactivity Disorder how to better control their attention. Various types of simulators (e.g., flight simulators) have demonstrated effectiveness in teaching some of the skills required to perform the task being simulated.

One of the organizations that relies most heavily upon videogames to teach is the U.S. military. The U.S. Army has a unit called the Program Executive Office for Simulation, Training, and Instrumentation (PEO STRI) with an annual budget of one billion dollars. This unit is responsible for implementing training through videogames that are designed to simulate military operations (Buckley & Anderson, 2006). The military simulators teach a variety of skills, such as how to fire different weapons, operate vehicles, interpret computer interfaces, military strategy, and teamwork. Various private organizations also use videogames for training purposes.

Although these videogame effects illustrate that videogames can exert a positive influence in many areas, both intentionally and unintentionally, there remain many other ways in which videogames could be applied in beneficial ways. Games could be designed to teach social skills to children experiencing social difficulties. It may also be possible to design videogames with psychotherapeutic applications. The benefits of videogames can apply to a broad range of skills, abilities, and general life practices, and can even occur in unintentional ways.

Negative videogame effects

Unfortunately, not all of the effects of videogames are positive. Videogames also have the potential to change behavior in undesirable ways. One of these ways that has received the most research attention is the potential for violent videogames to increase aggression. It is not particularly surprising, given the effectiveness of educational games in teaching various skills and information, that videogames with violent content can also teach their content to players.

Nature of the effects. Different research methods have yielded converging evidence that short term exposure to violent entertainment media produces immediate increases in aggression, and that repeated, long term exposure increases aggression across the lifespan (Anderson et al., 2003). Similar findings now exist in the videogame research literature (Anderson, Gentile, & Buckley, 2007). These research findings can be clearly and effectively explained by the General Aggression Model (GAM). This model is similar to the General Learning Model, and it likewise explains short term and long term effects of videogames. GAM more specifically addresses the processes that lead to aggression. According to GAM, when aggressive scripts, cognitions, or other knowledge structures become activated (either through short term situational priming or due to aggression-related per- sonological factors) and a person is mildly provoked, they are more likely to act aggressively. This action will often be interpreted as excessive by the target of their aggression, which can lead to an aggression-escalation cycle. Thus violent videogames can increase aggression either through the short term activation (i.e., priming) of aggression related knowledge structures or through long term increases in the accessibilty of such knowledge struc- tures (i.e., the development of an aggressive personality). Even then, it will take some form of provocation for violent behavior to be evoked, but such provocations are common in the day-to-day experiences of most people, and violent videogames increase the likelihood of an aggressive response.

A common question about violent videogame effects is whether they are stronger than the effects that have been found for violent television and films. There are several reasons, based on social psychological theory, to believe this to be the case (see Table 3.2). First, theory suggests that iden- tification with an aggressor makes an individual more likely to behave aggressively in the future. Videogames force a player to identify with the aggressor because the player is controlling them. This is similar to the active–passive distinction from the general learning model, in that the active role of a videogame player leads to better learning of the violent con- tent. This increased identification with the aggressor is likely to make the rewards for the portrayed violence more direct and salient as well.

Violent videogames may also have a stronger effect on aggressive behav- ior than films or television because these games often allow the player to rehearse the entire aggression sequence. A player may be required to look for threats, identify them, make a decision, and take aggressive action in a game, whereas television or film observer may not rehearse all of these steps in watching a film or television show. By developing more complete aggressive scripts, future aggressive behavior becomes more likely.

Table 3.2. Are violent videogames worse than violent television/films?

Reasons they might be:
– Identification with the aggressor
– Active participation
– Rehearsal of the entire aggression sequence
– Violence is directly rewarded
– Rate of violence is much higher

The overall rate of violence tends to be higher in violent videogames than violent films and television shows. Even films and television shows with generally violent themes often spend a decent amount of time in non-violent plot development. Many videogames, on the other hand, contain non-stop violence. This difference in the quantity of violence is likely to make the effect of videogame violence stronger than that of television and film.

Strength of the evidence. Despite the consistent finding in the research literature that violent videogames increase aggression, many people outside the research field have not accepted this conclusion. The scientific knowledge of the relationship between media violence and aggression is most accurately reflected in meta-analyses. Meta-analysis is a statistical technique for combining the results of many studies that test the same general hypothesis (e.g., violent videogames increase aggression). Meta-analyses quantify the overall findings of the literature, leaving less potential for reviewer bias than narrative literature reviews. A recent review of the literature, including review of relevant meta-analyses, found "unequivocal evidence that media violence increases the likelihood of aggressive and violent behavior in both immediate and long-term contexts" (Anderson, Berkowitz, Donnerstein, Huesmann, Johnson, Linz, Malamuth, & Wartella, 2003, p. 81). This same conclusion now applies specifically to violent videogame effects (Anderson, Gentile, & Buckley, 2007).

Of course, in any research domain studies typically find somewhat varying results. The media violence domain is no different in this regard. To a great extent, differing outcomes are merely the result of chance factors. Other factors include use of different measures and different methodologies. Recent reviews of the violent videogame literature have revealed that the relative quality of the research methodology also explains some of the differences in results. Some studies of videogame violence have had serious methodological flaws, such as the use of "violent" videogames that are not actually violent, the use of "non-violent" videogames that contain a substantial amount of violence, the use of violent and non-violent games that differed in other important ways, or studies that used an inappropriate measure of aggression (e.g., trait aggression as the primary dependent measure in a short term experimental study). Meta-analysis has demonstrated that studies with such methodological flaws yield smaller effect sizes for the relationship between videogame violence and aggression than studies without such flaws. This finding remains true regardless of whether the studies were using aggressive behavior, hostile affect, physiological arousal, or prosocial behavior (which is inversely related to videogame violence) as the dependent measure (Anderson, Carnagey, Flanagan, Benjamin, Eubanks, & Valentine, 2004). In other words, poor methodology leads to underestimates of the effect of videogame violence on aggression (see Figure 3.3).

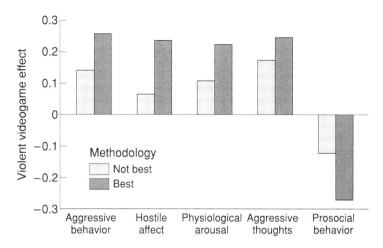

Figure 3.3. Meta-analysis of videogame violence effects on five outcome variables: Effects of Best versus Not Best methodology.

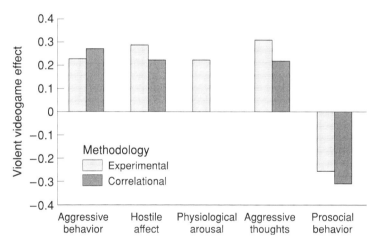

Figure 3.4. Meta-analysis of videogame violence effects on five outcome variables: Best studies by experimental versus correlational method.

Not only is there a clear link between videogame violence and aggression, there is also strong evidence that this relationship is causal (i.e., playing violent videogames causes aggression). Many of the studies which have tested this hypothesis have used experimental methodology, which allows for stronger conclusions of causality to be made than correlational research, though correlational and experimental research on media violence yields similar effect sizes (Anderson et al., 2004; see Figure 3.4). There is also some *longer* {

evidence based on longitudinal studies that repeated exposure to violent videogames increases aggression over time (Anderson et al., 2007).

Despite such evidence of the causal nature of the relationship between violent videogames and aggression, there is a particularly large amount of resistance by many people to accept this relationship. This is due, in large part, to the differences in the usage of the concept of causality between media violence researchers and the general public. Scientific researchers in many disciplines use the concept of causality in a probabilistic fashion. That is, if a particular variable influences the likelihood that some specific outcome will occur, it can be said to cause that outcome. Another commonly used form of causality is necessary and sufficient causality. Necessary causality means that a given outcome can only occur if a particular level of a specific variable is present. Sufficient causality means that if that particular level of the variable is present, the outcome will always be produced.

People generally do not have trouble accepting probabilistic causality in medical contexts. For example, it is widely accepted that smoking cigarettes *causes* cancer, despite the fact that this relationship clearly does not match the necessary and sufficient form of causality. Not everyone who smokes cigarettes gets cancer (indicating that smoking is not a sufficient cause of cancer) and not everyone who gets cancer has smoked cigarettes (indicating that smoking is not a necessary cause of cancer).

But many non-scientists (and many scientists as well) have difficulty applying probabilistic causality to social psychological contexts, especially when the causal relationship is one which they find disfavorable. Many cigarette smokers and the tobacco industry once used the necessary and sufficient form of causality to argue against the effects of cigarette smoking on cancer. The same type of argument is now used by some videogame players and the videogame industry to discount the causal effect of videogame violence on aggression. Thus, we hear obviously invalid arguments of the form: "I've played violent videogames [smoked cigarettes] for many years, and have never killed anyone [have not gotten lung cancer]. Therefore, playing violent videogames [smoking cigarettes] cannot cause aggression [lung cancer]."

Research has shown the effect of videogame violence on aggression to be moderately strong (see Figure 3.5). The effect size of this relationship is sufficient to warrant public concern. To put this effect size into perspective, note that it is larger than effect sizes found for the impact of asbestos exposure on cancer, the effect of homework on grades, calcium intake on bone mass, nicotine patch use on smoking cessation, lead exposure on reductions in children's IQ, secondhand smoke on cancer, and condom use on succeptibility to HIV (Anderson et al., 2004). These effects serve as useful comparisons for the videogame violence effects, in that all of these effects are of general public concern (see Figure 3.6). The relationship between

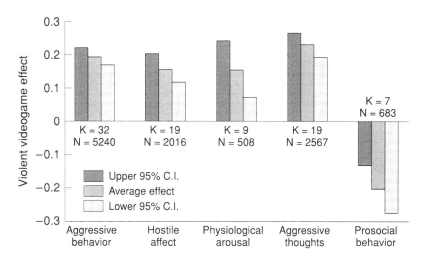

Figure 3.5. Meta-analysis of videogame violence effects on five outcome variables: Overall.

K = number of independent samples.

N = total number of participants.

C.I. = the upper and lower 95% confidence intervals.

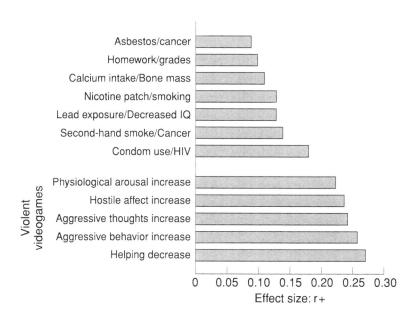

Figure 3.6. How big are violent videogame effects?

variables such as violent videogame use and aggression does not have to be large in order to be deserving of public concern, because so many people are exposed to it and because the outcome (aggression) is of sufficient societal importance that even moderate effects are worthy of attention and concern.

Aggression is an important variable in part because factors that increase aggression, such as violent videogames, can increase extreme forms of aggression (i.e., violent behavior). Although it is unethical to use severe violence as a dependent measure in experimental research, correlational data suggests that playing such games is predictive of violent behavior. Taken together with the findings of experimental research (which relies on other forms of aggression such as setting punishment levels), this suggests that playing violent videogames causes an increase in the probability that someone will behave violently.

Public Policy and Videogames

Some resistance to the findings of violent videogame researchers is due to concern that acknowledging such effects means that it will be necessary to ban those videogames. This is a misconception of the meaning of the research findings. The question of whether or not such a policy is necessary is not a scientific one. In order to create public policies to deal with videogames in light of the findings on violent videogames, it is necessary to understand the role that science plays in public policy (Gentile & Anderson, 2006).

One of the primary roles of science in public policy is to provide factual answers (or as close to factual answers as the science is capable of providing) to key questions. In order to fulfill this role, science must have good theory. This theoretical basis must have an empirical basis in the form of scientific studies that provide data to support the theory. The scientific tests of a theory may lead to revisions of the theory. Based on the current scientific theories, scientists are able to answer some public policy questions. For example, scientists can comment on whether a specific public policy is or is not likely to prove successful at achieving a specific result. For example, the question of whether *Midnight Basketball* (an inner-city program for organizing basketball games among youth that are at risk for committing crimes) is likely to be effective at reducing inner-city crime can be addressed by scientists within the framework of established scientific theory.

Science cannot be the only factor determining public policies. Other factors including legal issues, personal values, and political realities, go into shaping public policies as well (see Figure 3.7). Personal values are a particularly important factor in shaping policy. For example, personal values

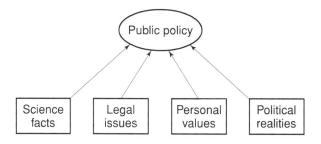

Figure 3.7. The role of science in public policy.

influence public policy decisions about gun control laws. Even if there were indisputable evidence that stricter gun control laws would reduce homicide rates, one could still argue against having such laws. If a person valued less-restricted access to guns more than they valued low homicide rates, such a position could be logical.

There are several ways that the effects of violent media on children can be reduced, primarily by reducing exposure. We have described three pillars of responsibility for such action (Gentile & Anderson, 2003). First, the television, film, and videogame industries need to accurately label their products to indicate the content. They must also educate parents about the meaning of this labelling system. These industries should also maintain ethical marketing practices, ensuring that their advertisements are not aimed at children for whom the games are inappropriate based on their age. The second pillar of responsibility lies with the retail and rental industry. Once media is accurately labelled regarding its content, these industries can enforce appropriate restrictions on the distribution of such media. Third, parents should educate themselves about the meanings of the ratings systems used to label television, films, and videogames. Parents also need to learn why both the content of videogames and the amount of play are important in determining the effects these games produce. Parents also need to act on this knowledge if they are to reduce the negative impact that videogames can have on their children.

Conclusion

It is clear that videogames can be very effective teaching tools. The General Learning Model explains how videogames exert their influence on players. Games can have a variety of positive effects on their players, both in general, unintended ways as well as in terms of deliberately teaching specific knowledge and skills. Unfortunately, along with these positive effects comes the potential for videogames to exert a negative influence on their players. For example, research indicates that violent videogames produce both short term and long term increases in aggression. Science alone cannot resolve the question of how public policy should deal with such negative effects, though there are ways that videogame industries, retailers, and parents can work to reduce these harmful effects.

Acknowledgments

This chapter is largely based on a presentation by Craig Anderson at the Children's Learning in a Digital World conference, which took place on August 19 and 20, 2005 at Brock University, St. Catharines, Ontario, Canada.

References

Abrams, A. (1986, January). *Effectiveness of interactive video in teaching basic photography skills.* Paper presented at the Annual convention of the Association for Educational Communication and Technology, Las Vegas, NV.

Anderson, C. A. (1989). Temperature and aggression: Ubiquitous effects of heat on the occurrence of human violence. *Psychological Bulletin, 106,* 74–96.

Anderson, C. A., Anderson, K. B., Dorr, N., DeNeve, K. M., & Flanagan, M. (2000). Temperature and aggression. *Advances in Experimental Social Psychology, 32,* 63–133.

Anderson, C. A., Berkowitz, L., Donnerstein, E., Huesmann, L. R., Johnson, J. D., Linz, D., et al. (2003). The influences of media violence on youth. *Psychological Science in the Public Interest, 4,* 81–110.

Anderson, C. A., & Bushman, B. J. (2001). Effects of violent video games on aggressive behavior, aggressive cognition, aggressive affect, physiological arousal, and prosocial behavior: A meta-analytic review of the scientific literature. *Psychological Science, 12,* 353–359.

Anderson, C. A., & Bushman, B. J. (2002). Human aggression. *Annual Review of Psychology, 53,* 27–51.

Anderson, C. A., Carnagey, N. L., Flanagan, M., Benjamin, A. J., Eubanks, J., & Valentine, J. C. (2004). Violent video games: Specific effects of violent content on aggressive thoughts and behavior. *Advances in Experimental Social Psychology, 36,* 199–249.

Anderson, C. A., Gentile, D. A., & Buckley, K. E. (2007). *Violent video game effects on children and adolescents: Theory, research, and public policy.* Oxford, UK: Oxford University Press.

Anderson, C. A., & Huesmann, L. R. (2003). Human aggression: A social-cognitive view. In M. A. Hogg & J. Cooper (Eds.), *Handbook of Social Psychology* (pp. 296–323). London: Sage.

Anderson, K. B., Anderson, C. A., Dill, K. E., & Deuser, W. E. (1998). The interactive relations between trait hostility, pain, and aggressive thoughts. *Aggressive Behavior, 24,* 161–171.

Berkowitz, L. (1990). On the formation and regulation of anger and aggression: A cognitive-neoassociationistic analysis. *American Psychologist, 45,* 494–503.

Berry, G. E. (1997). Information processing in anxiety and depression: Attention responses to mood congruent stimuli. *Dissertation Abstracts International, 58*(2-B), 967.

Bower, G. H. (1978). Emotional mood as a context for learning and recall. *Journal of Verbal Learning and Verbal Behavior, 17,* 573–585.

Buckley, K. E., & Anderson, C. A. (2006). A theoretical model of the effects and consequences of playing video games. In P. Vorderer & J. Bryant (Eds.), *Playing video games: Motives, responses, and consequences* (pp. 363–378). Mahwah, NJ: Lawrence Erlbaum.

Carnagey, N. L., Anderson, C. A., & Bushman, B. J. (2006). The effect of video game violence on physiological desensitization to real-life violence. *Journal of Experimental Social Psychology, 43*(3), 489–496.

Corbett, A. T., Koedinger, K. R., & Hadley, W. (2001). Cognitive tutors: From the research classroom to all classrooms. In P. S. Goodman (Ed.), *Technology enhanced learning* (pp. 235–263). Mahwah, NJ: Lawrence Erlbaum.

Deshpande, S. W., & Kawane, S. D. (1982). Anxiety and serial verbal learning: A test of the Yerkes-Dodson law. *Asian Journal of Psychology and Education, 9,* 18–23.

Gentile, D. A., & Anderson, C. A. (2003). Violent video games: The newest media violence hazard. In D. Gentile (Ed.), *Media violence and children* (pp. 131–152). Westport, CT: Praeger.

Gentile, D. A., & Anderson, C. A. (2006). Violent video games: Effects on youth and public policy implications. In N. Dowd, D. G. Singer, & R. F. Wilson (Eds.), *Handbook of children, culture, and violence* (pp. 225–246). Thousand Oaks, CA: Sage.

Gentile, D. A., & Gentile, J. R. (2005, April). *Violent video games as exemplary teachers.* Paper presented at the 2005 Society for Research in Child Development Biennial Conference, Atlanta, GA.

Ghinea, G., & Chen, S. Y. (2003). The impact of cognitive styles on perceptual distributed multimedia quality. *British Journal of Educational Technology, 34,* 393–406.

Green, C. S., & Bavelier, D. (2003). Action video game modifies visual selective attention. *Nature, 423,* 534–537.

Huesmann, L. R. (1986). Psychological processes promoting the relation between exposure to media violence and aggressive behavior by the viewer. *Journal of Social Issues, 42,* 125–139.

Huesmann, L. R. (1997). Observational learning of violent behavior: Social and biosocial processes. In A. Raine & P. A. Brennan (Eds.), *Biosocial bases of violence. NATO ASI series: Series A: Life sciences, Vol. 292* (pp. 69–88). New York: Plenum Press.

Kahn, K. (1999, June). *A computer game to teach programming.* Paper presented at the National Educational Computing Conference, Atlantic City, NJ.

Kunst-Wilson, W. R., & Zajonc, R. B. (1980). Affective discrimination of stimuli that cannot be recognized. *Science, New Series, 207,* 557–558.

Lieberman, D. A. (1997). Interactive video games for health promotion: Effects on knowledge, self-efficacy, social support, and health. In R. L. Street Jr., & W. R. Gold (Eds.), *Health promotion and interactive technology: Theoretical applications and future directions. LEA's communication series* (pp. 103–120). Mahwah, NJ: Lawrence Erlbaum.

Lieberman, D. A. (1998, July). *Health education video games for children and adolescents: Theory, design, and research findings.* Paper presented at the Annual Meeting of the International Communication Association, Jerusalem, Israel.

Lieberman, D. A. (2006). What can we learn from playing interactive video games? In P. Vorderer & J. Bryant (Eds.), *Playing computer games: Motives, responses, and consequences.* Mahwah, NJ: Lawrence Erlbaum.

Mischel, W., & Shoda, Y. (1995). A cognitive-affective system theory of personality: Reconceptualizing situations, dispositions, dynamics, and invariance in personality structure. *Psychological Review, 102,* 246–268.

Murphy, R. F., Penuel, W. R., Means, B., Korbak, C., Whaley, A., & Allen, J. E. (2002). *E-DESK: A review of recent evidence on the effectiveness of discrete educational software.* (Prepared for Planning and Evaluation Service, US Department of Education.) Menlo Park, CA: SRI International.

Rosser, J. C. Jr., Lynch, P. J., Haskamp, L. A., Yalif, A., Gentile, D. A., & Giammaria, L. (2004, January). *Are video game players better at laparoscopic surgery?* Paper presented at the Medicine Meets Virtual Reality Conference, Newport Beach, CA.

Schachter, S., & Singer, J. (1962). Cognitive, social, and physiological determinants of emotional state. *Psychological Review, 69,* 379–399.

Schneider, W., & Shiffrin, R. M. (1977). Controlled and automatic human information processing: I. Detection, search, and attention. *Psychological Review, 84,* 1–66.

Squire, K. (2003). Video games in education. *International Journal of Intelligent Simulations and Gaming, 2,* 1.

Standen, P. J., & Cromby, J. J. (1996). Can students with developmental disability use virtual reality to learn skills which will transfer to the real world? In H. J. Murphy (Ed.), *Proceedings of the Third International Conference on Virtual Reality and Persons with Disabilities.* Northridge, CA: California State University Center on Disabilities.

Todorov, A., & Bargh, J. A. (2002). Automatic sources of aggression. *Aggression & Violent Behavior, 7,* 53–68.

Tremblay, R. E. (2000). The development of aggressive behaviour during childhood: What have we learned in the past century? *International Journal of Behavioral Development, 24,* 129–141.

Winograd, K. (2001). Migrant families: Moving up with technology. *Converge, 4,* 16–18.

Ybarrondo, B. A. (1984). A study of the effectiveness of computer-assisted instruction in the high school biology classroom. Idaho. (ERIC Document Reproduction Service No. ED265015).

Yerkes, R. M., & Dodson, J. D. (1908). The relation of strength of stimulus to rapidity of habit formation. *Journal of Comparative Neurology & Psychology, 18,* 459–482.

Chapter 4

Videogame Addiction:
Fact or Fiction?

Mark D. Griffiths

The popularity of videogames as a leisure phenomenon has become an ever-increasing part of many people's lives. Videogames are widely marketed to adults and children and are readily available in most countries around the world. This leisure activity, however, has recently become the target of criticism within the media. There have been a growing number of reports about excessive use of videogames by both children and adults (often referred to as "joystick junkies") to the extent that some users are being identified as videogame addicts This concept of "videogame addiction" is a relatively new concept that is currently causing many to rethink more traditional views about what constitutes addiction. Although the concept of "videogame addiction" appears to have its supporters in the media, there is much skepticism within the academic community—especially among those working in the field of addiction research. For many in the academic environment, the concept of videogame addiction seems farfetched, particularly if their concepts and definitions of addiction are based on the criteria typically associated with addictions to psychoactive drugs. Despite the predominance of drug-based definitions of addiction, there is now a growing movement which views a number of *behaviors* as potentially addictive. For example some have identified gambling, computer game playing, exercise, sex, and now the Internet as potentially addictive behaviors. Such diversity in addictive agents (drugs or behaviors) has led to new all-encompassing definitions of what constitutes addictive behavior.

The first step in expanding the definition of addiction to include videogaming requires a full examination of what we know and what we need to know about videogaming behavior. Specifically, research into the area of videogame addiction needs to be underpinned by three fundamental questions: (1) What is addiction? (2) Does videogame addiction exist? (3) If videogame addiction exists, what are people actually addicted to?

What Is Addiction?

This first question continues to be a much-debated question both among psychologists within the field of addiction research as well as those working in other disciplines. For many years, I have operationally defined addictive behavior as any behavior that features all the core components of addiction. For example, throughout my own research examining the psychology of gambling, I have consistently argued that excessive gambling is no different from alcoholism or heroin addiction in terms of the core components of addiction (i.e., salience, mood modification, tolerance, withdrawal, conflict, relapse, etc.). If it can be shown that a behavior like pathological gambling can be a bona fide addiction then there is a precedent that any behavior which can provide continuous rewards in the absence of a psychoactive substance can be potentially addictive (i.e., a behavioral as opposed to a chemical addiction). Such a precedent "opens the floodgates" for other excessive behaviors to be theoretically considered as potential addictions (such as videogames).

It has been alleged for almost 25 years that social pathologies exist among excessive videogame players. For instance, Soper and Miller (1983) claimed "videogame addiction" was like any other behavioral addiction and consisted of a compulsive behavioral involvement, a lack of interest in other activities, association mainly with other addicts, and physical and mental symptoms when attempting to stop the behavior (e.g., the shakes). More recently, such addictions (including addictions to the Internet and slot machines) have been termed "technological addictions" (Griffiths, 1995a, 1996a) and have been operationally defined as non-chemical (behavioral) addictions that involve excessive human–machine interaction. They can either be passive (e.g., television) or active (e.g., computer games), and usually contain inducing and reinforcing features which may contribute to the promotion of addictive tendencies (Griffiths, 1995a). Technological addictions can thus be viewed as a subset of behavioral addictions (Marks, 1990) and feature core components of addiction first outlined by Brown (1993) and modified by Griffiths (1996b), i.e., salience, mood modification, tolerance, withdrawal, conflict, and relapse. It is my contention that any behavior (e.g., videogame playing) that fulfills these six criteria is therefore operationally defined as an addiction. In the case of videogame addiction it would be:

Salience—This occurs when videogame play becomes the most important activity in the person's life and dominates their thinking (preoccupations and cognitive distortions), feelings (cravings), and behavior (deterioration of socialized behavior). For instance, even if the person is not actually playing on a videogame they will be thinking about the next time that they will be.

Mood modification—This refers to the subjective experiences that people report as a consequence of engaging in videogame play and can be seen as a coping strategy (i.e., they experience an arousing "buzz" or a "high" or paradoxically tranquilizing feel of "escape" or "numbing").

Tolerance—This is the process whereby increasing amounts of videogame play are required to achieve the former mood modifying effects. Thus for someone engaged in videogame playing, they gradually build up the amount of the time they spend engaged in the behavior.

Withdrawal symptoms—These are the unpleasant feeling states and/or physical effects which occur when videogame play is discontinued or suddenly reduced. These include the shakes, moodiness, irritability, etc.

Conflict—This refers to the conflicts between the videogame player and those around them (interpersonal conflict), conflicts with other activities (job, schoolwork, social life, hobbies, and interests) or from within the individual themselves (intrapsychic conflict and/or subjective feelings of loss of control) which are concerned with spending too much time engaged in videogame play.

Relapse—This is the tendency for repeated reversions to earlier patterns of videogame play to recur and for even the most extreme patterns typical of the height of excessive videogame play to be quickly restored after periods of abstinence or control.

Does Videogame Addiction Exist?

Having operationally defined addiction above, it is my belief that videogame addiction does indeed exist but that it affects only a very small minority of players. There appear to be many people who use videogames excessively but are not addicted as measured by these (or any other) criteria.

If Videogame Addiction Exists, What Are People Actually Addicted To?

The third question is perhaps the most interesting and the most important when it comes to research in this field. What are people actually addicted to? Is it the interactive medium of playing? Aspects of its specific style (e.g., an anonymous and disinhibiting activity)? The specific types of games (aggressive games, strategy games, etc.)? This has led to much debate among those working in this field. Research being carried out into Internet addiction may lead to insights about videogame addiction. For instance, Young (1999) has claimed that Internet addiction is a broad term covering a wide variety of behaviors and impulse-control problems. This is categorized by five specific subtypes:

Cybersexual addiction: compulsive use of adult websites for cybersex and cyberporn.
Cyber-relationship addiction: overinvolvement in online relationships.
Net compulsions: obsessive online gambling, shopping, or day-trading.
Information overload: compulsive web surfing or database searches.
Computer addiction: obsessive computer game playing (e.g., *Doom*, *Myst*, *Solitaire*, etc.)

I have argued (Griffiths, 1999, 2000a) that many of these excessive users are not "Internet addicts" but just use the Internet excessively as a medium to fuel other addictions. Put very simply, a gambling addict or a computer game addict who engages in their chosen behavior online is not addicted to the Internet. The Internet is just the place where they engage in the behavior. However, in contrast to this, there are case study reports of individuals who appear to be addicted to the Internet itself (e.g., Young, 1998; Griffiths, 1996a, 1998, 2000b). These are usually people who use Internet chat rooms or play fantasy role-playing games—activities that they would not engage in except on the Internet itself. These individuals to some extent are engaged in text-based virtual realities and take on other social personas and social identities as a way of making them feel good about themselves. In these cases, the Internet may provide an alternative reality to the user and allow them feelings of immersion and anonymity that may lead to an altered state of consciousness. This in itself may be highly psychologically and/or physiologically rewarding. Obviously for those playing online computer games, these speculations may provide insights into the potentially addictive nature of computer games for those playing in this medium.

Other insights into the potentially addictive nature of videogames has come from research into slot machines. Both videogame machines and slot machines may be considered under the generic label of "amusement machines" (Griffiths, 1991a). The main difference between videogame machines and slot machines are that videogames are played to accumulate as many points as possible whereas slot machines are played (i.e., gambled upon) to accumulate money. I have suggested (Griffiths, 1991a) that playing a videogame could be considered as a non-financial form of gambling. Both types of machine (in the case of arcade games) require insertion of a coin to play, although the playing time on a slot machine is usually much less than on a videogame machine. This is because on videogames the outcome is almost solely due to skill, whereas on slot machines the outcome is more likely to be a product of chance. However, the general playing philosophy of both slot machine players and videogame players is to stay on the machine for as long as possible using the least amount of money (Griffiths, 1990a, 1990b). I have also argued that regular slot machine players play *with* money rather than for it, and that winning money is a means to an end (i.e., to stay on the machine as long as possible).

Besides the generic labeling, their geographical juxtaposition, and the philosophy for playing, it could be argued that on both a psychological and behavioral level, slot machine gambling and videogame playing share many similarities (e.g., similar demographic differences such as age and gender breakdown, similar reinforcement schedules, similar potential for "near miss" opportunities, similar structural characteristics involving the use of light and sound effects, similarities in skill perception, similarities in the effects of excessive play, etc.) (Griffiths, 2005a). The most probable reason the two forms have rarely been seen as conceptually similar is because videogame playing does not involve the winning of money (or something of financial value) and therefore cannot be classed as a form of gambling. However, the next generation of slot machines are starting to use video-game graphics and technology. While many of these relate to traditional gambling games (e.g., roulette, poker, blackjack, etc.) there are plans for developing video gambling games in which people would win money based on their game scores. This obviously gives an idea of the direction that slot machines and the gaming industry are heading.

Furthermore, there are a growing number of researchers who suggest that arcade videogames share some common ground with slot (gambling) machines including the potential for dependency (e.g., Brown & Robertson, 1993; Fisher, 1994; Griffiths, 1991a, 1993, 1997a, 2005a; Gupta & Derevensky, 1996; Wood, Griffiths, Chappell, & Davies, 2004). As Fisher and Griffiths (1995) point out, arcade videogames and slot machines share some important structural characteristics, these being:

- the requirement of response to stimuli which are predictable and governed by the software loop.
- the requirement of total concentration and hand–eye coordination.
- rapid span of play negotiable to some extent by the skill of the player (more marked in videogames).
- the provision of aural and visual rewards for a winning move (e.g., flashing lights, electronic jingles).
- the provision of an incremental reward for a winning move (points or cash), which reinforces "correct" behavior.
- digitally displayed scores of "correct behavior" (in the form of points or cash accumulated).

- the opportunity for peer group attention and approval through competition.

As with excessive slot machine playing, excessive videogame playing partly comes about by the partial reinforcement effect (PRE) (Wanner, 1982). This is a critical psychological ingredient of videogame addiction whereby the reinforcement is intermittent—that is, people keep responding in the absence of reinforcement hoping that another reward is just around the corner. Knowledge about the partial reinforcement effect gives the videogame designer an edge in designing appealing games. Magnitude of reinforcement is also important. Large rewards lead to fast responding and greater resistance to extinction—in short to more "addiction." Instant reinforcement is also satisfying.

Videogames rely on multiple reinforcements (i.e., the "kitchen sink" approach) in that different features might be differently rewarding to different people. Success on videogames comes from a variety of sources and the reinforcement might be intrinsic (e.g., improving your highest score, beating your friend's high score, getting your name on the "hall of fame," mastering the machine) or extrinsic (e.g., peer admiration). Malone (1981) has also reported that videogames are positively correlated to (i) a presence or absence of goals, (ii) the availability of automatic computer scores, (iii) the presence of audio effects, (iv) the random quality of the games, and (v) the degree to which rapid reaction times enhance game scores.

Empirical Research on Videogame Addiction

To date, there has been very little research directly investigating videogame addiction. Furthermore, almost all of it has concentrated on adolescents only. Shotton (1989) carried out a study specifically on "computer addiction" using a sample of 127 people (half being children, half adult; 96% male) who had been self-reportedly "hooked" on home videogames for at least five years. Seventy-five of these were measured against two control groups, and it was reported that the computer-dependent individuals were highly intelligent, motivated, and achieving people but often misunderstood. Following-up after five years, Shotton found that the younger cohort had done well educationally, gone on to university and then into high ranking jobs. However, Shotton's research was done with people who were familiar with the older generation of videogames that were popular in the earlier part of the 1980s. The videogames of the 1990s onwards may in some way be more psychologically rewarding than the games of a decade ago in that they require more complex skills, improved dexterity, and feature socially relevant topics and better graphics. Anecdotal accounts of greater psychological rewards could mean that the newer games are more "addiction inducing," although such an assertion needs empirical backing.

A more recent questionnaire study was undertaken by Griffiths and Hunt (1995, 1998) with almost 400 adolescents (12 to 16 years of age) to establish the level of "dependence" using a scale adapted from the DSM-III-R criteria for pathological gambling (American Psychiatric Association, 1987). Eight questions relating to the DSM-III-R criteria were adapted for computer game playing and examined a number of addiction components including:

1   salience ("Do you frequently play most days?")
2   tolerance ("Do you frequently play for longer periods of time?")
3   euphoria ("Do you play for excitement or a 'buzz'?")
4   chasing ("Do you play to beat your personal high score?")
5   relapse ("Do you make repeated efforts to stop or decrease playing?")
6   withdrawal ("Do you become restless if you cannot play?")
7   conflict ("Do you play instead of attending to school-related activities?"
8   conflict ("Do you sacrifice social activities to play?")

A cut-off point of four was assumed to indicate a participant was playing at dependent (i.e., addictive) levels at the time of the study. Scores on the adapted DSM-III-R scale indicated that 62 players (19.9%) were dependent on computer games (i.e., scored four or more on the scale). Furthermore, 7% of the sample claimed they played over 30 hours a week. The dependence score correlated with gender—that is, significantly more males than females were dependent. Dependence score also correlated with how often they played computer games, the mean session length playing time, and the longest single session playing time. Further analysis indicated that those dependent were significantly more likely to have started playing computer games to impress friends, because there was nothing else to do, for a challenge, and to meet friends. Dependent players were also significantly more likely to report aggressive feelings as a direct result of their computer game playing. There are a number of problems with the findings of this study. Although the criteria for the scale were all based on the different components of dependence common to other addictive behaviors (e.g., salience, euphoria, tolerance, withdrawal, conflict, etc.) it could be that these are less relevant for excessive computer game playing. There was also an assumption made that computer game playing was similar to gambling in terms of the consequences of excessive behavior.

Alternative explanations could be that excessive computer game playing cannot be conceptualized as an addiction at all or that the scale is more a measure of preoccupation rather than dependence. A replication study found very similar results (Griffiths, 1997b). It is also worth noting that 7% of the sample in Griffiths and Hunt's (1995, 1998) study claimed to play computer games for over 30 hours a week. Similar findings have also been reported in other studies (Fisher, 1994; Griffiths, 1997b; Parsons, 1995; Phillips, Rolls, Rouse, & Griffiths, 1995; Tejeiro-Delguero & Moran, 2002). However, it is worth noting that Charlton's (2002) factor analytic study of computer addiction showed a blurring of distinction between non-pathological high engagement and addiction. Therefore, it could alternatively be the case that there are very excessive gamers who show few negative consequences in their life.

There is no doubt that for a minority of children and adolescents, videogames can take up considerable time. Whether these studies suggest videogames may be addictive is perhaps not the most salient issue here. The question to ask is: What is the longitudinal effect of any activity (not just videogame playing) that takes up 30 hours of leisure time a week on the educational and social development of children and adolescents? At present we do not know the answer to this question. However, it is my contention that any child who engaged in any activity excessively (whether defined as an addiction or not) every day over a number of years from a young age, would have their social and/or educational development negatively affected in some way.

There is also the question that if videogames are addictive, then what is the addictive process? One potential way of answering this question is to produce possible theoretical accounts of videogame addiction and test the hypotheses empirically. McIlwraith (1990) proposed four theoretical models of television addiction in the popular and psychological literature that would seem good models to test the boundaries of videogame addiction. Substituting "videogame" for "television" in McIlwraith's account would leave the four explanations as thus:

That videogame addiction is a function of the videogame's effects on imagination and fantasy life—that is, people who play videogames to excess have poor imaginations.

That videogame addiction is a function of the videogame's effects on arousal level—that is, people who play videogames to excess either do so for its arousing or tranquilizing effects.

That videogame addiction is a manifestation of oral, dependent, or addictive personality—that is, people who play videogames to excess do so due to their inner personality as to opposed to the external source of the addiction.

That videogame addiction is a distinct pattern of uses and gratifications associated with the videogame medium—that is, people who play video-games to excess enjoy the physical act of playing or play only when they are bored, etc.

Few of these explanations for home videogame playing have been empirically studied, although some empirical evidence by Griffiths and Dancaster (1995), and evidence from arcade videogame addiction (Fisher, 1994) appears to support the second theoretical orientation, that videogame addiction is a function of the videogame's effects on arousal level. Recent research by Koepp, Gunn, Lawrence, Cunningham, Dagher, Jones, et al. (1998) demonstrated dopaminergic neurotransmission during the playing of a videogame. This may have implications for understanding the underlying addictive process in the playing of videogames. If it is accepted that videogame playing can be addictive then it is appropriate to look for the neural foundation of such behavior. Over recent years the role of the mesotelencephalic (nucleus accumbens) dopaminergic system that is constructed as a circuit between the midbrain and the forebrain (within the medial forebrain bundle) has been widely accepted as the neural substrate of reinforcement (Julien, 1995). The work has until now focused on modeling the psychopharmacological process of drug-seeking behavior.

In addition to neurochemical research, there are further reports of behavioral signs of videogame dependency among adolescents. Dependency signs reported include stealing money to play arcade games or to buy new games cartridges (Griffiths & Hunt, 1995; 1998; Keepers, 1990; Klein, 1984), truanting from school to play (Griffiths & Hunt, 1998; Keepers, 1990), not doing homework/getting bad marks at school (Griffiths & Hunt, 1998; Phillips et al., 1995), sacrificing social activities to play (Egli & Meyers, 1984; Griffiths & Hunt, 1998), irritability and annoyance if unable to play (Griffiths & Hunt, 1998; Rutkowska & Carlton, 1994), playing longer than intended (Egli & Meyers, 1984; Griffiths & Hunt, 1998) and an increase in self-reported levels of aggression (Griffiths, & Hunt, 1995). There is no doubt that for a minority of people (particularly adolescents) videogames can take up considerable time and that to all intents and purposes they are "addicted" to them. However, the prevalence of such an addiction is still of great controversy, as is the mechanism by which people may become addicted. This is one area where research appears to be much needed. The need to establish the incidence and prevalence of clinically significant problems associated with videogame addiction is of paramount importance. There is no doubt that clearer operational definitions are required if this is to be achieved.

It has been argued above that the only way of determining whether non-chemical (i.e., behavioral) addictions (such as videogame addiction) are addictive in a non-metaphorical sense is to compare them against clinical criteria for other established drug-ingested addictions. However, most people researching in the field have failed to do this, which has perpetuated the skepticism shown in many quarters of the addiction research community. The main problems with the addiction criteria suggested by most researchers in the field is that the measures used (i) have no measure of severity, (ii) have no temporal dimension, (iii) have a tendency to overestimate the prevalence of problems and (iv) take no account of the context of videogame use. There are also concerns about the sampling methods used. As a consequence, none of the surveys to date conclusively shows that videogame addiction exists or is problematic to anyone but a small minority. At best, they indicate that videogame addiction may be prevalent in a significant minority of individuals but that more research using validated survey instruments and other techniques (e.g., in-depth qualitative interviews) are required. Case studies of excessive videogame players may provide better evidence of whether videogame addiction exists because the data collected are much more detailed. Even if just one case study can be located it indicates that videogame addiction actually does exist—even if it is unrepresentative. There are case study accounts in the literature which appear to show that excessive videogame players display many signs of addiction (e.g., Keepers, 1990) including those that play online (e.g., Griffiths, 2000b; Griffiths, Davies, & Chappell, 2003, 2004a, 2004b). These case studies tend to show that the videogames are used to counteract other deficiencies and underlying problems in the person's life (e.g., relationships, lack of friends, physical appearance, disability, coping, etc.). Again, further work of a more in-depth qualitative nature is needed to confirm the existence of videogame addiction.

Excessive Videogame Play—Other Negative Consequences

Other indirect evidence of addictive and excessive play comes from the many health consequences that have been reported in the literature. The risk of epileptic seizures while playing videogames in photosensitive individuals with epilepsy is well established (e.g., Graf, Chatrian, Glass, & Knauss, 1994; Harding & Jeavons, 1994; Maeda, Kurokawa, Sakamoto, Kitamoto, Kohji, & Tashima, 1990; Millett, Fish, & Thompson, 1997; Quirk, Fish, Smith, Sander, Shorvon, & Allen, 1995). Graf et al. (1994) report that seizures are most likely to occur during rapid scene changes, and high intensity repetitive and flickering patterns. However, for many individuals, seizures during play will represent a chance occurrence without a causal link. Furthermore, there appears to be little direct link to excessive and/or addictive play because occasional players appear to be just as susceptible.

In addition to photosensitive epilepsy, the medical profession for over 20 years has voiced a number of concerns about videogame playing. Back in the early 1980s, rheumatologists described cases of "Pac-man's Elbow" and "Space Invaders' Revenge" in which players have suffered skin, joint, and muscle problems from repeated button hitting and joystick pushing on the game machines (Loftus & Loftus, 1983). Early research by Loftus and Loftus indicated that two-thirds of (arcade) videogame players examined complained of blisters, calluses, sore tendons, and numbness of fingers, hands, and elbows directly as a result of their playing. There have been a whole host of case studies in the medical literature reporting some of the adverse effects of playing videogames (see Griffiths, 2003, 2005b). These have included auditory hallucinations (Spence, 1993), enuresis (Schink, 1991), encoprisis (Corkery, 1990), wrist pain (McCowan, 1981), neck pain (Miller, 1991), elbow pain (Miller, 1991), tendosynovitis—also called "nintendinitis"—(Brasington, 1990; Casanova & Casanova, 1991; Reinstein, 1983; Siegal, 1991), hand–arm vibration syndrome (Cleary, McKendrick, & Sills, 2002), repetitive strain injuries (Mirman & Bonian, 1992), and peripheral neuropathy (Friedland & St. John, 1984). Admittedly, some of these adverse effects are quite rare and "treatment" simply involved non-playing of the games in question. In fact, the cases involving enuresis and encoprisis, the children were so engaged in the games that they did not want to go to the toilet. In these particular cases they were simply taught how to use the game's "pause" button!

There has also been some speculation that excessive play may have a negative effect on both heart rate and blood pressure. One study (Gwinup, Haw, & Elias, 1983) suggested that some individuals with cardiovascular disease could experience adverse effects. More recent research has highlighted both gender and ethnic differences in cardiovascular activity during game play (see Murphy, Stoney, Alpert, & Walker, 1995). Although some authors (e.g., Segal & Dietz, 1991) have suggested that game playing may lead to increased energy expenditure when compared with activities such as watching television, the energy increase identified is not sufficient to improve cardiorespiratory fitness.

Other speculative (i.e., non-empirically tested) negative aspects of videogame playing that have been reported include the belief that videogame play is socially isolating and prevents children from developing social skills (Zimbardo, 1982). For instance, Selnow (1984) reported that videogame players use the machine as "electronic friends." However, this does not necessarily mean that players play the machines instead of forming human friendships and interacting with their peer groups. Further to this, Colwell, Grady, and Rhaiti (1995) reported that heavy videogame players see friends more often outside school (and have a need for friends) more than non-heavy players. Rutkowska and Carlton (1994) reported there was no difference in "sociability" between high and low frequency players and reported that games foster friendship. This finding was echoed by Phillips et al. (1995), who found no difference in social interactions between players and non-players.

It has also been suggested that videogame playing may prevent children and adolescents from participating in more educational or sporting pursuits (Egli & Meyers, 1984; Professional Association of Teachers, 1994). In this context, it is worth noting that childhood obesity has also been linked with videogames. For instance, Shimai, Yamada, Masuda, & Tada (1993) found that obesity was correlated with long periods of videogame playing in Japanese children. This finding has also been found in young French children (Deheger, Rolland-Cachera, & Fontvielle, 1997). In the UK, Johnson and Hackett (1997) reported that there was an inverse relationship between physical activity and playing videogames in schoolgirls.

What is clear from the case studies displaying the more negative consequences of playing is that they all involved people who were excessive users of videogames. From prevalence studies in this area, there is little evidence of serious acute adverse effects on health from moderate play. Adverse effects are likely to be relatively minor, and temporary, resolving spontaneously with decreased frequency of play, or to affect only a small subgroup of players. Excessive players are the most at risk from developing health problems although more research appears to be much needed. The need to establish the incidence and prevalence of clinically significant problems associated with videogame play is of paramount importance. There is also no doubt that clearer operational definitions are required if this is to be achieved.

Taking all factors and variables into account and by considering the prevalence of play, the evidence of serious adverse effects on health is rare. An overview of the available literature appears to indicate that adverse effects are likely to affect only a very small subgroup of players and that frequent players are the most at risk from developing health problems. Those that game play does affect will experience subtle, relatively minor, and temporary effects that resolve spontaneously with decreased frequency of play. However, the possible long term effects and its relationship to conditions such as obesity have not been fully examined and must remain speculative.

Conclusions

This chapter has demonstrated that research into videogame addiction is a little-studied phenomenon. Obviously more research is needed before the debate on whether videogame addiction is a distinct clinical entity is decided. From the sparse research, it is evident that videogames appear to be at least potentially addictive. There is also a need for a general taxonomy of videogames as it could be the case that particular types of games are more addictive than others. Another major problem is that videogames can be played in lots of different ways including handheld consoles, personal computers, home videogame consoles, arcade machines, and on the Internet. It may be the case that some of these media for playing games (such as in an arcade or on the Internet) may be more addictive because of other factors salient to that medium (e.g., disinhibition on the Internet). Therefore future research needs to distinguish between excessive play in different media.

Research also demonstrates that males are the most excessive users of videogames (Griffiths, 1991b, 1993, 1997a; Kaplan, 1983); this again mirrors many other youth addictions (Griffiths, 1995b). Reasons as to why males play videogames significantly more than females have been generally lacking. Explanations may include:

1 The content of the games—Most videogames have traditionally contained masculine images (Braun, Goupil, Giroux, & Chagnon, 1986) although this is changing with the introduction of strong female lead characters like Lara Croft. Furthermore, videogames have been and continue to be predominantly designed by males for male consumers (Gutman, 1982) Although there have been "female" forms of game hardware and software introduced, e.g., *Ms. Pac-man* and Nintendo's *Game Girl*, there are fewer games designed specifically for females than those designed for males.

2 Socialization—Women are not encouraged to express aggression in public and feel uncomfortable with games of combat or war (Surrey, 1982). It could be that male domination of videogames is due more to the arcade atmosphere, its social rules and socialization factors than the games themselves.

3 Sex differences—Males, on average, perform better in visual and spatial skills (particularly depth perception) (Maccoby & Jacklin, 1974) and hand–eye coordination (Keisler, Sproull, & Eccles, 1983) which are essential to good game playing. Therefore, the average male player would be more likely to score higher than the average female player and thus be more likely to persist in playing.

It is also apparent that there are gender differences between the types of game played. For example, Griffiths and Hunt (1995) reported that males preferred "beat 'em ups" and "puzzlers" and that females preferred "platform" games. Another study by Griffiths (1997b) reported that males play more "beat 'em ups" and sport simulations, and that females play more "puzzlers" and "platformers." Although there are some slight differences in these findings, they do seem to suggest that males prefer the more aggressive type of games. In fact, Griffiths (1997b) went on to report that 42% of boys' favourite games were violent whereas only 9% of the girls' were. This was also echoed by Parsons (1995), who reported that females prefer less aggressive games than males, and that males prefer violence. More research is therefore needed into the relationship (if any) between violent videogames and potential addictiveness. There is also the question of developmental effects—that is, do videogames have the same effect regardless of age? It could well be the case that videogames have a more pronounced addictive effect in young children but less of an effect (if any) once they have reached their adult years. There is also the social context of playing— that is, does playing in groups or individually, with or against each other affect potential addictiveness of games in any way? These all need further empirical investigation.

It does appear that excessive videogame playing can have potentially damaging effects upon a minority of individuals who display compulsive and addictive behavior, and who will do anything possible to "feed their addiction." Such individuals need monitoring. Using these individuals in research would help identify the roots and causes of addictive playing and the impact of such behavior on family and school life. It would be clinically useful to illustrate problem cases, even following them longitudinally and recording developmental features of the adolescent videogame addict. This would help determine the variables that are salient in the acquisition, development, and maintenance of videogame addiction. It may be that videogame addiction is age related like other more obviously "deviant" adolescent behaviors (e.g., glue sniffing), since there is little evidence to date of videogame addiction in adults.

There is no doubt that videogame play usage among the general population will continue to increase over the next few years, and that if social pathologies (including videogame addiction) do exist then this is certainly an area for development that should be of interest and concern to all those involved in the addiction research field. Real-life problems need applied solutions and alternatives, and until there is an established body of literature on the psychological, sociological, and physiological effects of videogame playing and videogame addiction, directions for education, prevention, intervention, and treatment will remain limited in scope. The time has come for the addiction research community to take videogame addiction seriously.

References

American Psychiatric Association. (1987). *Diagnostic and statistical manual for mental disorders (third edition).* Washington, DC: American Psychiatric Association.

Brasington, R. (1990). Nintendinitis. *New England Journal of Medicine, 322,* 1473–1474.

Braun, C. M. J., Goupil, G., Giroux, J., & Chagnon, Y. (1986). Adolescents and microcomputers: Sex differences, proxemics, task and stimulus variables. *Journal of Psychology, 120,* 529–542.

Brown, R. I. F. (1993). Some contributions of the study of gambling to the study of other addictions. In W. R. Eadington & J. A. Cornelius (Eds.), *Gambling behavior and problem gambling* (pp. 241–272). Reno: University of Nevada Press.

Brown, R. I. F., & Robertson, S. (1993). Home computer and video game addictions in relation to adolescent gambling: Conceptual and developmental aspects. In W. R. Eadington & J. A. Cornelius (Eds.), *Gambling Behavior and Problem Gambling* (pp. 451–471). Reno: University of Nevada Press.

Casanova, J., & Casanova, J. (1991). Nintendinitis. *Journal of Hand Surgery, 16,* 181.

Charlton, J. P. (2002). A factor analytic investigation of computer "addiction" and engagement. *British Journal of Psychology, 93,* 329–344.

Cleary, A. G., McKendrick, H., & Sills, J. A. (2002). Hand-arm vibration syndrome may be associated with prolonged use of vibrating computer games. *British Medical Journal, 324,* 301.

Colwell, J., Grady, C., & Rhaiti, S. (1995). Computer games, self-esteem, and gratification of needs in adolescents. *Journal of Community and Applied Social Psychology, 5,* 195–206.

Corkery, J. C. (1990). Nintendo power. *American Journal of Diseases in Children, 144,* 959.

Deheger, M., Rolland-Cachera, M. F., & Fontvielle, A. M. (1997). Physical activity and body composition in 10-year-old French children: Linkages with nutritional intake? *International Journal of Obesity, 21,* 372–379.

Egli, E. A., & Meyers, L. S. (1984). The role of video game playing in adolescent life: Is there a reason to be concerned? *Bulletin of the Psychonomic Society, 22,* 309–312.

Fisher, S. E. (1994). Identifying video game addiction in children and adolescents. *Addictive Behaviors, 19*(5), 545–553.

Fisher, S. E., & Griffiths, M. D. (1995). Current trends in slot machine gambling: Research and policy issues. *Journal of Gambling Studies. Special Issue: Slot machine gambling, 11*(3), 239–247.

Friedland, R. P., & St. John, J. N. (1984). Video-game palsy: Distal ulnar neuropathy in a video game enthusiast. *New England Journal of Medicine, 311,* 58–59.

Graf, W. D., Chatrian, G. E., Glass, S. T., & Knauss, T. A. (1994). Video-game related seizures: A report on 10 patients and a review of the literature. *Pediatrics, 3,* 551–556.

Griffiths, M. D. (1990a). The acquisition, development and maintenance of fruit machine gambling in adolescence. *Journal of Gambling Studies, 6,* 193–204.

Griffiths, M. D. (1990b). The cognitive psychology of gambling. *Journal of Gambling Studies, 6,* 31–42.

Griffiths, M. D. (1991a). The observational analysis of adolescent gambling in UK amusement arcades. *Journal of Community and Applied Social Psychology, 1*, 309–320.

Griffiths, M. D. (1991b). Amusement machine playing in childhood and adolescence: A comparative analysis of video games and fruit machines. *Journal of Adolescence, 14*, 53–73.

Griffiths, M. D. (1993). Are computer games bad for children? *The Psychologist: Bulletin of the British Psychological Society, 6*, 401–407.

Griffiths, M. D. (1995a). Technological addictions. *Clinical Psychology Forum, 76*, 14–19.

Griffiths, M. D. (1995b). *Adolescent gambling.* London: Routledge.

Griffiths, M. D. (1996a). Internet "addiction": An issue for clinical psychology? *Clinical Psychology Forum, 97*, 32–36.

Griffiths, M. D. (1996b). Behavioural addictions: An issue for everybody? *Journal of Workplace Learning, 8*(3), 19–25.

Griffiths, M. D. (1997a). Video games and children's behaviour. In T. Charlton & K. David (Eds.), *Elusive links: Television, video games, cinema and children's behaviour* (pp. 66–93). Gloucester, UK: GCED/Park Publishers.

Griffiths, M. D. (1997b). Computer game playing in early adolescence. *Youth and Society, 29*, 223–237.

Griffiths, M. D. (1998). Internet addiction: Does it really exist? In J. Gackenbach (Ed.), *Psychology and the Internet: Intrapersonal, interpersonal and transpersonal applications* (pp. 61–75). New York: Academic Press.

Griffiths, M. D. (1999). Internet addiction: Internet fuels other addictions. *Student British Medical Journal, 7*, 428–429.

Griffiths, M. D. (2000a). Internet addiction—Time to be taken seriously? *Addiction Research, 8*, 413–418.

Griffiths, M. D. (2000b). Does Internet and computer "addiction" exist? Some case study evidence. *CyberPsychology and Behavior, 3*, 211–218.

Griffiths, M. D. (2003). The therapeutic use of videogames in childhood and adolescence. *Clinical Child Psychology and Psychiatry, 8*, 547–554.

Griffiths, M. D. (2005a). The relationship between gambling and videogame playing: A response to Johansson and Gotestam. *Psychological Reports, 96*, 644–646.

Griffiths, M. D. (2005b). Video games and health. *British Medical Journal, 331*, 122–123.

Griffiths, M. D., & Dancaster, I. (1995). The effect of Type A personality on physiological arousal while playing computer games. *Addictive Behaviors, 20*, 543–548.

Griffiths, M. D., Davies, M. N. O., & Chappell, D. (2003). Breaking the stereotype: The case of online gaming. *CyberPsychology and Behavior, 6*, 81–91.

Griffiths, M. D., Davies, M. N. O., & Chappell, D. (2004a). Online computer gaming: A comparison of adolescent and adult gamers. *Journal of Adolescence, 27*, 87–96.

Griffiths, M. D., Davies, M. N. O., & Chappell, D. (2004b). Demographic factors and playing variables in online computer gaming. *CyberPsychology and Behavior, 7*, 479–487.

Griffiths, M. D., & Hunt, N. (1995). Computer game playing in adolescenc: Prevalence and demographic indicators. *Journal of Community and Applied Social Psychology*, 5, 189–194.

Griffiths, M. D., & Hunt, N. (1998). Dependence on computer games by adolescents. *Psychological Reports*, 82, 475–480.

Gupta, R., & Derevensky, J. L. (1996). The relationship between gambling and video-game playing behavior in children and adolescents. *Journal of Gambling Studies*, 12, 375–394.

Gutman, D. (1982). Video games wars. *Video Game Player*, Fall 1982 (whole issue).

Gwinup, G., Haw, T., & Elias, A. (1983). Cardiovascular changes in video game players: Cause for concern? *Postgraduate Medicine*, 74, 245.

Harding, G. F. A., & Jeavons, P. M. (1994). *Photosensitive epilepsy.* London: MacKeith Press.

Johnson, B., & Hackett, A. F. (1997). Eating habits of 11- to 14-year-old schoolchildren living in less affluent areas of Liverpool, UK. *Journal of Human Nutrition and Dietetics*, 10, 135–144.

Julien, R. M. (1995). *A primer of drug action: A concise, nontechnical guide to the actions, uses and side effects of psychoactive drugs.* Oxford, UK: Freeman.

Kaplan, S. J. (1983). The image of amusement arcades and differences in male and female video game playing. *Journal of Popular Culture*, 16, 93–98.

Keepers, G. A. (1990). Pathological preoccupation with video games. *Journal of the American Academy of Child and Adolescent Psychiatry*, 29, 49–50.

Keisler, S., Sproull, L., & Eccles, J. S. (1983). Second class citizens. *Psychology Today*, 17(3), 41–48.

Klein, M. H. (1984). The bite of Pac-man. *Journal of Psychohistory*, 11, 395–401.

Koepp, M. J., Gunn, R. N., Lawrence, A. D., Cunningham, V. J., Dagher, A., Jones, T., et al. (1998). Evidence for striatal dopamine release during a video game. *Nature*, 393, 266–268.

Loftus, G. A., & Loftus, E. F. (1983). *Mind at play: The psychology of video games.* New York: Basic Books.

Maccoby, E. E., & Jacklin, C. N. (1974). *The psychology of sex differences.* Stanford, CA: Stanford University Press.

Maeda, Y., Kurokawa, T., Sakamoto, K., Kitamoto, I., Kohji, U., & Tashima, S. (1990). Electroclinical study of video-game epilepsy. *Developmental Medicine and Child Neurology*, 32, 493–500.

Malone, T. W. (1981). Toward a theory of intrinsically motivating instruction. *Cognitive Science*, 4, 333–369.

Marks, I. (1990). Non-chemical (behavioural) addictions. *British Journal of Addiction*, 85, 1389–1394.

McCowan, T. C. (1981). Space Invaders wrist. *New England Journal of Medicine*, 304, 1368.

McIlwraith, R. (1990, August). *Theories of television addiction.* Paper presented at the American Psychological Association, Boston.

Miller, D. L. G. (1991). Nintendo neck. *Canadian Medical Association Journal*, 145, 1202.

Millett, C. J., Fish, D. R., & Thompson, P. J. (1997). A survey of epilepsy-patient perceptions of video-game material/electronic screens and other factors as seizure precipitants. *Seizure, 6,* 457–459.

Mirman, M. J., & Bonian, V. G. (1992). "Mouse elbow": A new repetitive stress injury. *Journal of the American Osteopath Association, 92,* 701.

Murphy, J. K., Stoney, C. M., Alpert, B. S., & Walker, S. S. (1995). Gender and ethnicity in children's cardiovascular reactivity: 7 years of study. *Health Psychology, 14,* 48–55.

Parsons, K. (1995, April). *Educational places or terminal cases: Young people and the attraction of computer games.* Paper presented at the British Sociological Association Annual Conference, University of Leicester.

Phillips, C. A., Rolls, S., Rouse, A., & Griffiths, M. (1995). Home video game playing in schoolchildren: A study of incidence and patterns of play. *Journal of Adolescence, 18,* 687–691.

Professional Association of Teachers. (1994). *The street of the Pied Piper: A survey of teachers' perceptions of the effects on children of the new entertainment technologies.* Derby, UK: PAT.

Quirk, J. A., Fish, D. R., Smith, S. J. M., Sander, J. W., Shorvon, S. D., & Allen, P. J. (1995). First seizures associated with playing electronic screen games: A community based study in Great Britain. *Annals of Neurology, 37,* 110–124.

Reinstein, L. (1983). de Quervain's stenosing tendosynovitis in a video games player. *Archives of Physical and Medical Rehabilitation, 64,* 434–435.

Rutkowska, J. C., & Carlton, T. (1994, April). *Computer games in 12- to 13-year-olds' activities and social networks.* Paper presented at the British Psychological Society Annual Conference, University of Sussex.

Schink, J. C. (1991). Nintendo enuresis. *American Journal of Diseases in Children, 145,* 1094.

Segal, K. R., & Dietz, W. H. (1991). Physiologic responses to playing a video game. *American Journal of Diseases of Children, 145,* 1034–1036.

Selnow, G. W. (1984). Playing video games: The electronic friend. *Journal of Communication, 34,* 148–156.

Shimai, S., Yamada, F., Masuda, K., & Tada, M. (1993). TV game play and obesity in Japanese school children. *Perceptual and Motor Skills, 76,* 1121–1122.

Shotton, M. (1989). *Computer addiction?: A study of computer dependency.* London: Taylor & Francis.

Siegal, I. M. (1991). Nintendonitis. *Orthopedics, 14,* 745.

Soper, W. B., & Miller, M. J. (1983). Junk time junkies: An emerging addiction among students. *School Counsellor, 31,* 40–43.

Spence, S. A. (1993). Nintendo hallucinations: A new phenomenological entity. *Irish Journal of Psychological Medicine, 10,* 98–99.

Surrey, D. (1982). "It's like good training for life." *Natural History, 91,* 71–83.

Tejeiro-Dalguero, R. A. T., & Moran, R. M. B. (2002). Measuring problem video game playing in adolescents. *Addiction, 97,* 1601–1606.

Wanner, E. (1982). The electronic bogeyman. *Psychology Today, 16*(10), 8–11.

Wood, R. T. A., Griffiths, M. D., Chappell, D., & Davies, M. N. O. (2004). The structural characteristics of video games: A psycho-structural analysis. *CyberPsychology and Behavior, 7,* 1–10.

Young, K. (1998). *Caught in the Net: How to recognize the signs of Internet addiction and a winning strategy for recovery.* New York: Wiley.

Young, K. (1999). Internet addiction: Evaluation and treatment. *Student British Medical Journal, 7,* 351–352.

Zimbardo, P. (1982). Understanding psychological man: A state of the science report. *Psychology Today,* 16, 15.

Chapter 5

Meeting the Needs of the Vulnerable Learner

The Role of the Teacher in Bridging the Gap Between Informal and Formal Learning Using Digital Technologies

Laurence Peters

"I never try to teach my students anything. I only try to create an environment in which they can learn." (Einstein, as quoted in Prensky, 2001a, p. 71)

This chapter explores the role of learner self-identity in relation to formal and informal learning. It also examines the part digital technologies play in both these contexts. In particular I highlight how difficult it is for both students and their teachers to break free of the notion that the only "real learning" and knowledge is to be found in "formal learning," defined as the information transmitted in lecture fashion by the teacher and found in text-books and approved by teachers in the form of assignments, grades, and assessments. By contrast, "informal learning" can be defined as "any activity involving the pursuit of understanding, knowledge, or skill which occurs outside the curricula of educational institutions, or the courses or workshops offered by educational or social agencies" (Livingstone, 2001, p. 51).

One does not have to be a disciple of Foucault to understand the importance of the wall between institutionally sanctioned learning and what exists beyond it. Clearly informal learning is perceived by most teachers and students as standing at some distance from its formal counterparts. It is not too much of an exaggeration to conclude that informal learning is just not seen as part of the "school's business"—and so, not surprisingly, it is widely ignored. Neither the progressive era of education nor its modern renaissance in the 1960s could do much to scale that barrier, as informal learning continues to be defined in opposition to school, whether it is incidental (finding out something by accident), socialized (learning without knowing you are, as with table manners or language), or intentional (picking up a book). Informal learning, particularly the socialized kind that leads to most children's ability to master grammar of any language by the age of 4 without formal instruction, has a more powerful reach than formal learning. Yet its potential is seldom tapped by schools which continue to regard "real learning" as the transactions carried on in the classroom and controlled by the teacher. For example, few honors are available to children who have not just learned computer functions and applications but also how to repair and service them, or who can play advanced videogames. Rather these children may be identified as "techies" or at worst "nerds" or "geeks."

The power of digital technologies is that they lend themselves to informal learning and as such pose a challenge to the conventional orthodoxy that formal learning is the only real and valid kind that can be accepted in schools. One of the better explanations for why this state of affairs continues to exist has been offered by David Tyack and Larry Cuban (1995). They coined the phrase "the grammar of schooling" to explain the way various concepts such as the "lesson period," and the notion of a curriculum that needs to be "covered" and assessed within certain defined parameters, got started some time in the nineteenth century and became considered as the normal way schools, teachers, and students operated. Given this context it is not surprising that, for example, students' obvious interest in videogames should be sidelined by schools even when some educational aspects of certain games have been well described.[1] A leading advocate for a more game-driven curriculum, Marc Prensky (2005a), is engaged in an uphill battle to convince his colleagues as to their value. Commenting on how bestselling games deliver on their promises of exciting children's imagination, a place where students can continuously reinvent themselves, he contrasts that with the realities in classrooms:

> Rather than being empowered to choose what they want ("Two hundred channels! Products made just for you!") and to see what interests them ("Log on! The entire world is at your fingertips!") and to create their own personalized identity ("Download your own ring tone! Fill your iPod with precisely the music you want!")—as they are in the rest of their lives—in school, they must eat what they are served. (Prenksy, 2005a, p. 64)

Increasingly this type of control over technology—and the ways that students use it to learn informally—creates tensions, particularly in the high school setting. Prensky argues passionately that students want engagement—the same level they gain from computer games in their learning:

> In my view, it's not "relevance" that's lacking for this generation, it's engagement. What's the relevance of Pokémon, or Yu-Gi-Oh!, or American Idol? The kids will master systems ten times more complex than algebra, understand

systems ten times more complex than the simple economics we require of
them, and read far above their grade level—when the goals are worth it to
them. (Prenksy, 2005a, p. 64)

Notwithstanding many prestigious reports that would seem to underscore
Prensky's belief that the high school experience in particular is a source of
profound boredom for many teenagers (e.g., Bridgeland, Dilulio, & Morison, 2006), there appear to be few takers for Prensky's challenge and no
major software manufacturer out there willing to jump into the school
market to produce an educational game on the same kind of scale as say, for
example, *Grand Theft Auto*. It is still the student who must conform to the
demands of formal education, not the other way around. The learning styles
and strategies developed as a result of being part of the digital generation
often have to be sacrificed to the requirements of reading textbooks, listening to lectures, and raising hands when the teacher asks for a response.

It is therefore not a big surprise to find a close link between higher numbers of bored and disengaged youngsters, poor grades, and increased
dropout rates (Bridgeland et al., 2006). The resulting loss of talent is stag-
gering. Despite the lip service that is paid to such nostrums that "children
are our future," a "mind is a terrible thing to waste," and a widespread appre-
ciation that everyone (following Howard Gardner's 1983 popular book)
uses one of a number of distinct "learning styles," most of which are not
deployed in schools—the educational system casts off 16-year-olds in their
thousands and pays no real penalty for forsaking them—arguably it gains
the advantage of higher per capita test scores and smaller class sizes. On
the student end, the price to be paid in terms of a long term feeling of failure is enormous since the stigma of failure continues to haunt the student
throughout their lifetimes even if they decide, as they rarely do, to return to
school or take adult education courses. Their personalities and identities,
shaped in so many ways by the new technologies, are not given much room
to develop within the more confining environment of formal learning, and
they tend to give up and perceive themselves as "failed learners." Bandura
(1993) has traced how a cyclical process is begun when students constantly
fail to reach teacher expectations. He argues that the resulting frustration
lowers self-efficacy and makes students more likely to give up (Bandura,
1993).

The argument advanced here centers on our need to do more for the youth
that disengage early and asks us to examine the opportunities that digital
technologies present to re-engage a generation of informal learners who
cannot find satisfactory ways to apply their skills in the formal learning
context. The argument, therefore, has three prongs. First, informal learning is a place where most students can succeed. Rather than dismissing this

insight as too common an outcome to take seriously, we should be doing more to draw these students into the formal curriculum by recognizing how informal learning can build confidence as well as knowledge vital to success for all students who wish to develop skills and interests over a lifetime. Second, schools dismiss a need for students to perceive themselves as confident independent learners at their own peril—since research suggests that self-efficacy and confidence are critical elements if students are to grow into strong independent learners (Graham & Weiner, 1996). Third, for the group that can most benefit from informal learning, disadvantaged students (whom I shall, for reasons set out below, also call "vulnerable learners"), more effort to find spaces within the curriculum is necessary in order for them to develop success as informal learners. Teachers in such environments need to find ways to connect disadvantaged students' informal understandings with the formal curriculum.

The reason for the term *vulnerable learner* is to see those most at risk of academic failure as students who in their own eyes have already failed. There is no need at this time to dwell on the well-documented linkage between self-perception and failure, beginning with the famous Pygmalion study and in more recent years revealing itself in self-sabotaging tendencies of minorities who are not supposed to do well on tests like the SAT (e.g., Rosenthal & Jacobson, 1968). Suffice to say that this research strand is repeatedly overlooked or ignored in our willingness to keep sorting and labeling students despite the negative ramifications. The apparent consensus that early educational experiences determine later ones—as in the aphorism "if at first you don't succeed, you don't succeed" (Tuckett, 1997)— may be something of an overgeneralization, but not by much (Gorard, Rees, Fevre, & Welland, 2001). For example, many working-class students have what Selwyn, Gorard, and Williams(2001) refer to as a "deep reluctance" to continue their formal education because of the widely held perception that it is unrelated to the "real world" of making a living. They tend to perceive the academic world as not representative of their lives and realities.

The most common reasons for the vulnerable learner's proximity to failure is an early loss of self-confidence, an internalized feeling that they are "stupid" for not being able to do math or read at an early age (Chapman & Tunmer, 2003). This then clouds their appetite for taking on much extra effort if they find a subject or topic difficult—after all, they are stupid— so why could they be expected to understand x or y—goes the logic. It is not that more secure formal learners develop quite sophisticated strategies to solve unfamiliar problems, although sometimes they do. In many cases, they just know they can learn and have the confidence it takes to ask for help from teachers, from parents, peers, and in some cases tutors (Loranger, 1994). To change that unproductive dynamic means changing fundamentally their orientation to knowledge. We need to place vulnerable learners in more situations where they do not see themselves as exercising any "smartness" or being judged and revealing again they are stupid. In other words, we need to place them in settings where they retain control over their own learning, a place where they can shed their old identity as the not-so-smart student and forget who they are supposed to be as they enjoy the natural process of learning they knew before they entered school, the activity known as play. In the sections that follow, I describe a fascinating illustration of how learning becomes play and vice versa with a description of a unique experiment involving computer learning in an Indian village. I then try to uncover some of the critical features that make such informal learning successful and then conclude with how those elements might be applied in conventional classrooms, with the additional support of some technology-based interventions as an enabler of some more effective strategies that can be used by vulnerable learners.

National statistics suggest that a large number of those vulnerable students are in fact minorities who in many urban areas now have a one in two chance of graduating high school (Vail, 2004). The question is, can we find a way forward? The path to success is not, I would argue, employing more failed traditional instructional methods most clearly typified by the all-purpose phrase "drill and practice," but to start from a recognition that today's average college graduates have spent over 10,000 hours playing videogames and only 5,000 hours reading (not to mention 20,000 hours watching TV) (Prensky, 2001b). Not addressing the needs of "digital natives" (to use Marc Prensky's phrase) is to risk further failure and loss of hope.

Informal Learning: Informal Play: A Case Study of Informal Learning in an Indian Village

Imagine a dusty and remote Indian village. Against one wall sits a computer kiosk crowded with children (see Figure 5.1)—all scrambling for a turn on the computer as if it were a videogame—some voices are shouting out advice to the lucky few at the front of the line, others are yelling for their turn. Soon it is clear the children are teaching each other how to control and operate the computer to find out information, play games, and generally impress each other with their skills. The excitement of finding how spontaneously children learn basic computer skills has been turned into a 2002 *Frontline* documentary. The person behind the idea, Indian Institute Chief Scientist, Sugatra Mitra, has always been fascinated with the use of technology to assist children learning. He tells his story to the *Frontline*

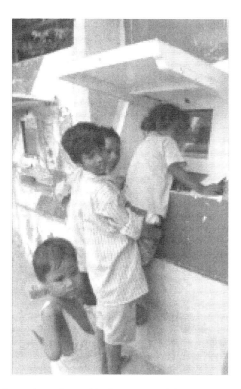

Figure 5.1. From the Hole in the Wall Education Ltd. http://www.hole-in-the-wall. com/ensuring-impact.html.

documentary team this way: "In 1988, I had written a very short paper to say that maybe children are capable of learning a whole bunch of things on their own, and specifically, perhaps computers. I got taken with my idea. But nobody else did." Eleven years later he found an opportunity to implement the idea when his company was exploring how to use kiosks to provide customers with new web based services.

> The idea had nothing to do with children. It was because kiosks were expected to become big business. Since I was heading R&D, I got the job to see how to build a kiosk. It was then a natural move to see what would happen if we built a kiosk in a village square, and the rest they say is history. (From Rory O'Connor, producer of the *Frontline*/World segment "The Hole in the Wall," October, 2002, http://www.pbs.org/frontlineworld/stories/india/connection. html; see Figure 5.2).

Mitra now refers to his experiment as "Minimally Invasive Education," as compared to traditional classroom learning. Mitra describes it as

Figure 5.2. From http://www.pbs.org/frontlineworld/stories/india/connection. html.

Note: Other photos can be obtained at http://www.niit.com/niit/ContentAdmin/images/ sugata/gallery3/index.htm and Dr Mitra: http://www.niit.com/niit/ContentAdmin/images/ sugata/gallery1/index.htm).

an alternative form of education. It's kind of primitive in the sense that if we were in a pack and three of us knew how to hunt then the rest of us need to know how to cook—you know something like that—whereas the formal education system says everyone needs to be an average hunter and an average cook. (King, 2004, p. 3)

He acknowledges it is difficult to integrate any of these approaches inside the formal curriculum He points out, for example, that while individual students may pick up things it is not true to say that the group learns everything in the same way:

... unlike the formal education system where you have an average achievement and fairly small deviation. Everybody in class knows approximately the same things. In the kiosks there is a remarkable growth in the average knowledge but there is also a very large standard deviation, which means that some children are learning something completely different from others. (King, 2004, p. 3)

The "Hole in the Wall" experiment is such a startling one partly because it runs so counter to the traditional way we understand education as a process of sitting down passively at a desk and either listening to a teacher or reading a book. There are no rules here, only options: to engage in an unstructured open-ended activity where no one can predict what will happen with any certainty—or not. Disengagement is much harder than engagement given the pressure of the peer group, at turns pushing you forward to understand and to integrate, and then at others forcing you to the front as the group begins to decide on what to do with the new almost magical machine.

Reasons Why Formal Learning Does not Work for Vulnerable Learners

How do we translate any of the insights to be derived from the "Hole in the Wall" experiment to modern classrooms? We must begin by understanding why in too many instances formal learning—in other words traditional teaching methods—fail to connect with vulnerable learners. A good example of vulnerable learners these days are adolescent, particularly minority, boys who lag in reading. In their book *"Reading Don't Fix No Chevys,"* Smith and Wilhelm (2002) explore some reasons for boy's lack of prowess in reading as opposed to subjects like math and science. Through some expertly conducted case studies, the authors suggest that teachers are conducting a monologue, excluding boys and their emerging need to declare who they are as people by following a course of study in which they have no real interest and which has little relevance to their lives. This might be considered by most educators as tough luck—that is the way it has been through the ages; kids don't get choices in what they want to study. The point here is that schools often do not make a real effort to connect students' experiences with the formal curriculum—not even when the choice of curriculum content is not written in stone. The authors make a compelling case for teachers not to see themselves as teachers of content but to help "students independently engage with content" (p. 113). Such "content" might take a variety of forms—for example, Bam, an African-American 11th grader featured in *"Reading Don't Fix No Chevys"* feels that his real self—as expressed in poetry, rap, emails, and personal Internet searching—is completely disconnected from the one he presents in school. "You feel you can say anything you want to" on the computer, but like another student, Robert (a 10th-grade African-American), he rejected much of school writing—which he perceived to be more about correctness than expression. Robert viewed reading in English as being "too superficial, as jumping from topic to topic, as being about texts instead of ideas, and not being useful" (p. 202).

Smith and Wilhelm (2002) refer back to an entire tradition of writings that link identity with choice and control, starting with the great philosopher

Alfred North Whitehead. Whitehead believed that knowledge begins with interest—what the philosopher referred to as "romance." Cultivating student interests, according to Whitehead (1961), is the necessary first step toward assisting them to be knowledgeable. For the boys interviewed in *"Reading Don't Fix No Chevys,"* the computer represents a gateway to follow and develop their interests in a way school rarely made possible. When students feel they are in control of their own learning there is deeper engagement and, as Greene (1988) points out, an opportunity to deepen self identity.

Reaching Vulnerable Learners Without Disrupting the "Grammar of Schooling"

The conflict between the grammar of schooling (to use once again Tyack and Cuban's useful phrase, 2005) and the need for vulnerable learners to regain a measure of control over their learning environment has made it inevitable that many vulnerable students disengage from school. Running parallel to this trend is the way technology (particularly the Internet) has not been made widely available as a resource, resulting in growing frustration among students. In many schools, much of students' engagement with the Internet happens "outside of schools and outside of teacher direction" (Levin, Arefeh, Lenhart, & Rainie, 2002, p. 23). What are some productive ways we might use some of the strengths of informal learning while still living within the grammar of schooling?

Let me suggest three possible applications of technology in the school context that would emphasize informal learning:

1 Designing educational games that really are as good as the best video-games—speed, challenge and individual problem solving and control.
2 Creating more spaces outside of the school curriculum where students can engage in more informal learning such as "computer clubhouse"-type operations.
3 Developing more collaborative activities using technology that enable students to work together in groups and collaborate with teachers and interested adults.

Educational Games

Educational games offer an extremely promising way to bridge formal and informal learning, but so far the promise has not met the reality. There are very few games that have been developed that can come near the quality of the best videogames. Advocates for educational videogames argue that the current use of technology in schools "has had little to do with transformation and far more to do with its principal appeal to educational administrators: its unprecedented capabilities for surveillance, control, and documentation—all basically forms of record-keeping—and so of 'educational *accountability*'" (DeCastell & Jenson 2003, p. 48). The same authors recommend a "digital re-tooling of curriculum by asking . . . how we can devise educative engagements which immerse students in the least pedantic, the most demanding, and the most engaging forms of intelligent participation in fields and forms of human endeavor?" (p. 52). It is a utopian-sounding challenge and we still seem a distance away from achieving anything close to this goal.[3]

There is of course some danger that we could be looking for a solution in the wrong place. If we burden the educational game with having to "teach" a certain set of academically valued content and skills we may well be destroying the potential of the game to be attractive to the user. Clearly, the game has to be less about solving teacher's dilemmas and more about addressing learners' need for some kind of role-playing experience. What may be needed is less the perfect "killer app game"—the one that teaches a year of physics in a two-hour game—and more one that enables teacher and student to discuss what the student has experienced in the game and use that conversation to recognize the skills and knowledge that the student gained as a result of the game. The agenda here is building learner confidence and enabling a student to be more in control of the conversation as a result of that experience than he or she would otherwise be. Because games are played in groups the peer group can play a more active role and have improved interaction with the teacher.

Computer Clubhouse

Another way to reach vulnerable learners is of course in the out-of-school hours, and a leading digitally based approach here is the Computer Clubhouse, which was started in 1993 by the Computer Museum in Boston in collaboration with MIT. There are now over 100 Computer Clubhouses worldwide. The goal of the Computer Clubhouse is to provide youth with access to resources, skills, and experiences that can help them succeed (see their website at http://www.computerclubhouse.org/). The basic idea is that students play the building bricks such as Lego to build robots and other gadgets, learning what they need to know through peer group interaction as well as through adult mentors. Mitchell Resnick of MIT and colleagues (a founder and leading advocate for the Computer Clubhouse concept) write that students, particularly the disadvantaged, need to have an environment in which all their creative interests are supported as they rarely are in schools (Resnick, Rusk, & Cooke, 1998).

This approach works only if the environment supports a great diversity of possible projects and paths. Perhaps the most respected figure in this tradition is the late John Holt, who argued that for children to successfully learn they need to see adults work on their projects and act as mentors as they once did in an age before mass schooling. As Holt wrote (1977, p. 5.): "I'm not going to take up painting in the hope that, seeing me, children will get interested in painting. Let people who already like to paint, paint where children can see them." Collaboration takes on a whole new dimension in this type of environment—instead of students being placed into groups and told to collaborate, Resnick argues that communities "emerge" over time. Design teams form informally, coalescing around common interests. Communities are dynamic and flexible, evolving to meet the needs of the project and the interests of the participants. A large green table in the middle of the Clubhouse acts as a type of village common, where people come together to share ideas, visions, information, and even food. Resnick and his team seem not to be interested in connecting these concepts to formal learning, preferring instead to think about schooling in an entirely different light so the classroom resembles more the clubhouse than the other way around.

While institutionally it may be important for Computer Clubhouses to be viewed as separate from schools, there is no reason why a computer clubhouse concept cannot be built into schools. Places where students, particularly vulnerable students, can go to engage in some serious play—build a robot or construct a car that can traverse rocky terrain, etc.—could be a place where immature or wounded self-identifies can be nurtured once the vulnerable learner gains some feelings of self-respect and regard from an adult who respects him or her as a successful learner. The point here is that time is used not to cram more facts and drill more skills but to develop confidence and play—and an opportunity to take on a challenge and be successful completing the task.

Conclusion

Given the need for more practical advice following the large numbers of students for whom formal education fails with increasingly dire consequences for the individuals involved and for our society in general, it would seem that the movement towards advocating the introduction of more informal approaches to learning should be stronger. Alas it is not—we do not have in the US or Europe the counterpart to the folk high school tradition that emerged first in Norway in the latter part of the nineteenth century and quickly spread through the rest of Scandinavia. In the Norwegian folk high school, attendance is voluntary, tuition is free and there are no tests or admission requirements. Currently there are 82 such schools in Norway that operate in a 33-week year from August through to May. As Harrington, Kopp, and Schimmel (2003) point out, "The pedagogical emphasis is on self-development through peer interaction, open discussion and dialogue" (p. 124). Each school has defined a different mix of subject areas from art and radio journalism to organic agriculture, childcare, and travel and tourism. "Folk high school teachers are selected not only for their competence in specific subject areas but their ability to instill, through example, the love for learning, community responsibility and individual growth hands-on experience" (p. 125). For many vulnerable students some time working in these areas in an environment that encourages confidence building and personal development is clearly something that is needed. It is an unfortunate consequence of the dominant accountability movement that it is harder to imagine any such system of youth development from taking root in the US—as indeed in most of the developed countries. We must continue to work with what we have— a promising range of technologies that whether the school likes it or not will force teachers to recognize student's capabilities to create worthwhile content and engage in new ways with media and subject matter. We can refer here to the growth of podcasting and the rapid way that teachers are finding ways to modify their own classrooms to accommodate not just the ubiquitous iPod but also a host of other micro technologies, from the Palm Pilot to smaller digital video cameras. The important first step is to realize that media saturated environments don't spell doom for student creativity. They can enable students to become more inspired if the teacher is to transfer more control to the student and harness the enthusiasm for the media and the desire to play more adult roles to advance curriculum goals.

Learner self-identity is a fragile thing—once lost it is very difficult to regain. Teachers bear a great deal of responsibility, particularly in the early grades, for shaping that identity and getting the child ready for lifelong learning—not just giving a grade on a test.

As Frank Smith (1998) reminds us,

> It is a frightening thought for many teachers that their students are learning all the time. Without any forgetting. And the students can't help it. They even learn things they might be better off not learning. The problem in school is not that many students aren't learning, but what they are learning. They may not learn what their teachers teach them, but their teachers may not be teaching them what they think they are teaching. To find out what students

actually learn, look at the way they leave school. If they leave thinking that "school things"—such as reading, writing, mathematics, or history—are boring, difficult and irrelevant to their lives and that they are "dummies" this is something they have learned both in school and outside. They learn to be non readers, or that they are nonspellers, or that they can't do mathematics. They learn who they are. If they learn they are leaders or geniuses (or clowns or fools) they behave accordingly. (p. 10)

The key to success in teaching is in being able to connect abstract thought with concrete experience, to represent new knowledge and new information (and practices and skills) in a way that connects with the student's accumulated body of experience. Informal learning can help bridge that often yawning divide that too frequently schools refuse to acknowledge is there. Smith (1998) reminds us about the need to start afresh. When Bruner (1966) observes the complex interaction among a certain tribe in Africa, we can perhaps see the kind of direction we have to go in. Among the Kung people of Africa, Bruner describes a different form of education from the way we often define "instruction":

Among hunting-gathering humans there is constant interaction between adult and child, adult and adolescent, adolescent and child. Kung adults and children play and dance together, sit together, participate in minor hunting together join in song and story telling together . . . one virtually never sees an instance of "teaching" taking place outside of the place where the behavior to be learned is relevant. (pp. 150–151)

For better and worse we can—and have to—do it differently. Digital technologies may provide us another opportunity to start over.

Notes

1   Shreve (2005) suggests that games are viewed by their developers as "a supplement, not a replacement, for good, old-fashioned teaching" and quotes a game publisher as saying that "We see this not as the only way to teach history but as part of the whole process that will include lecture, textbook reading, and paper writing. But it will greatly enrich the process of doing all those things" (p. 31).

2   From http://www.pbs.org/frontlineworld/stories/india/thestory.html. For a copy of the video, see http://www.globalvision.org/program/how/how.html. For more information on the "Hole in the Wall" experiment, see Hole in the Wall Education Ltd.'s website at http://www.hole-in-the-wall.com/index.html.

3   Harvard University's Chris Dede's own project using NSF funding involves the design and study of "a multi-user virtual environment (MUVE) that uses digitized museum resources to enhance middle school students' motivation and learning of higher order scientific inquiry skills, as well as standards-based knowledge

in biology and ecology." http://muve.gse.harvard.edu/muvees2003/documents/ Dede_Games_Symposium_AERA_2005.pdf (Retrieved, August 30, 2006).

References

Bandura, A. (1993). Perceived self-efficacy in cognitive development and functioning. *Educational Psychologist, 28*, 117–148.

Bridgeland, J. M., Dilulio, J. J., & Morison, K. B. (2006). The silent epidemic: Perspectives of high school dropouts. Retrieved from http://www.civicenterprises. net/pdfs/thesilentepidemic3-06.pdf

Bruner, J. (1966). *Toward a theory of instruction*. Cambridge, MA: Belknap Press.

Chapman, J. W., & Tunmer, W. E. (2003). Reading difficulties, reading-related self-perceptions, and strategies for overcoming negative self-beliefs. *Reading and Writing Quarterly, 19*, 5–24.

DeCastell, S., & Jenson, J. (2003). Serious play: Curriculum for a post-talk era. *Journal of the Canadian Association for Curriculum Studies, 1*, 47–52.

Gardner, H. (1983). *Frames of mind: The theory of multiple intelligences*. New York: Basic Books.

Gorard, S., Rees, G., Fevre, R., & Welland, T. (2001). Lifelong learning trajectories: Some voices of those "in transit." *International Journal of Lifelong Education, 20*(3), 169–187.

Graham, S., & Weiner, B. (1996). Theories and principles of motivation. In D. C. Berliner & R. C. Calfee (Eds.), *Handbook of educational psychology* (pp. 63–84). New York: Simon & Schuster Macmillan.

Greene, M. (1988). *The dialectic of freedom*. New York: Teachers College Press.

Harrington, C. L., Kopp, T., & Schimmel, K. S. (2003). Lessons from the Norwegian folk high school tradition, *International Education Journal, 4*(2). Retrieved from http://ehlt.flinders.edu.au/education/iej/articles/v4n2/harring/paper.pdf

Holt, J. (1977). On alternative schools. *Growing without Schooling, 17*, 5. Cambridge, MA: Holt Associates.

King, B. M. (2004). Access, culture and a "Hole in the Wall." Retrieved from http:// www.niit.com/niit/ContentAdmin/images/sugata/Interaction%20media-hole%20in%20the%20wall.pdf

Levin, D., Arefeh, S., Lenhart, A., & Rainie, L. (2002). The digital disconnect: The widening gap between Internet-savvy students and their schools. Research Report. Retrieved from http://www.pewinternet.org/report_display.asp?r=67

Livingstone, D. (2001). Adults' informal learning: Definitions, findings, gaps and future research, *New Approaches to Lifelong Learning (NALL) Working Papers* #21-2001. Retrieved from http://www.nall.ca/res/21adultsifnormallearning.htm

Loranger, A. L. (1994). The study strategies of successful and unsuccessful high school students. *Journal of Reading Behavior, 26*(4), 347–360.

Prensky, M. (2001a). *Digital game-based learning*. Toronto: McGraw-Hill.

Prensky, M. (2001b). Digital natives, digital immigrants. *On the Horizon, 9*(5), 1–6. Retrieved from http://www.marcprensky.com/writing/Prensky%20-%20Digital %20Natives,%20Digital%20Immigrants%20-%20Part1.pdf

Prensky, M. (2005a). "Engage me or enrage me": What today's learners demand. *EDUCAUSE Review, 40*(5), 60–65.

Prensky, M. (2005b). *Don't bother me mom—I'm learning: How computer and video games are preparing your kids for 21st century success and how you can help.* New York: Paragon House.

Resnick, M., Rusk, N., & Cooke, S. (1998). The computer clubhouse: Technological fluency in the inner city. In D. A. Schon, B. Sanyal, & W. J. Mitchell (Eds.), *High technology and low-income communities.* Cambridge, MA: MIT Press.

Rosenthal, R., & Jacobson, L. P. (1968). *Pygmalion in the classroom: Teacher expectation and pupils' intellectual development.* New York: Holt, Rinehart, & Winston.

Selwyn, N., Gorard, S., & Williams, S. (2001). Digital divide or digital opportunity? The role of technology in overcoming social exclusion in U.S. education. *Educational Policy, 15*(2), 258–277.

Shreve, J. (2005, April). Let the games begin, *Edutopia*, 29–31. Retrieved from http://www.edutopia.org/magazine/ed1article.php?id=art_1268

Smith, F. (1998). *The book of learning and forgetting.* New York: Columbia University.

Smith, M. W., & Wilhelm, J. D. (2002). *"Reading don't fix no Chevys": Literacy in the lives of young men.* Portsmouth, NH: Heinemann.

Tuckett, A. (1997, March 14). An election shopping list for lifelong learning. *Times Education Supplement*, p. 32.

Tyack, L., & Cuban, L. (1995). *Tinkering toward utopia: A century of public school reform.* Cambridge, MA: Harvard University Press.

Vail, K. (2004, November). Rethinking high schools. *American School Board Journal, 191*(11). Retrieved from http://www.asbj.com/2004/11/1104coverstory.html

Whitehead, A. N. (1961). *The adventure of ideas.* Cambridge, UK: Cambridge University Press.

Part II

Formal Learning with Technologies: Opportunities and Challenges

Introduction

Eileen Wood, Bowen Hui, and Teena Willoughby

The classroom is undoubtedly one of the most important and consistent formal learning contexts across the world. Children around the world attend schools, and for many children, especially those in developing nations or in underprivileged homes, schools present the major or only opportunity to become exposed to and interact with technology (e.g., Specht et al., 2002; Wood, Willoughby, Specht, Stern, Cavalcante, & Child, 2002). As computer technology becomes an integrated part of school curricula, it becomes increasingly important to create and evaluate effective software. It also is critical that we understand the interaction between what software designers state their software can do and the corresponding underlying cognitive operations that are actually evoked when software is engaged. Designing effective, well-grounded software and implementing computers into the formal learning context of the classroom are the key foci of the chapters in this section of the book.

An important consideration regarding the use of computers in formal learning environments is that the technology provides value-added learning experiences. Specifically, formal learning environments can provide a rich, interesting, and diverse context for learning. Computer technology has the potential to offer learners opportunities that exceed those available through traditional classroom instruction. Specific examples include software that automatically adapts to individual learners' needs and multimedia presentations that allow for simulations not possible in classrooms. In addition, the level of youth engagement afforded by computers with well-designed software exceeds that of some traditional formal learning contexts. It is important, however, that software effectively use the technological resources available rather than simply become a poor adaptation of a task that could just as easily be performed within the regular classroom context. To be maximally effective, therefore, software has to match the demands and needs of the learning context, the needs and interests of individual learners, and use the technology well.

At present there is an abundance of available software from both commercial and privately generated sources. Some of this software may have tremendous appeal and learning potential; however, there are caveats. One concern with available software is that although claims are made regarding the content, learning goals, and expected outcomes (e.g., promotes memory, creativity, teaches reading, etc.), there is no regulatory body that oversees software production to ensure the veracity of the claims that may be made in the software packaging. Similarly, little formal evaluation may have been conducted prior to releasing the software, leaving the user or educator to determine whether the stated goals or claims are substantiated or how these claims are realized through the software.

What is needed is high quality software development that is pedagogically and theoretically sound, adequately evaluated, and technologically sophisticated. In addition, the structural design of the software should be relatively similar across applications, particularly to avoid challenges for young learners. Most importantly, the software design should match the claims made by the designers. The chapters in this section of the text present software and applications that meet these goals. Prior to exploring these software applications, however, we present an example of an analysis we conducted with existing commercial software for very young learners (i.e., preschool and kindergarten age). Our goal was two-fold— first, to explore similarities in structural or navigational design across game applications, and second, to examine whether the cognitive components promised as outcomes by the developers (e.g., promotes memory and reading skills) were truly supported by the software.

In total, we sampled six games: Disney *Winnie the Pooh* preschool, Disney *Winnie the Pooh* kindergarten, *Reader Rabbit* preschool, *Reader Rabbit* kindergarten (from The Learning Company), Edmark *Trudy's Time and Place House*, and Edmark *Sammy's Science House*. Our goal was to identify a generic canonical navigation structure that might help to map out the commonalities across games, so that the structural path of games would become more evident and more accessible (Hui, Wood, & Willoughby, 2005a). In this structure, we identified three major components: the core, context, and peripheral (see Figure Iii.1) (Hui et al., 2005a, 2005b).

The core component consists of the "navigation screen" leading to various activities. The navigation screen serves to provide a "landscape" or layout of the activities in the game. From here the user may select an available activity to play from an assortment of options. The user may switch from one activity to another via the navigation screen. The core component is the basis of these games because a user would spend most of the time in individual activities and traveling in the navigation screen. The other components are peripheral to the overall game.

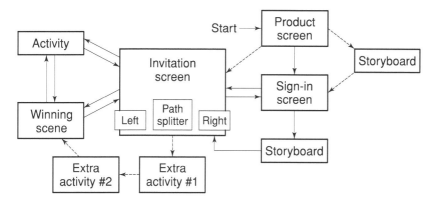

Figure Iii.1 Canonical navigation structure

The second component of the canonical structure, the context component, permits and encourages children to explore and complete individual activities. This structure can be mapped in the following ways. Some games keep a record of the user's activity performance history, so they require the users to sign into the game. This step is accomplished at the "sign-in screen," where new users enter their game identity or select one from an existing profile. A new user would listen to the storyboard—which describes the purpose of the game and serves as the motivation for completing the various game activities. After signing-in, the user is brought to the navigation screen and the game playing starts. Incremental progress is monitored through the successful completion of tasks within activities. For example, once a task is completed, students receive a small reward that leads toward the final goal. Once all the small rewards have been collected, students enter the "winning screen" where they watch a winning animation as a celebration of their effort. Thereafter, students may continue playing different activities for fun or for skill practice. Together, these screens make up the context component of the canonical structure, since they contribute to motivating the children to explore and complete individual activities.

The third major component is the peripheral structure, which extends the storyboard and the navigational screen by giving more control to the child in the exploration process (e.g., through more choices or options). However, careful design in separating the navigation screen is required so that the child remains spatially oriented. The peripheral structure also makes the game more realistic and challenging by having extra activities after collecting the immediate rewards. The contextual and peripheral structure increases the student's incentive to play the educational activities, but does not require additional skills.

Each of these major components serves different purposes, and each of the game companies in this study used a different combination of components. Specifically, Edmark software provided the core navigational structure, Disney software provided a goal-oriented context around the core structure—after the student signs into the game, a story is told outlining a particular objective (e.g., in the preschool version where the child has to help Pooh organize a surprise birthday party for Eeyore). Pooh travels around the navigation screen to tell everyone about the party. At each activity, the student's task is to help prepare a birthday present. Once all the characters are ready with a present, everyone gathers together to celebrate the occasion.

Finally, software from The Learning Company (*Reader Rabbit*) provided a structure that elaborated on the storyboard, navigation screen, and extraneous activities beyond the goal. Specifically, after the student is introduced to the main characters, signs into the game, and watches the story unfold, the student is brought to a navigation screen that splits into multiple paths. As the alternatives are explored, the student receives a reward (e.g., a yellow brillite after completing each activity). When five yellow brillites have been collected, the student enters the mountain to blow the pirates' boat off. This final task is complicated by requiring the student to accomplish two small activities before arriving to the winning scene. In order to represent these unique features in our generic model we merged some of the complex structures into one component, for example, the multiple navigation screens in *Reader Rabbit*. As a result, we arrived at a canonical game structure that underlies these four games.

Importantly, children who master the navigation structure of one product should be able to transfer this knowledge to other software by the same company and across companies to some extent, especially those with simpler structures. In order to develop effective software, it is clear that the design needs to be systematic and clearly accessible to the learner. Having a generic template of structures allows learners, even very young ones, to transition between software with greater ease.

In addition to the structural features, the content of software has to be relevant, accurate, and interesting. It is critical that the "interesting" activities in the software map onto specified cognitive, emotional, or social variables. For example, if the software is designed to promote early literacy skills, then the games or activities should contain exercises which strengthen these skills. In a further analysis of the software, we constructed cognitive taxonomies for skills such as emergent reading, memory, and language development consistent with the target areas purportedly supported by the software. Currently, we are mapping the specific activities present in the software onto the taxonomies to see which if any specific functions the games actually addressed. For example, both *Reader Rabbit* and *Winnie the Pooh* claimed to promote reading. When we examined the taxonomy we identified that in the *Winnie the Pooh* software, a game called "Kanga's Alphabet Soup" supported letter-name matching ("L" equals the sound for the letter l) for capital and lowercase letters. This is one of the fundamental skills required for emergent readers.

Similarly, with *Reader Rabbit*, there were a range of games that supported a number of emergent reading skills including letter-name matching, sight word recognition, rhyming, and blending. Within the software packages, some skills appeared at the preschool and kindergarten levels and some skills only at one level. There were more emergent reading skills identified in the *Reader Rabbit* software than in the *Winnie the Pooh* software. Also of interest, there were other domains where only some of the reported skills identified in the taxonomies were supported in the software. Clearly, packages designed for formal education contexts need to be precise with respect to the skills that can be developed in the software, and the software needs to be explicit about the match between activities and skill development in order to maximize the effective use of the software for learners with different needs.

Researchers have been sensitive to ensuring the development of high quality and relevant software for children. For example, the chapters written by Abrami et al. (chapter 6) and Nesbit and Winne (chapter 7) introduce software packages designed to facilitate learning. In both of these chapters, there is considerable attention to structure and content and the need to ensure that the software is pedagogically appropriate for formal educational environments. Abrami et al.'s chapter identifies software interventions that promote the development of basic skills (e.g., a balanced reading program for children called ABRACADABRA) as well as software programs that allow learners and educators to maintain digital records and evaluate academic performance (e.g., e-portfolios).

The chapter by Nesbit and Winne examines software designed to facilitate learning across subject domains, called *gstudy*. The impetus behind this software is to develop self-directed learning behaviors in learners. This software package is a key element also in fostering higher-order information literacy skills. Interventions like these are critical in allowing learners to strengthen their information literacy, critical thinking and learning skills across the curriculum.

The chapters by Abrami et al. and Nesbitt and Winne focus on rigorously designed software packages that support learners as they develop understanding and skills. An additional recent innovative program explores instruction through the Internet. Specifically, Kafai and Giang in chapter 8 demonstrate how Internet applications, drawing on a naturally engaging environment, can be used to provide an important alternative instructional format. They discuss how multi-user virtual environments (MUVEs), in particular *Whyville*, can offer both science play and learning activities to thousands of players through a primarily informal learning experience. Kafai and Giang argue that MUVEs have the potential to lead to greater engagement and understanding of science and technology ideas.

Learning by exploration is also a key fundamental concept in the work discussed by diSessa in chapter 9. diSessa outlines the best intellectual possibilities and opportunities offered by new-media literacies for reinventing or redesigning fundamental scientific principles. diSessa convincingly argues that the ability to transform the way that science and mathematics are taught will increase young children's motivation for learning these subjects.

The final two chapters in this section examine some of the supports and limitations experienced by both learners and educators when using technology. Specifically, Desjarlais, Willoughby, and Wood (chapter 10) examine the importance of identifying potential challenges that learners may experience when interacting with the Internet. In particular, learners with little domain knowledge may experience difficulties when conducting searches, identifying relevant information, and/or integrating information within and across individual websites. Desjarlais et al. discuss why learners with low domain knowledge experience these challenges with the Internet, and outline supports that can be provided to facilitate their learning.

Educators also play a critical role in children's learning with technologies. We explore the knowledge and experiences of educators in chapter 11 by Mueller, Wood, and Willoughby. These authors summarize educators' perceptions about their technological skills. In addition, there is discussion of the potential supports and barriers to the integration of technology within the school system. This chapter distinguishes between having access to technology and using it effectively as an integrated part of instruction. As such, this work has important implications for policy with respect to the design and implementation of in-service and technological support programs for educators.

In summary, there have been extensive technological advancements in software capability and in access to information on the Internet. As a result, there are exciting new opportunities for enhancing formal learning contexts for children. The challenge, however, continues to be how to ensure that these technologies are used effectively in the classroom. In fact, children's learning with technologies in informal settings often may be more sophisticated than what they experience at school. To effectively understand and use technologies, therefore, we need to pay attention to both formal and informal learning technologies. The two sections of this book provide a balance in understanding informal (Part I) and formal (Part II) learning contexts.

References

Hui, B., Wood, E., & Willoughby, T. (2005a, June). *Canonical navigation structure for children's software.* Presentation at the Canadian Language & Literacy Research Network (CLLRNet) 4th Annual Network Conference, Toronto, Ontario.

Hui, B., Wood, E., & Willoughby, T. (2005b, August). *Developing a taxonomy of cognitive skills required in young children's software.* Presentation at the Children's Learning in a Digital World Conference, Brock University, St. Catharines, Ontario.

Specht, J., Wood, E., & Willoughby, T. (2002). What early childhood educators want to know about computers. *Canadian Journal of Learning and Technology, 28,* 31–40.

Wood, E., Willoughby, T., Specht, J., Stern-Cavalcante, W., & Child, C. (2002). Developing a computer workshop to facilitate computer skills and minimize anxiety for early childhood educators. *Journal of Educational Psychology, 94,* 164–170.

Chapter 6

Using Technology to Assist Children Learning to Read and Write

Philip C. Abrami, Robert Savage, C. Anne Wade, Geoffrey Hipps, and Monica Lopez

In the 1980s and early 90s, when Robert Slavin addressed whole school reform and the problems of struggling readers in a program called Success for All (SFA), we followed the developments with interest. Because the research evidence on SFA in the United States was impressive, we arranged to bring the program to Canada as a pilot project and went on to investigate its effectiveness in a Montreal school. Chambers, Abrami, Massue, and Morrison (1998) showed the project could be implemented effectively but there were practical concerns about maintaining and expanding SFA in Canada. Chief among these was cost. In the United States, Title I federal funds are used to provide additional resources to inner city and impoverished schools, those with the highest percentage of at-risk and struggling readers. The full implementation of SFA depends on these resources, including funding at each school for a full-time program facilitator and tutors to work with approximately 30% of the students who fall behind their peers learning to read.

With an emerging interest in the uses of technology for learning, we turned our attention to the development of a tool—the Reading Computer Assisted Tutor or Reading CAT (Chambers, Abrami, McWhaw, & Therrien, 2001) to help ameliorate the funding problems. This prototype, or proof of concept, was designed both to reduce the costs associated with tutoring in SFA and to increase its effectiveness. The success of the Reading CAT led us to develop *Alphie's Alley* (AA), an interactive multimedia learning tool used by tutors and tutees simultaneously to help struggling readers learn. As we gained experience with AA, we realized we needed to develop a second reading tool, ABRACADABRA, for use in Canada which was not tied to a particular curriculum, and which was flexible and modular, allowing teachers in different provinces to use the tool to meet local needs. Simultaneously, we have undertaken the research and development of e-portfolio, a multimedia environment for the creation of student work designed to assist in the development of student reading and writing skills by encouraging their self-regulation.

We describe each of these tools in separate sections outlining the key ideas that define them and the evidence we have to date on their effectiveness. We begin with a brief summary of the state of the research evidence on educational technology and provide an overview of the Centre for the Study of Learning and Performance (CSLP) Software Design Principles as one way to explain our approach to using technology to help children learn to read and write.

Research on Technology in the Schools

Enthusiasm for, as well as apprehension regarding, the use of technology for learning appears widespread as we herald the arrival of the information age. To some, computer technology can be used as a powerful and flexible tool for learning (Harasim, Hiltz, Teles, & Turoff, 1995; Lou, Abrami, & d'Apollonia, 2001; Scardamalia & Bereiter, 1996). Indeed, there is sufficient optimism in the potential of technology to have a positive impact on learning that governments have established task forces and dedicated substantial research funds to identifying and promoting ways to deliver or enhance instruction with the use of technology. At the same time, there is sufficient skepticism about the use of technology to improve learning and beliefs that it may even represent serious threats to education (Healy, 1998; Russell, 1999). For example it is believed that an imbalance between computer skills and essential literacy skills may be created; technology dependencies and isolation may be fostered rather than independent and interdependent learners; and the joy and motivation to learn may be eroded, replaced by frustration with failed equipment. Many teachers hold beliefs concerning the usefulness of information and communication technologies (ICT) that parallel their attitudes towards any change to teaching and learning, be it through government-mandated reform or societal pressure. "If the computer can accomplish the task better than other materials or experiences, we will use it. If it doesn't clearly do the job better, we will save the money and use methods that have already proven their worth" (Healy, 1998, p. 218).

Technology Integration and Student Achievement

What has the research evidence revealed about the impact of technology integration, broadly defined, on student learning? There are now numerous narrative as well as quantitative reviews exploring the primary research on the impact of computer use on student achievement. The summaries vary: Some suggest positive impacts on student learning, while others are more equivocal, suggesting the evidence does not yet justify concluding that technology impacts positively and pervasively on student learning.

There are numerous examples of promising results. Kulik and Kulik (1989) cited several reviews that found positive effects of computer-based instruction on student performance, with a range of gains from .22 standard deviations to as high as .57 standard deviations. Schacter (1999) cited several studies that reported achievement, motivation, and engagement were higher for students in a technology-enriched environment. In their meta-analysis, Waxman, Lin, and Michko (2003) found positive, albeit small, effects of teaching with technology on student outcomes. Sivin-Kachala and Bialo (2000) included studies that reported gains in the areas of language arts and reading, mathematics, science and medicine, social studies, foreign and second language acquisition, and programming languages such as LOGO. Kulik (2003) found that most studies looking at the impact of the word processor on student writing have shown improved writing skills, as well as a positive impact on teaching programs in math, and in the natural and social sciences. Goldberg, Russell, and Cook (2003) conducted a meta-analysis looking at the effect of computer technology on student writing from 1992 to 2002. Results suggested that students who used computers when learning to write produced written work given standardized grades that were 0.4 standard deviations better than the grades given to the written work of students who did not use computers. Coley, Cradler, and Engel (2000) conclude that drill-and-practice forms of computer-assisted instruction can be effective in producing achievement gains in students.

In contrast, studies of more pedagogically complex uses of technology generally have been less conclusive, offering only promising and inviting educational vignettes (Coley et al., 2000). Fuchs and Woessmann (2004) initially found positive effects of home computer use on math achievement. After adjusting for family background and school characteristics, they found "the mere availability of computers at home is negatively related to student performance in math and reading, and the availability of computers at school is unrelated to student performance" (p. 17). Ungerleider and Burns (2002), reviewing mostly Canadian research, found little methodologically rigorous evidence of the effectiveness of computer technology in promoting achievement, motivation, and metacognitive learning and on instruction in content areas in elementary and secondary schools. Ungerleider and Burns (2002) also emphasized that student academic achievement does not improve simply as a result of having access to computers in the classroom without concurrent changes to instruction. More recently, Abrami, Bernard, Wade, Schmid, Borokhovski, Tamim, and others (2005) catalogued the arguments about learning with technology in Canada from multiple perspectives. Like Ungerleider and Burns, Abrami et al. (2005) concluded there was a great deal of enthusiasm but less sound evidence of the positive effects of educational technology.

We share the concerns of these researchers that methodologically sound studies must be undertaken with proper experimental and statistical controls to advance knowledge in this domain. We also believe it is important to conduct longitudinal investigations of pervasive and ubiquitous attempts at technology integration. And finally, we believe that there is a need for evidence-based software tools and include that as fundamental to our design principles.

The Centre for the Study of Learning and Performance

The Centre for the Study of Learning and Performance (CSLP) has taken on the challenge of combating the literacy problem. Established in 1988 and based at Concordia University, Montreal, Quebec, the CSLP is a research center consisting of over 50 principal members, research collaborators and/ or associates, 16 support staff, and over 100 graduate students.

A core principle of all our research and development is evidence-based practice. That is, we strive to use the best available evidence to design our tools, collect empirical evidence to validate and refine our tools, and consider the final tools as research vehicles to further our understanding of how children learn and teachers teach. The CSLP has developed Software Design Principles (See Table 6.1) to guide us through the creation of pedagogically sound tools.

Alphie's Alley: Electronic Performance Support for Success for All Literacy Tutors

According to Chambers, Abrami, Slavin, Cheung, & Gifford (2007) and Chambers, Slavin, Madden, Abrami, Tucker, Cheung, et al. (2007), since it first began to be used in education, technology has been primarily applied as a replacement for teacher instruction. Applications of instructional television and video have focused on the use of programs intended to teach in themselves. Computer applications have primarily engaged students with tutorial, drill, and practice, or writing software that they use independently of the teacher. In reading, these strategies have had inconsistent effects (e.g., Kulik, 2003; Torgerson, & Zhu, 2003).

Researchers at the Success for All Foundation and Concordia University

Table 6.1. The CSLP software design principles.

---

1. Research

1.1. All aspects of tool development should be based on peer-reviewed empirical research evidence, refined on the basis of research evidence, and then serve as the basis for collecting new evidence about teaching and learning using technology.

1.2. Emphasis should be placed on supporting meaningful motivational and learning outcomes.

1.3. Tool design should consider what is known about the processes and contexts of learning and instruction.

2. Design

2.1. We should strive to achieve the highest standards of excellence and lowest programming, interface, and instructional design error rates in the field of application and use.

2.2. Designs should be appealing and easy to learn and use.

2.3. Tools should be designed to address the specified goals of the target audience.

2.4. To the extent possible, tools should be inclusive and conform to universal design principles.

2.5. Technical support should be readily available and integral where possible.

2.6. Professional development, with an emphasis on pedagogy, should be readily available and integral where possible.

2.7. Design should emphasize adoption and use by the largest possible audience with a balance between the state of the practice and the state of the art.

2.8. Assumptions about physical (e.g., input devices) and cognitive skills (e.g., memory/attention, problem solving, self-regulation, etc.) interpersonal (e.g., collaboration), and other skills needed to use the tools for learning should be specified by design and validated (e.g., via transfer to novel tasks) either before or during development.

2.9. To the extent possible and appropriate, tools should be flexible and reusable.

3. Ethics

3.1. The intellectual property is owned by the CSLP unless otherwise specified by contractual agreements with funders.

3.2. All those who made a contribution will receive appropriate recognition.

3.3. Tools should reflect the values of universal human rights by avoiding any form of media that would be seen to unfairly marginalize a segment of our society.

4. Community

4.1. We encourage and support design and development by collaboration among CSLP members with diverse backgrounds and skills.

4.2. Input from the stakeholders should be sought throughout design, development, and testing.

4.3. Tools should be scalable and sustainable with minimal post-production cost.

4.4. Tools should be distributed not-for-profit with a philanthropic purpose in mind.

---

have developed and evaluated quite different strategies for the use of video and computer technology. These researchers have created strategies that embed the use of technology in teacher instruction, using technology as a tool for the teacher rather than a substitute. Two applications of this concept have been developed: embedded multimedia, in which video content is interspersed in teachers' lessons, and computer-supported tutoring, in which human tutors use computers to help structure their interactions with struggling first graders. Both of these applications are applied to enhance outcomes of the SFA beginning reading program, Reading Roots (Slavin & Madden, 2001), and evaluated in comparison to the SFA program without technology.

The SFA Tutoring Process

SFA tutoring can be described as a cyclical process with three main components: assessment, planning, and daily tutoring (see Figure 6.1). Tutors begin by assessing students to identify their strengths and weaknesses in reading. Then, based on the results of this assessment, tutors create an instructional plan to work with each student for a period of two weeks. Creating this plan involves identifying the reading skills to focus on during tutoring and selecting instructional activities to address (teach and practice) those skills. Finally, tutors implement their plan during daily 20-minute sessions. As they work daily with the students, tutors also monitor and record student progress. At the end of the two-week period, they reassess the students.

In the traditional tutoring sessions, much paperwork is required from the tutors, bringing unneeded complications to what should be powerful one-on-one tutoring sessions. Tutors, often uncertified volunteers, are also expected to perform complex tasks such as analyzing assessment results, and planning effective tutoring sessions for each tutee, all while keeping accurate records of tutee progress. The combination of this complex process with the excessive paperwork leads, in some instances, to poor program implementation, especially by the inexperienced tutors. Computer-supported tutoring was the selected strategy to address these implementation problems in tutoring and enhance the overall effect of the tutoring process. *Alphie's Alley* (after Alphie the Alligator, a central character in the SFA beginning reading program) is a computer program designed to guide tutors through the different stages of the tutoring process, facilitating the implementation of complex tasks like assessment and instructional planning, and enhancing the daily tutor–tutee interaction with interactive multimedia activities.

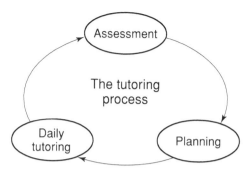

Figure 6.1. Assessment, planning, and daily tutoring.

Electronic Performance Support Systems: A Framework for the Design of *Alphie's Alley*

The design of *Alphie's Alley* followed Gery's (1991) concept of an Electronic Performance Support System (EPSS). An EPSS is an interactive program that is intended to both train and support the novice user in the performance of a task (Wild, 2000). Everything needed to complete this task—information, software, expert advice, guidance, and learning experiences—is integrated and available, ideally leading to improved time to performance (time needed for a novice to perform like a more experience colleague), improved worker productivity, and minimal support and intervention by others (Brown, 1996). Table 6.2 summarizes the central elements and attributes of an EPSS (Gery, 2002).

The goal of *Alphie's Alley* as an EPSS is to promote SFA program fidelity by providing a computer environment where all the steps of the tutoring process can be implemented. Each step in the process is structured, simplified, and supported. Implementing the tutoring process with *Alphie's Alley* also reduces the paperwork and automates the record keeping previously required from tutors. Table 6.3 summarizes the support features in the different modules of the system.

Although some task automation is included in *Alphie's Alley* as part of the support features, our discussions on artificial intelligence (based on Everson, 1995; Mandl & Lesgold, 1988; Mitchell & Grogono, 1993) concluded that adaptive branching was undesirable given the fact that we do not envisage the computer replacing a human tutor. Because our goal is to use the computer and the SFA tutor skills in concert for the progress of the child, we decided to enhance the computerized diagnostic and assessment activities toward a front-end complexity that will simplify the tutor's record-keeping and memory skills so his or her full attention can be devoted to the child.

Table 6.2. Design principles of electronic performance-support systems.

EPSS Elements	Gery's (1991) EPSS Attributes
Task Structuring	• Establish and maintain a work, process, or task context. • Structure work process: progress performers through best-practice performance of a process, activity, or task. • Aid in goal establishment: help people determine what to do in a certain situation. • Provide evidence for task progression: users know what they have done and what they have to do next. • Reflect natural work situations, including natural language. • Employ consistent visual conventions, language, positioning, navigation, and other system behavior (interface design).
Knowledge and Data	• Contain embedded knowledge on the interface, accessible from the interface, or in the underlying rules, relationships, and logic programmed into the software. • Institutionalize best practices or current best approach. • Inform about the consequences of actions, decisions, and the failure to act or decide. • Observe performer actions and provide contextually relevant feedback and information and advice.
Support Tools and Resources	• Provide support resources at the time of need and without breaking the context. • Provide layered support resources to accommodate diverse performer motivations, time, and existing knowledge or skill. • Automate tasks including deliverable creation (e.g., automatically generated reports, communications, outputs, etc.). • Provide alternative view of the interface to allow varying amount of structure and freedom to users who require more or less guidance and task structuring.

The computer analyzes the collected data and provides possible paths of instruction for the tutors.

In the development of the computer-based tutoring activities we incorporated elements of the American Psychological Association's Fourteen Learner-Centered Principles (APABEA, 1997) to ensure maximum understanding and capability on the part of the child by developing ways to enhance learner control of, and peak the child's interest in reading for predominantly intrinsic reasons. For example, cognitive and metacognitive

Table 6.3. Alphie's Alley support features.

Modules	Support Features
Tutor Professional Development	• Tutorial on the purpose and the "how to" for the different modules of the tool. • Description of all Reading Roots tutoring goals and objectives addressing the following questions: What is it? Why is it important for learning to read? How do you work on it? (Video clips of expert tutors working on these objectives.) • Video clips of expert tutors explaining/modeling key elements of tutoring: tutor qualities, goal setting, praising, fading support, re-reading stories. • Instructional demos of all computer-based activities available in *Alphie's Alley*.
Assessment	• Computer walks tutor/student through the assessment until enough information is determined to create a tutoring plan. • Just-in-time tutor prompts and directions for assessment of different objectives. • Student progress is stored in a database to inform the creation of the tutoring plan.
Planning	• Computer suggests instructional plan based on student assessment results. • Computer guides tutor through the planning process (select objectives, select activities, communicate plan to teacher). • Just-in-time support for the selection of objectives (What?—Why?—How? / video clips of expert tutors working on different objectives). • Database of paper-based and computer-based activities provides multiple choices for tutoring plan development.
Tutoring Activities	• Access to pen and paper (on screen) and computer-based activities selected in the tutoring plan. • Computer-based activities: – Provide practice appropriate to the student level (based on assessment results). – Increase student motivation. – Provide just-in-time support for tutor role (Tutor Street). – Provide appropriate scaffolding (model for tutors). – Keep record of student progress.

factors were addressed by how we incorporated the student goal-setting process, how we integrated the content of the paper-based SFA curriculum as animated visual aids, and how we scaffold the students skill development in various activities.

The design of the professional development module was informed by the cognitive models of professional development based on Learning First Alliance (2000), in which aspects of cognitive apprenticeship (Collins, Brown, & Newman, 1989) and self-regulated learning (Randi & Corno, 2000) both find a place. Our selection of what aspects of professional development have the most impact, such as a focus on content, were also informed by recent work by Garet, Porter, Desimone, Birman, and Yoon (2001).

Alphie's Alley Software

As students are identified as at-risk and placed into tutoring, they are formally assessed to determine their reading level (see Figure 6.2). Since the assessment can be a fairly long process, depending on the level of the student, the tutor can leave and return to where she/he was at any time, not burdening the student with lengthy questioning.

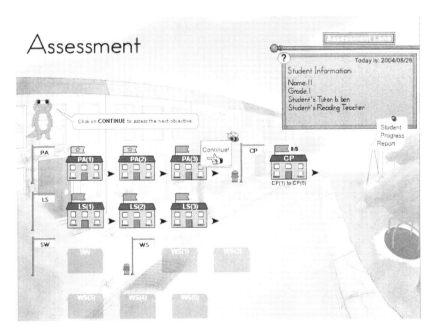

Figure 6.2. Assessment interface.

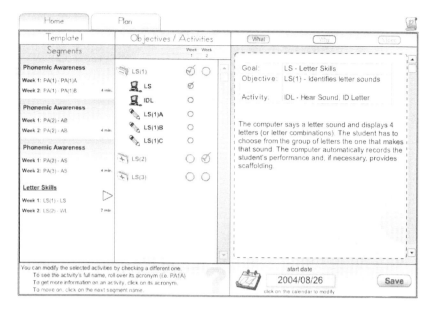

Figure 6.3. Planning interface.

After a predetermined number of objectives have been assessed, the computer generates a plan for the student, consisting of 10 sessions (see Figure 6.3). It should be noted that a tutor can change a plan, thus overriding the computer-generated items. A plan consists of a series of instructional activities that the student will work on to improve her/his literacy skills. There are 19 computer-based activities and over 60 pen and paper activities that can be accessed from the software. Using the planning module, the tutor can view or create a plan according to the identified difficulties, access information for the activities, and view the objectives in need of mastery. The planning template also allows the tutor to make comments on student performance after every session.

Once the plan is complete the tutor can then accesses the activity section (see Figure 6.4) and have the student work on the designated activities. Each activity's difficulty level is determined by the assessment; as each student masters items within the activity new levels are achieved. For many activities, the validity of the answer is entirely dependent on the tutor. For this reason we have created a keypad that allows the tutor to enter student responses without crowding the space of the student. After the 10 sessions are completed, the student is reassessed and the cycle begins again.

Figures 6.5 and 6.6 are screen captures from two activities: Sequencing (see Figure 6.5) where the student must place events from a story in

Figure 6.4. Activity menu.

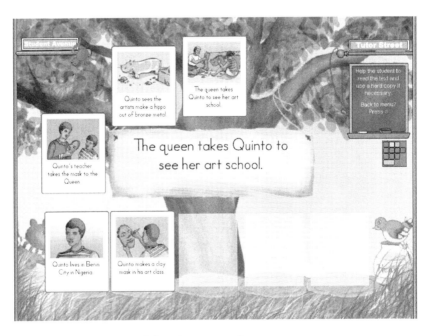

Figure 6.5. Sequencing and shared story questions.

Figure 6.6. Sequencing and shared story questions.

the correct order, and Shared Story Questions where the student's comprehension of a story is demanded. Other activities that support the SFA instructional objectives are described in Table 6.4.

Every section of the software contains a guide that prompts the tutor how to proceed. The just-in-time information is contextual and always kept to a minimum so as not to be distracting. It is a dynamic reminder of the support options that the tutor can access at any given time. In addition, just-in-time video vignettes are embedded in *Alphie's Alley* in order to provide professional development for tutors who need support with particular aspects of tutoring as specific difficulties and challenges arise.

Research Evidence

A recently completed study (Chambers, Abrami et al., 2007) of *Alphie's Alley* employed a true experimental design. A total of 25 high-poverty Success for All schools located throughout the US participated in the study. In each, first graders identified for tutoring services were randomly assigned to be tutored either with or without *Alphie's Alley*. Tutors within each school were also randomly assigned to treatments. A total of 412 first graders who

Table 6.4. Alphie's Alley's computer-based activities.

Activity name	Skill
Auditory blending	Ability to hear individual phonemes and blend sounds into words.
Auditory segmenting	Ability to hear a word and separate each sound.
Letter sounding	Identifies (reads) letter sounds.
Id letter	Identifies (reads) letter sounds by choosing the correct letter.
Word level blending	Reads words by using the blending strategy.
Word level spelling	Spells words by breaking into separate sounds.
Sentence level spelling	Writes sentences by spelling words using the strategy of breaking into separate sounds.
Shared story questions	Answers Shared Story or Treasure Hunt question with evidence (oral); makes reasonable predictions with evidence from text.
Story event sequencing	Identifies the story elements by sequencing main events in a story.
Organizer	Identifies the story elements (characters, setting, problem, sequence of events, and solution) with prompting (oral).
Sight words	Recalls essential sight words.
Story preparation	Answers 'WH" questions for a story.
Sentence level spelling	Spells words by using the strategy of breaking them into separate sounds.
Tracking	Reads from left to right; reads with one-to-one word correspondence; reads without losing place or skipping words.
Word level decoding	Uses sound blending to read unknown words in text.
Fluency	Reads words accurately; reads words smoothly; reads with expression, using punctuation appropriately.
Comprehension	Recognizes and attempts to correct word errors in text (clarifies words); recognizes when sentence or passage doesn't make sense and attempts to clarify.
Story questions: evidence and prediction	Makes reasonable predictions with evidence from text.

Table 6.5. Effect sizes for reading measures reported in Chambers, Abrami, et al. (2007).

Test	Effect size	Label
Woodcock letter–word identification	+0.45	Large
Word attack	+0.31	Moderate
DIBELS fluency	+0.23	Moderate
Grey oral reading test	+0.18	Small
Passage comprehension	+0.05	Small

Note: Effect sizes of less than 0.2 are "small," 0.2 to 0.4 are "moderate" and above 0.5 are "large," and reflect real-world importance of findings, not just "statistical significance."

received tutoring were identified for the study. Results varied depending on ratings of the quality of implementation of the tutoring model. All tutors were rated on a three-point scale from "fully implemented" to "not implemented." Here we will focus on the 203 children in high implementing schools. Effects strongly favored the children who received the computer-assisted tutoring. Significant positive effects were found on Woodcock Letter–Word Identification and Word Attack, and on DIBELS Fluency (see Table 6.5). Directionally positive but non-significant differences were found on the Grey Oral Reading Test and Passage Comprehension.

The results of this study strongly support the effectiveness of the *Alphie's Alley* computer-supported tutoring model when it is well implemented. The findings are especially noteworthy given that they show reading gains made beyond the paper and pencil tutoring programme in SFA (a well established and demonstrably effective program) and not compared to a "no treatment" control, where we speculate the large effects found here would be even larger.

Observations of the computer-supported tutoring sessions, conversations, and questionnaire results from tutors (Schmid, Tucker, Jorgensen, Abrami, Lacroix, & Nicoladou, under review) also showed very positive attitudes toward *Alphie's Alley*, but it took many of the schools several months to fully implement the program with fidelity. With tutors experienced with the software, the percentage of tutors doing high quality implementations would surely rise, and the positive outcomes seen in this study for high implementers only could come to characterize outcomes for more of the tutors.

ABRACADABRA: A Balanced Reading Approach for Canadians Designed to Achieve Best Results for All

The United States is not alone in having too many children and adults who cannot read well. Canada is generally seen as a literate developed nation, with a well-developed and successful education infrastructure, and consequently a thriving economy. Like all impressions, however, it is important to go deeper and explore the evidence. How well then is Canada really doing in terms of literacy? The well-respected OECD Program for International Student Assessment (OECD, 2000) measured how well young adults around the world are prepared to meet the challenges of today's knowledge societies. The average performance of Canadian students was in the upper quartile on the PISA measures of reading (OECD, 2000; Statistics Canada, 2004). Nevertheless the same report noted that *27.6% of those students tested performed at or below Level 2*. These students encountered basic difficulties in "Locating straightforward information, making low-level inferences of various types, working out what a well-defined part of a text means, and using some outside knowledge to understand it" (OECD, 2000; Statistics Canada, 2004).

Such basic difficulties, played out across the nation, have a significant impact on the economic well-being of all Canadians. Recently the results of national and international surveys—the Adult Literacy and Life Skills (ALLS) survey by Statistics Canada and the Organisation for Economic Co-operation and Development (OECD) disseminated by the Canadian Council on Learning (2007)—suggested that almost half of adult Canadians have only low level literacy skills. The survey set five levels of literacy, with level 3 considered to be the minimum level of skill required in today's society. Results showed that only 58% of Canadians achieved level 3 or above in the category of prose literacy. The ALLS survey was conducted in Canada, the United States, Italy, Norway, Switzerland, Bermuda, and the state of Nuevo León, Mexico. More than 23,000 Canadians took part in the survey that tested prose and document literacy, numeracy, and problem-solving skills. In addition the survey showed that there has been virtually no improvement in Canada's results since the previous surveys.

Paul Cappon, President and CEO of the Canadian Council on Learning, responded to these findings (2007) by arguing that there is an urgent need to develop a more cohesive approach to ensure that Canadian adults have the literacy, numeracy, and analytical skills they need to reach their full potential He drew specific attention to the urgent need to understand why our current literacy and learning programs are not succeeding in order to develop more effective approaches. These crucial aims are pursued below in an exploration of what is known about effective reading interventions.

Research on Literacy

It is now generally agreed that the strongest evidence for developing effective educational policy comes from summaries of randomized control studies or RCTs (e.g., Reynolds, 2001). Such RCT designs, if well implemented, are true experiments that provide the clearest possible internal validity (i.e., they offer genuine proof of a causal connection between variables). Furthermore, a well-designed study in one part of the world can then be replicated in perhaps dozens of other universities and research centers around the world. Finally, secondary meta-analyses of all available studies can lead to the highest confidence in the internal and external validity of evidence described. Such research designs are routine in medicine, but sadly have not been common in education (e.g., Sebba, 1999).

One area where such progress in the use of RCT designs has taken place is in cognitive approaches to reading research. Over the past 30 years or so there has been a massive growth in the availability of primary research in this field. Consequently there has been an emergence of both narrative and statistical meta-analyses of evidence in reading research (e.g., Ehri, Nunes, Willows, Schuster, Yaghoub-Zadeh, & Shanahan, 2001; Hall & Harding, 2003; Kuhn & Stahl, 2003; Rack, Snowling, & Olson, 1992; Torgerson & Zhu, 2003; Troia, 1999; Van Izjendoorn & Bus, 1994; Wolf & Bowers, 1999). This has in turn led to the development of clear evidence-based approaches to interventions aimed at all aspects of literacy from word-recognition through to fluency and advanced text comprehension and nuances of meaning-construction (e.g., Ehri et al., 2001, Troia, 1999).

The strongest forms of reading research are those that are both well designed and that have been repeatedly replicated. A good example of this approach is the National Reading Panel report (NRP, 2000, and see also Pressley, 1998; Pressley, Wharton-McDonald, Allington, Block, Morrow, Tracey, et al., 2001; Taylor, Pearson, Clark, & Walpole, 2000). In addition, interventions must be comprehensive or balanced. Truly balanced approaches emphasize reading skills such as: *phonemic awareness*—word reading and spelling accuracy, phonological awareness, and letter–sound (and grapheme–phoneme) knowledge; *fluency* and automaticity; and *comprehension*—sequencing previewing and prediction; and an emphasis on meta-cognition (reflection on knowledge). Dozens of studies worldwide have shown these techniques to be effective in improving literacy when used as part of a classroom approach that also includes the fostering of: on-task activities, student self-regulation, connections across curricular themes, and between home and school (see e.g., Hall & Harding, 2003 for a recent review).

We are, therefore, in a position now where we really do know what to do to enhance early literacy. For example, we know that effective preventative reading programs in Grade 1 that involve structured phonics, word rec-ognition, and letter–sound knowledge training that are over-learned and repeatedly connected to the end goal of text reading for meaning are one of several important elements of balanced literacy approaches that will also involve explicit attention to fluency and to a host of strategies for under-standing and evaluating texts (e.g., Pressley, 1998). So what prevents progress in literacy at a national and international level? The problem is, to a large degree, one of implementation. One issue that prevents fuller imple-mentation of evidence-based programs is that such programs are frequently prohibitively expensive. Allington (2004), for example, has argued in an influential paper in *Educational Leadership* that the costs of current reading programs in the US (some $500,000 per typical school) effectively prevents full literacy for all ever taking place.

The application of evidence about collaborative group-based learning pro-vides a partial solution to this financial problem (see e.g., Savage, 2006). In such a context, one might also for a moment stop and imagine what massive impact the availability of a flexible, comprehensive, entirely evidence-based intervention program, that is entirely free at the point of delivery, would make. What if such a tool also incorporated ongoing professional develop-ment, multiple assessment, and recording tools? Such a system would be a massive contribution to the improvement of national literacy, with far-reaching social and economic consequences. ABRACADABRA is just such a system.

ABRACADABRA Design Methodology

The creation of a large application like ABRACADABRA is a complex pro-cess. In an effort to exercise our design principles the CSLP practices an iterative design and development methodology in which a multidiscipli-nary team conducts formative evaluation and formal research, works with the community at large for guidance, and designs pedagogically sound tools based on the evidence. This process culminates in working versions of ABRACADABRA and the cycle of research and development begins again.

ABRACADABRA is an evidence-based tool in at least three senses:

1 *The content of ABRACADABRA learning activities is derived directly from systematic reviews of evidence about what works in reading and spelling.* For example, there is a huge body of evidence that reciprocal teaching techniques involving meta-cognitive skills of prediction, sequencing, and summarizing can improve reading comprehension (e.g., Ehri et al., 2001; Pressley, 1998). These skills are, therefore, integrated in all story elements. See Table 6.6 for

Table 6.6 Sample from the ABRACADABRA research matrix: comprehension

Skill Area	Comprehension					
Skill	Story elements	Comprehension monitor	Sequencing	Prediction	Summarizing	Vocabulary
Activity title	Who, where, and what happened?	Find the word that doesn't belong	Place these events in order	What happened next		
Story titles						
Bean Sprouts	✕	✕	✕			✕
I Can Move	✕					✕
Open My Eyes	✕					✕
Feelings	✕					✕
Red Hen	✕	✕	✕	✕	✕	✕
Dove and Ant	✕	✕	✕	✕	✕	✕
Frogs and Well	✕	✕	✕	✕	✕	✕
Darryl	✕	✕				✕
Henny-Penny	✕	✕	✕	✕	✕	✕
Billy Goats	✕	✕	✕	✕	✕	✕
Waterfalls	✕		✕	✕	✕	✕

the Comprehension section of the research and content matrix developed from research studies and used to guide the creation of specific ABRACADABRA activities.

These applied evidence-based approaches of constructing and applying evidence matrices are taken to all stories in ABRACADABRA and for all text-, word-, and fluency-level activities.

2 ABRACADABRA is based on the experience gained by working with part-ners to develop technological tools. Specifically, we have gained much expertise from designing, developing, testing, and scaling early literacy software, *Alphie's Alley*, for the Success for All Foundation. As noted, a recently completed study (Chambers, Abrami et al., 2007) of *Alphie's Alley* strongly supports the effectiveness of the computer-assisted tutoring model when it is well implemented.

ABRACADABRA is also based on the research on emerging reading skills in English conducted by a member of the CSLP, Dr. Robert Savage. For example, Savage and Carless (2005) report that there are consistent data across a host of longitudinal and intervention studies showing the theoretical and practical importance of awareness of small speech sounds (phonemes) as an early foundation for developing effective reading skills. Phonemic activities are accordingly incorporated in screening tasks for "at-risk" poor readers and in early ABRACADABRA reading intervention activities. Exactly the same approach will be taken to the application of research on emerging reading skills now emerging in the French-speaking world with the help of our French language and literacy experts.

3 ABRACADABRA is developed and improved based upon the CSLP's design principles and evidence from direct intervention in schools. Our strong belief in evidence-based practice, our guiding design standards, our adherence to ethical responsibilities, and our commitment to working with the community are evident in all stages of the developing this application.

The ABRACADABRA Application

ABRACADABRA is a web-based application that allows teachers to expose children to literacy building skills that they must have to be successful readers. Still in its infancy, the completed site will contain stories, activities, assessment features, a communication device, and a reporting module. It will offer a flexible solution to literacy development where teachers can customize learning for individuals and groups of students. ABRACADABRA also offers multimedia professional development material to help teachers understand the importance of research-based literacy skills and how this application can be successfully used in the classroom.

The ABRACADABRA web application can be viewed at http://grover. concordia.ca/ABRA/"version1/abracadabra.html. Figure 6.7 demonstrates the ABRACADABRA chooser where users can match skill-building activities with leveled stories.

The following two screenshots show how we have created meaningful contexts by establishing the relationship between the content within the stories and the content within an activity. The "Blending Train" activity (Figure 6.8) for example, contains the word *red*, which is directly taken from the story The Little Red Hen (Figure 6.9). Wherever possible the text

Figure 6.7. ABRACADABRA chooser.

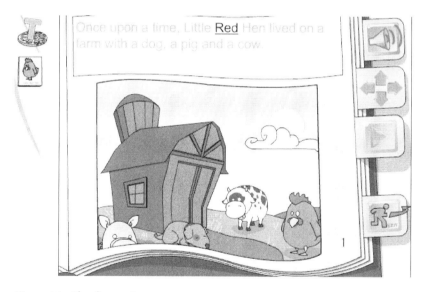

Figure 6.8. Blending train.

(words and sentences) from the stories are used in the activities, as well as a visual representation of the story within the activity.

The Professional Development Module, represented in Figure 6.10, is intended to support teachers in both the development of literacy skills for beginning readers, and the use of the website. This module contains short video clips that present information in a just-in-time fashion. The fact that

Figure 6.9. The Little Red Hen.

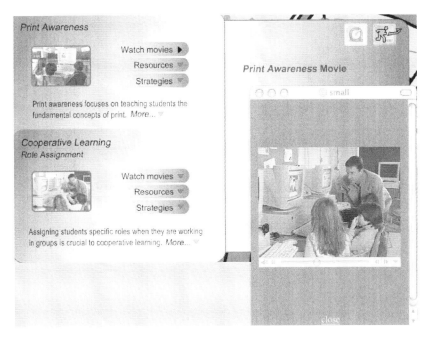

Figure 6.10. Professional development module screen shot.

teachers respond best to other teachers speaking with a real-world perspective was considered in our design.

The video clips explain each literacy skill, what it looks like in a real setting, and (where appropriate) what it looks like when students are lacking the skill. Future development will include extension activities and animated demonstrations of each activity—not only to help the student understand the navigation and the particular skill, but also to provide another avenue for training the teacher.

ABRACADABRA Research

Formative evaluation

In summer 2003, a group of trained Masters students facilitated groups of children (four at a time) using the ABRACADABRA prototype (http://grover. concordia.ca/ABRA/school/) and then observed their responses to the system. This provided preliminary evidence that practicing skills on the computer was viable, popular (with children, parents, and teachers), and children showed clear signs of improvement. This demonstrated that children discuss texts they have shared on a computer in small groups when prompted to do so by the computer.

Pilot intervention (2004–2005)

Current cognitive-developmental models of early reading rest on the assumption that accurate word recognition is a crucial co-requisite of skilled reading comprehension (e.g., Ehri, 1995). Phonological awareness appears to be necessary but not sufficient for reading acquisition (Brady & Shankweiler, 1991; Byrne, 1998; Ehri, et al., 2001; Goswami & Bryant, 1990; Gough, Ehri, & Treiman, 1992; Hulme & Snowling, 1997; Metsala & Ehri, 1998; Share, 1995). Beyond the general consensus, accounts that emphasize larger rhyme units and use of analogy strategies early in learning to read (Goswami, 1999) can be contrasted with models that emphasize smaller grapheme-to-phoneme units in early reading (Ehri, 1992, 1995). Rhyme-based models (Goswami, 1999; Goswami & Bryant, 1990) emphasize analysis of a syllable into the initial consonant or consonants (e.g., *back* might be analyzed into *b—ack*). The linguistic term *rime* refers specifically to the sub-syllabic unit containing the vowel and terminal consonants(s) and is used hereafter. Models based on smaller grapheme-to-phoneme correspondences (hereafter GPCs) emphasize analysis of all constituent phonemes of a syllable (e.g., *back* segmented into *b—a—ck*).

Phonological awareness training studies are often derived from the same cognitive-developmental models of reading described above that emphasize either rime- or phoneme-based units. Thus some studies have investigated the use of small grapheme to phoneme units (e.g., Solity, Deavers, Kerfoot, Crane, & Cannon, 1999, 2000; Stuart, 1999; Vellutino, Scanlon, Sipay, Small, Pratt, Chen, et al., 1996) while other studies have taught larger rime body units (e.g., Bradley, & Bryant, 1985; Gaskins, Downer, Anderson, Cunningham, Gaskins, & Schommer, 1988; Greaney, Tunmer, & Chapman, 1997; White & Cunningham, 1990; Wise, Olson, & Treiman, 1990). Both rime-based and phoneme-based models of intervention have provided some support for their efficacy. However many intervention studies are "horse race" models, contrasting *either* rime- *or* phoneme-based training with philosophically distinct methods of reading (e.g., Iversen & Tunmer, 1993) or with untaught controls (e.g., Ball & Blachman, 1991; White & Cunningham, 1990).

Comparative studies of rime- versus phoneme-based programs may provide a better way of evaluating the role of rimes and phonemes. When overall reading ability is considered, several short term studies have reported equivalent improvements for rime- and phoneme-based programs (e.g., Haskell, Foorman, & Swank, 1992; O'Shaughnessy & Swanson, 2000; Sullivan, Okada, & Niedermeyer, 1971). Recent longer term intervention studies suggest that intense phoneme-based interventions are superior to mixed phonic approaches that include rime awareness (Christensen & Bowey, 2005; Hatcher, Hulme, & Snowling, 2004; Solity et al., 1999, 2000). Savage, Carless, and Stuart (2003) describe a rime- and phoneme-based training study delivered over eight weeks by schools' own para-professionals to 6-year-olds "at-risk" of reading difficulties. They reported clear advantages in decoding nonsense words in all interventions, with subtle variations in phonological skills across interventions. This suggests that all children used a GPC strategy to decode nonsense words. The methodology would also be strengthened by the inclusion of standardized measures of change in reading ability, and longer term follow-ups of the retention of gains over time. ABRACADABRA provides an excellent vehicle for exploring these qualitatively different approaches as it delivers an equivalent curriculum in an entirely impartial manner. This intervention is described in detail below.

We view ABRACADABRA as an active tool that can be used to guide further research on what constitutes best practice in computer-based literacy development as well as an excellent general resource for teachers that reflects best practice as we currently know it. We, therefore, used the first pilot intervention not only to test the overall effectiveness of the application but also to explore different sub-questions about reading instruction. In the first phase of our research we focused to a large degree on word rec-

Table 6.7. ABRACADABRA intervention groupings.

Grouping	Intervention
Intervention A	Along with comprehension, fluency, and writing tasks, these groups of students *focused on a progression from sentences to words to rimes.*
Intervention B	Along with comprehension, fluency, and writing tasks, these groups of students *focused on phoneme-level blending and segmenting activities.*
Comparison Group	A second group acted as unseen control for the duration of the study. This group remained in the classroom and received classroom language arts instruction.

ognition, as this is crucial to early reading success, though we also explored the effects of ABRACADABRA on the development of comprehension and fluency skills.

The pilot intervention consisted of small groups of students, each randomly assigned to intervention A or B (See Table 6.7). Students were removed from their class during language arts period to work on the ABRACADABRA program. The two intervention syllabuses were identical in terms of time (20 minutes four times per week) and group size; the children were also of equivalent initial ability (across all classes). Each group also received identical comprehension, fluency tasks.

A note of caution concerning interpretation: These data are the result of a pilot study of the ABRACADABRA prototype, and should be interpreted accordingly. Particular caution is necessary in analyzing the contrasts of intervention A and B, as effects may reflect implementation differences (e.g., in the extent and delivery of activities as implemented on the pilot version of ABRACADABRA) rather than structural linguistic differences between rhyme- and phoneme-based intervention. Table 6.8 summarizes our findings from this pilot study.

Complying with our Software Design Principle 1.1, ABRACADABRA will ". . . serve as the basis for collecting new evidence about teaching and learning using technology." We have used the results of these data to return to both the design of the intervention and the design of the software. Accordingly we have focused particular and intensive development activity on improving the word analysis and word-reading activities. We have some empirical evidence that our rime-based games appear to be working well at the word level and are "pacey," lively, and popular. Overall, the results suggest both

Table 6.8. ABRACADABRA pilot study summary of results.

Effect	Effect Size	Definition	ABRACADABRA
Phonological Processing Speed	Moderate	These are "pure" processing tasks such as naming objects or letters as fast as possible. Efficiency here is closely linked to fluency in reading and spelling.	Children in intervention and comparison groups improved on these measures. Children in Intervention A did particularly well here!
Reading Vocabulary	Small to moderate	These are skills such as isolated word reading and reading isolated words for meaning.	All children improved here. Children in both Intervention A and B did better here than children in the comparison groups!
Word Analysis Skills	Small	These are skills such as segmenting a syllable into its sounds (e.g., c a—t) or sounding out unfamiliar words.	All children improved here but children taught using riming skills (Intervention A) improved to a modest additional degree.
Text-level Comprehension	Small	These are skills such as independently reading and then responding to questions on a sentence or a passage.	Children taught explicit decoding skills (Intervention B) showed strongest effects here.

pedagogical and technical developments that were incorporated into the next stages of development and evaluation. We have also focused on adding appropriate depth and progression to the phonemic activities and going back to basic research to explore maximally effective approaches. We have thus created an explicit decoding skills module as well as enhanced letter–sound knowledge activities. The technical specifications of certain activities such as phoneme blending have been improved to allow appropriate pace to learning activities. This will allow us to make a fair comparison of the effects of rime- and phoneme-based interventions in larger and more formal evaluations in the future. We will also modify the already successful text reading and processing speed-related elements further to aim for even stronger text-level comprehension activities and even larger effects on reading.

We will continue to operate within the cycle of research, development, and research in order to build ABRACADABRA as a tool that will be used for practical and scholarly benefits. The CSLP is currently conducting a larger version of our pilot study in six Quebec schools with a sample of over 150 students. This important process will help us continue the development of ABRACADABRA as well as allow us to adapt it to support other issues in literacy development such as ESL, French, and older struggling readers.

e-Portfolio Software

A portfolio is a purposeful collection of student work that tells the story of a student's effort, progress, and/or achievement in one or more areas (Arter & Spandel, 1992; MacIsaac & Jackson, 1994). Danielson and Abrutyn (1997) identified three main types of portfolios: working, showcase, and assessment. Working (also known as "process" or "learning") portfolios contain works in progress, track student learning over time, and may be temporary because students move on to either an assessment or showcase portfolio. Showcase portfolios exhibit the student's best work. They are generally used to demonstrate the level of accomplishment that the student has attained. Students often use showcase portfolios during college applications or for professional employment purposes. Assessment portfolios are structured and standardized with "the content of the curriculum determining what students select for their portfolios" (Danielson & Abrutyn, 1997, p. 5).

In the past, portfolios were collections of work stored in binders, file folders, or boxes. Today, computers are used as an effective tool for developing and storing portfolios given their ability to store and process large quantities of content, and because they can effectively support and guide the portfolio process. These computer-based portfolios are called digital or electronic portfolios (e-portfolios). The advantages of using digital portfolios include:

- Digital portfolios provide an effective means for cataloguing and organizing learning materials, better illustrating the process of learner development.
- Students can easily integrate multimedia materials, allowing them to use a variety of tools to demonstrate and develop understanding. (This may be especially advantageous for at-risk children whose competencies may be better reflected through these authentic tasks.)
- Students can develop their information and communication technology skills through the creation of multimedia work and use of the tool.
- Student work becomes easy to share with peers, teachers, parents, and

others, and lets students and others provide feedback through a single electronic container.

- Digital portfolios provide remote access to work for students to complete homework or when otherwise learning at a distance from school.
- Digital portfolios provide remote access to student work for teachers for review and assessment purposes.
- Digital portfolios provide an opportunity for greater and improved communication with parents.

The LEARN (2005) has identified five stages to the portfolio process for print-based or digital portfolios: (1) collection, (2) selection, (3) reflection, (4) evaluation, and (5) celebration. See: http://www.learnquebec.ca/en/content/pedagogy/portfolio. These stages are analogous to those laid out by Danielson and Abrutyn (1997) for developing portfolios. In the collection stage, teachers and students work together to save artefacts that represent successes and opportunities for growth. In the selection stage, teachers and students review and evaluate the saved artefacts and jointly decide which of those artefacts best demonstrate the achievement of learning goals. At the reflection stage, students articulate their thinking about each piece in the portfolio. Students evaluate their own growth over time as well as discover any gaps in their development. This stage is undoubtedly the most crucial and it is what enables portfolios to become lifelong learning tools. In the evaluation stage students compare their reflections to their preset goals and other achievement standards and indicators, and set learning goals for the future. Finally, in the celebration—or as Danielson and Abrutyn (1997) call it, the presentation stage—students share their portfolios with their peers. This is the stage where appropriate public commitments can be made to encourage collaboration and commitment to professional development and lifelong learning (Barrett, 2001).

Proponents of socio-cognitive models emphasize that to develop effective self-regulated learning strategies "students need to be involved in complex meaningful tasks, choosing the products and processes that will be evaluated, modifying tasks and assessment criteria to attain an optimal challenge, obtaining support from peers, and evaluating their own work" (Perry, 1998, p. 716). When students use portfolios, they assume more responsibility for their learning, better understand their strengths and limitations, and learn to set goals (Hillyer & Ley, 1996). Educators believe that portfolios allow students to think critically, and become active, independent, and self-regulated learners (Mills-Courts & Amiran, 1991; Perry, 1998).

Self-regulated learners are individuals who are metacognitively, motivationally, and behaviorally active participants in their own learning. A main feature of self-regulated learning is *metacognition*. Metacognition refers to the awareness, knowledge, and control of cognition. The three processes which make up metacognitive self-regulation are planning, monitoring, and regulating. Other aspects of self-regulated learning include time management, regulating one's own physical and social environment, and the ability to control one's effort and attention.

Planning involves setting educational goals and outcomes as well as task analysis. Self-regulated learners set specific learning or performance outcomes and then monitor the effectiveness of their learning methods or strategies and respond to their evaluations. Self-*monitoring* is essential in enhancing learning. It helps students focus their attention on and discriminate between effective and ineffective performance; it reveals inadequate learning strategies. It improves time management as well.

Regulating one's physical and social environment includes study environment management and help seeking. Management of study areas requires locating a place that is quiet and relatively free of visual and auditory distractions so that one can concentrate. Once identified with dependency, substantial evidence now indicates that seeking assistance from others, particularly in the form of elaborated explanations, is valuable and can subsequently lead to autonomous learning.

Time management involves scheduling, planning, and managing one's study and production time.

Effort regulation is the ability to maintain focus and effort towards goals despite potential distractions and setbacks. Effort regulation reflects a commitment to completing one's learning goals by directing and regulating one's energy toward them. Effort regulation is more generally associated with a belief in effort–outcome covariation which, in general, is the belief that success in learning is caused by personal effort and not personal ability, luck, or task difficulty.

Portfolios can provide evidence of student self-regulation. Students may review their own work and then modify learning goals as a result of such reflection. The process of reflection is what makes portfolios a tool for life-long learning and professional development rather than a mere collection of work (Foote & Vermette, 2001). The student needs to be able to make a direct connection between each submission in the portfolio and an intended learning goal. The student needs to be able to explain why a specific submission was placed within the portfolio. Barrett (2004) further confirms the importance of this idea when she says "the artifacts need to be accompanied by the learner's rationale, or their argument as to why these artifacts constitute evidence of achieving specific goals, outcomes, or standards" (p. 3). Bereiter and Scardamalia (1989) mention that portfolios encourage the pursuit of personal cognitive learning goals, what they call intentional learning. Portfolios prompt students to look back, to digest and debrief, and to review what happened so that they can set new goals and determine next steps (Camp, 1992). In an attempt to demonstrate the effects of reflection, Sweidel (1996) asked students self-reflective questions about their study strategies and found that at the end of the semester they were able to identify relationships between the process and the outcome of their studying.

Wade and Yarbrough (1996) elaborate on the pedagogical value of using portfolios as a learning tool. Portfolios are developmental in their nature, since a portfolio represents a certain period of students' growth and learning. Portfolios should not be solely used for short term goal attainment since they are the culmination of long term learning outcomes. Portfolios are doubly valued in that they offer both the teachers and the students the opportunity of dyadic interaction. A portfolio allows the student the opportunity to reflect and record learning process while offering teachers an authentic integrative approach of evaluating student growth and achievements as well as acting as a feedback mechanism for their teaching practices. Portfolios are also interactive in that they enable students to share their work with their teachers and peers, thus seeking guidance or suggestions. In this way, the development and establishment of the portfolio may be seen as a form of collaboration.

Alternative or authentic assessment is any type of assessment in which students construct or create a response to a question or a task. In traditional assessment, students choose or select a response from a given list, such as multiple choice, true/false, or matching. Alternative assessments may include short-answer questions, essays, performance assessment, oral presentations, exhibitions, and paper-based or electronic portfolios.

Well-designed alternative assessments elicit high level thinking and the demonstration of skills and competencies relevant to the complex tasks learners face in realistic situations. Alternative assessments, such as portfolios, have the potential to reflect a competency and not an abstraction of a competency (i.e., a numerical or letter grade). In addition, holistic appraisals allow for flexible and creative demonstration of competencies such that the "whole is greater than the sum of the parts." Finally, alternative assessment may be especially useful for encouraging learning improvement and self-regulated learning.

However, the evaluation of responses to alternative assessments may be especially time consuming to score and judgments may be idiosyncratic and lacking in dependability or repeatability. Using scoring keys or rubrics helps increase the accuracy of scoring but may not eliminate it entirely. Parents, in particular, seem to have difficulty interpreting the results of alternative assessments especially when they are used for the purposes of summative evaluation.

Portfolios help students become involved in the evaluation of their own learning (Fenwick & Parsons, 1999). Given that the use of portfolios allows students to choose and organize the kinds of content they want to include, this engages the students in the evaluation and assessment process. Contrary to traditional testing methods, which do not readily reflect student growth, portfolios may demonstrate learning gains and thus promote authentic learning.

Prior Research on Portfolios

As a precursor to our involvement with digital portfolios, Kakkar, Zitkute, and Abrami (2000) explored whether paper-based educational portfolios assist the processes of self-regulation. To this end, a mixed-method study was employed to investigate student self-regulation in high context, low context, and non-portfolio classrooms.

We found several important differences in portfolio pedagogy between the high and low context portfolio classrooms. Data from the low context portfolio classrooms indicated that student self-regulatory processes remain unchanged within a four-month period in a low-portfolio environment; this was congruent with our original predictions. In fact, we found that students in the low context portfolio classroom scored similar to students in the non-portfolio classrooms.

We also found that there were some significant positive changes in the area of personal achievement orientation and academic-related perceptions in the high context portfolio classrooms. With regards to alternative assessment, there was a strong focus on student progress and personal achievement throughout the portfolio process. There was less of a focus on student outcomes on specific tasks and more on long term projects. In this present study, however, this type of assessment strategy did create some level of stress and anxiety for the students. This often occurred because students had not completed the portfolio work in time.

Portfolios are touted as an excellent pedagogical tool, yet before large-scale portfolio implementation continues we need to re-examine why and how we use them. In this study, we noticed some change in the expected direction but not as much as we expected.

First, it appears that the transition is not a ready one from more traditional modes of instruction and assessment to portfolio processes and assessment. Despite their willingness, effort, and preparation—which was both genuine and substantial—our small sample of teachers in the low context classroom did not entirely abandon more traditional classroom practices. Likewise students in portfolio classrooms struggled, in some ways yearlong, with portfolio activities and responsibilities. Yet there were significant changes that occurred consistent with students increasing their self-regulation—a sign of hope. We speculate that the demands on both student and teacher of the portfolio classroom are greater than in more traditional, teacher-centered classrooms, especially during a time of transition from other ways of teaching and learning.

Second, portfolios place greater emphasis on the process of learning and different emphasis on the outcomes of learning than traditional methods of instruction and assessment. The discomfort of students with portfolios may signal their struggle with self-regulating their learning because they have not fully accepted its precepts, due perhaps to the demands placed on them externally for traditional achievement gains. Alternatively, they may not wish to accept the risks associated with the personal responsibility of regulating their own learning to achieve success. The struggle is difficult and change may neither be asked for nor accepted willingly.

The findings of this study have important implications for practice. Combining traditional and portfolio pedagogy in a similar environment does not encourage self-regulatory processes in students. Instead, it seems to create confusion for students trying to understand what is expected of them in both traditional and portfolio projects.

On the other hand, a high context portfolio environment does not guarantee high self-regulatory processes. The high-portfolio context which focuses on meaningful tasks, peer support, numerous self-reflection activities, flexibility for choosing projects to work on, and teacher guidance seems to increase self-regulatory processes only slightly.

On the basis of this evidence, we believe the following is worth exploring. First, the use of portfolios should be a school-based or board- (district-) based initiative. Both students and teachers should believe that the change to portfolios is widespread and a regular part of the school routine. Second, the use of portfolios should begin early in students' educational experience and not be short-lived. The processes of self-regulation and approaches to pedagogy which portfolios support require time for younger students to learn and effort for older students to make the transition from traditional, teacher-directed methods. Third, teachers need to develop facility with portfolio processes and they should be supported with appropriate professional development. Fourth, electronic portfolios may provide additional means to scaffold teachers and students in the portfolio process and better encourage self-regulation. This research and these reasons helped us develop the CSLP's electronic portfolio software tool.

The CSLP e-Portfolio Software

The CSLP's bilingual, web-based, database-driven e-portfolio software may be considered as both a process (or learning) and showcase portfolio tool for students. The software has been developed with PHP as the programming language using the MySQL database. It is currently installed on the servers of seven English school boards; approximately 40 teachers will use the software with their students this year. Various French boards are also considering partnering with us, along with a variety of international users. The e-portfolio package (with plug-ins and manuals) is downloadable through our FTP site. The software may be viewed at: http://doe.concordia. ca/cslp/ICT-ePortfolio/php

Structure of the software

The administrator environment: In this environment, the administrator (a school board technician or the board RÉCIT) must enter the various settings for school, teacher, and student records, within their school board. Data can be imported directly into the database for schools, classes, teachers, and student records.

The teacher environment: In this environment teachers are able to link the students in a given school to their own classes, set up a class homepage, set up specific subject areas or topics which will be linked to individual student work, define their questions to be used for student reflection and conferencing within specific subjects or topics, store shared work such as text or multimedia files to be viewed by all the students within their class, access students' process and showcase portfolios, and display/print out student work. Each page has a help button that opens a window with the in-context help related to this screen. This helps teachers to better understand the structure and functionalities of the software.

The Student Environment: This environment can really be considered the heart of the software, as it is here where students perform all the commands offered within the software. These include the selection of an interface from a dozen templates, the creation of new work, the editing of existing work; the setting of learning goals; the reflection on work; the conferencing on work with a peer, teacher, or parent; the selection of items to be sent to the showcase; and the viewing and customization of their showcase portfolio (see Figures 6.11 to 6.14). The student may click on a piece to view or listen to the work. The inclusion of a recorder allows students to read directly into their portfolio, and, for younger students, to record their reflections and conferences. Multimedia work such as a Quicktime movie, Powerpoint presentation or images may also be attached to a piece of work.

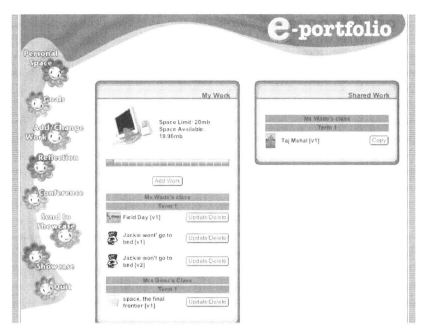

Figure 6.11. Student environment—add work.

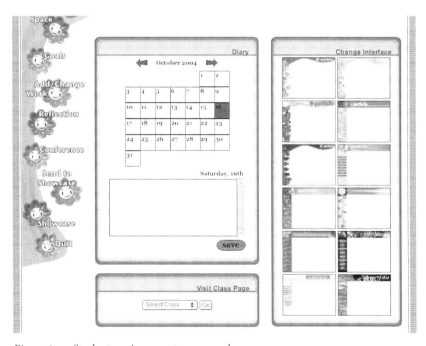

Figure 6.12. Student environment—personal space.

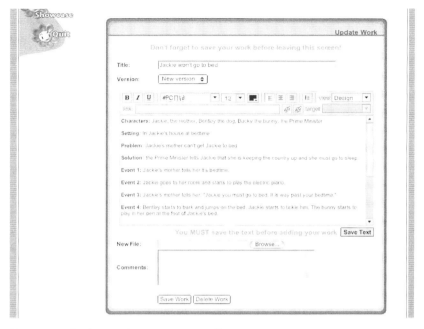

Figure 6.13. Student environment—text editor.

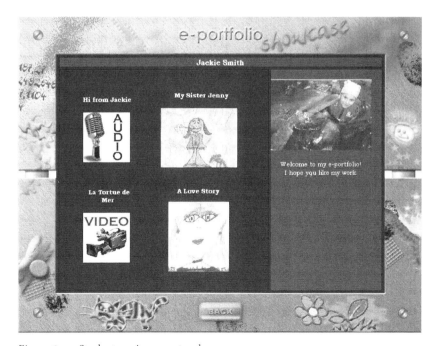

Figure 6.14. Student environment—showcase.

Non-Quebec users: Because the software was designed within the framework of the Quebec Education Programme, it uses the cycle system. Student work is linked to the cycle in which the student is enrolled. Thus, when a student enters the second level of their cycle, they may view their work from the previous year. However, given interest for use of the software outside of the province, the CSLP has also designed a non-Quebec version that operates according to grades.

Validation and Future Work

Each year, the RÉCIT have solicited teachers from each of their boards to collaborate with us in an attempt to learn more about how technology can be applied to the portfolio process. Professional Development Initiative Grants were requested from the Quebec Ministry of Education to fund release time for participating teachers. This provided the opportunity to organize swap and share days that allowed the teachers to come together and share portfolio projects, and discuss issues and challenges faced in the classroom. Additionally, focus groups were organized to obtain feedback on our software. The CSLP prepared annual reports summarizing these sessions. See http://www.learnquebec.ca/en/content/pedagogy/portfolio/archive to view the Case Study Reports.

Our team's activities in 2005–2006 will be guided by four main objectives:

1   To work with our partner school boards, the LEARN, and English Language Arts consultants, to create an intensive "portfolio" culture within a sample of Quebec English research schools. We hope to learn more about the core processes which underlie the use of portfolios and about effective online professional development material as revealed in the scholarly literature;
2   To work towards the full integration of three existing tools into one suite of bilingual, evidence-based portfolio process tools designed for different age groups within Quebec schools;
3   To ensure that adequate bilingual material is provided within the software to support teacher/student use of the software and teachers' understanding of the fundamental processes supported by the software; and
4   To obtain feedback about the software from the teachers and to learn about the quantity/quality of the use of the software in the pilot research schools.

In subsequent years we will follow students over two years, beginning in Cycle 2 (Grades 1 and 2). We will examine 18 classrooms (three per board) where digital portfolios are not used (control group), and 18 (three per board) classrooms where e-Portfolio is integrated (experimental group) into the Language Arts curriculum. We will employ a number of measures, including the Academic Self Regulated Learning (Ryan & Connell, 1989) and the Technology Implementation Questionnaire (Wozney, Venkatesh, & Abrami, 2006) to explore teacher and student use of e-portfolios and to understand how to best support teacher professional development.

Conclusion

The CSLP believes that our approach to research, development, and dissemination—which focuses on evidence-based practice—provides opportunities for our partners in particular and the educational community in general to have active input into all phases of these projects. It will also provide them with ownership over the outcomes and genuine opportunities to reap the benefits of effective pedagogical practices aimed at increasing literacy and, subsequently, a reduction in school dropouts. We will continue to function within our software design principles and we will continue to use an iterative process of research, design, development, and further research, learning from our own experiences and transferring such knowledge into practice.

We welcome others to use our tools and partner with us in research and development.

Acknowledgments

An earlier version of this chapter was presented at the Children's Learning in a Digital World Conference, August 19 and 20, 2005 at Brock University, St. Catharines, Ontario, Canada.

The projects described here were supported by grants from the US Interagency Educational Research Initiative, Social Sciences and Humanities Research Council, Norshield Foundation, Chawkers Foundation, Industry Canada, Fonds Québecois de la Recherche sur la Societé et la Culture, and Valorisation Recherche Québecois. The authors are solely responsible for the contents of this chapter.

References

Abrami, P. C., Bernard, R. M., Wade, C. A., Schmid, R. F., Borokhovski, E., Tamim, F., et al. (2005). *A state of the field review of e-learning in Canada: A rough sketch of the evidence.* Montreal, Quebec: Centre for the Study of Learning and Performance, Concordia University.

Allington, R. (2004). Setting the record straight. *Educational Leadership, 61,* 22–25.

American Psychological Association Work Group of the Board of Educational Affairs [APABEA]. (1997). *Learner-centred psychological principles: A framework for school reform and redisgn.* Washington, DC: American Psychological Association.

Arter, J. A., & Spandel, V. (1992). Using portfolios of student work in instruction and assessment. *Educational Measurement: Issues & Practice, 11*(1), 36–44.

Ball, E. W., & Blachman, B. A. (1991). Does phoneme awareness training in kindergarten make a difference in early word recognition and developmental spelling? *Reading Research Quarterly, 26*(1), 49–66.

Barrett, H. C. (2001). Electronic portfolios. In A. Kovalchick & K. Dawson (Eds.), *Educational technology: An encyclopedia.* Santa Barbara, CA: ABC-Clic.

Barrett, H. C. (2004, April). *Differentiating electronic portfolios and online assessment management systems.* Paper presented at the annual meeting of the American Educational Research Association, San Diego, CA.

Bereiter, C., & Scardamalia, M. (1989). Intentional learning as a goal of instruction. In L. B. Resnick (Ed.), *Knowing, learning, and instruction: Essays in honor of Robert Glaser* (pp. 361–392). Hillsdale, NJ: Lawrence Erlbaum.

Bradley. L., & Bryant, P. E. (1985). *Children's reading problems.* Oxford, UK: Blackwell.

Brady, S. A., & Shankweiler, D. P. (Eds.). (1991). *Phonological processes in literacy: A tribute to Isabelle Y. Liberman.* Hillsdale, NJ: Lawrence Erlbaum.

Brown, L. A. (1996). *Designing and developing electronic performance support systems.* Newton, MA: Digital Press.

Byrne, B. (1998). *The foundations of literacy: The child's acquisition of the alphabetic principle.* Hove, UK: Psychology Press.

Camp, R. (1992). Portfolio reflections in middle and secondary school classrooms. In. K. B. Yancey (Ed.), *Portfolios in the writing classroom* (pp. 61–79). Urbana, IL: National Council of Teachers of English.

Canadian Council on Learning (2007). *State of Learning in Canada: No time for complacency.* Ottawa, Ontario: Canadian Council on Learning.

Cappon, Paul (2007, January 26). Speaking notes: Launch of *State of Learning in Canada.* Vancouver, BC. Retrieved from http://www.ccl-cca.ca/CCL/Newsroom/Speeches/Cappon_State_of_Learning_in_Canada_Report20070126.htm

Chambers, B., Abrami, P. C., Massue, F. M., & Morrison, S. (1998). Success for all: Evaluating an early-intervention program for children at risk of school failure. *Canadian Journal of Education, 23*(4), 357–372.

Chambers, B., Abrami, P. C., McWhaw, K., & Therrien, M. C. (2001). Developing a computer-assisted tutoring program to help children at risk learn to read. *Educational Research and Evaluation, 7*(2–3), 223–239.

Chambers, B., Abrami, P. C., Slavin, R. E., Cheung, A., & Gifford, R. (2007). *Computer-assisted tutoring in Success For All: Reading outcomes for first graders.* Manuscript submitted for publication.

Chambers, B., Slavin, R. E., Madden, N. A., Abrami, P. C., Tucker, B. J., Cheung, A., et al. (2007). *Technology infusion in Success for All: Reading outcomes for first-graders.* Manuscript submitted for publication.

Christensen, C. A., & Bowey, J. (2005). The efficacy of orthographic rime, grapheme–phoneme correspondence and implicit phonics approaches to teaching decoding skills. *Scientific Studies of Reading, 9,* 327–350.

Coley, R. J., Cradler, J., & Engel, P. K. (2000). *Computers and the classroom: The status of technology in U.S. schools.* Princeton, NJ: Policy Information Center, Educational Testing Service.

Collins, A., Brown, J. S., & Newman, S. E. (1989). Cognitive apprenticeship: Teaching the crafts of reading, writing, and mathematics. In L. B. Resnick (Ed.), *Knowing, learning, and instruction. Essays in honor of Robert Glaser* (pp. 453–494). Hillsdale, NJ: Lawrence Erlbaum.

Danielson, C., & Abrutyn, L. (1997). *An introduction to using portfolios in the classroom.* Alexandria, VA: Association for Supervision and Curriculum Development.

Ehri, L. C. (1992). Reconceptualizing the development of sight word reading and its relationship to recoding. In P. B. Gough, L. C. Ehri, & R. Treiman (Eds.), *Reading acquisition* (pp. 107–142). Hillsdale, NJ: Lawrence Erlbaum Associates.

Ehri, L. C. (1995). Phases of development in learning to read by sight. *Journal of Research in Reading, 18*(2), 116–125.

Ehri, L., Nunes, R. S., Willows, D., Schuster, B. V., Yaghoub-Zadeh, Z., & Shanahan, T. (2001). Phonemic awareness instruction helps children learn to read: Evidence from the national reading Panel's meta-analysis. *Reading Research Quarterly, 36*(3), 250–287.

Everson, H. T. (1995). Modeling the student in intelligent tutoring systems: The promise of a new psychometrics. *Instructional Science, 23,* 433–452.

Fenwick, T. J., & Parsons, J. (1999). A note on using portfolios to assess learning. *Canadian Social Studies, 33*(3), 90–92.

Foote, C. J., & Vermette, P. J. (2001). Teaching portfolio 101: Implementing the teaching portfolio in introductory courses. *Journal of Instructional Psychology, 28*(1), 31–37.

Fuchs, T., & Woessmann, L. (2004, November). *Computers and student learning: Bivariate and multivariate evidence on the availability and use of computers at home and at school.* CESifo Working Paper number 1321.

Garet, M. S., Porter, A. C., Desimone, L., Birman, B. F., & Yoon, K. S. (2001). What makes professional development effective? Results from a national sample of teachers. *American Educational Research Journal, 38*(4), 915–945.

Gaskins, I. W., Downer, M., Anderson, R. C., Cunningham, P. M., Gaskins, R. W., & Schommer, M. (1988). A metacognitive approach to phonics: Using what you know to decode what you don't know. *Remedial and Special Education, 9,* 36–41.

Gery, G. (1991). *Electronic performance support systems: How and why to remake the workplace through the strategic application of technology*. Boston: Weingarten Publications.

Gery, G. (2002). Achieving performance and learning through performance centered systems. *Advances in Developing Human Resources*, 4(4), 464–478.

Goldberg, A., Russell, M., & Cook, A. (2003, February). The effect of computers on student writing: A meta-analysis of studies from 1992 to 2002. *The Journal of Technology, Learning and Assessment*, 2(1). Retrieved from http://www.staff. ucsm.ac.uk/rpotter/ict/research/effects-writing.pdf

Goswami, U. C. (1999). Causal connections in beginning reading: The importance of rhyme. *Journal of Research in Reading*, 22, 217–240.

Goswami, U. C., & Bryant, P. E. (1990). *Phonological skills and learning to read*. London and Hove: Lawrence Erlbaum.

Gough, P., Ehri, L. C., & Treiman, R. (Eds.). (1992). *Reading acquisition*. Hillsdale, NJ: Lawrence Erlbaum.

Greaney, K. T., Tunmer, W. E., & Chapman, J. W. (1997). Effects of rime-based orthographic analogy training on the word recognition skills of children with reading disability. *Journal of Educational Psychology*, 89(4), 645–651.

Hall, K., & Harding, A. (2003). A systematic review of effective literacy teaching in the 4 to 14 age range of mainstream school. In *Research Evidence in Education Library*. London: EPPI-Centre, Social Sciences Research Unit, Institute of Education.

Harasim, L., Hiltz, S. R., Teles, L., & Turoff, M. (1995). *Learning networks: A field guide to teaching and learning on-line*. Cambridge, MA: MIT Press.

Haskell, D. W., Foorman, B. R., & Swank, P. R. (1992). Effects of three orthographic/ phonological units on first-grade reading. *Remedial and Special Education*, 13(2), 40–49.

Hatcher, P., Hulme, C., & Snowling, M. J. (2004). Explicit phonological training combined with reading instruction helps young children at risk of reading failure. *Journal of Child Psychology and Psychiatry and Allied Disciplines*, 45, 338–358.

Healy, J. M. (1998). *Failure to connect: How computers affect children's minds—for better and worse*. New York: Simon & Schuster.

Hillyer, J., & Ley, T. C. (1996). Portfolios and second graders' self-assessments of their development as writers. *Reading Improvement*, 133, 148–159.

Hulme, C., & Snowling, M. (1997). *Dyslexia: Biology, cognition and intervention*. London: Whurr.

Iversen, S., & Tunmer, W. E. (1993). Phonological processing skills and the reading recovery program. *Journal of Educational Psychology*, 85, 112–126.

Kakkar, M., Zitkute, L., & Abrami, P. C. (2000, May). *Student learning in a portfolio classroom*. Paper presented at the Fifth Annual EvNet Conference, Cornwall, Ontario.

Kuhn, M. R., & Stahl, S. A. (2003). Fluency: A review of developmental and remedial practices. *Journal of Educational Psychology*, 95, 3–21.

Kulik, J. A. (2003, May). *Effects of using instructional technology in elementary and secondary schools: What controlled evaluation studies say*. Final Report. Arlington, VA: SRI International. Retrieved from http://www.sri.com/policy/csted/reports/sandt/it/Kulik_ITinK-12_Main_Report.pdf

Kulik, J. A., & Kulik, C.-L. C. (Eds.). (1989). Instructional systems [Special Issue]. *International Journal of Educational Research: Meta-Analysis in Education*, *13*(3), 277–289.

Learner-Centered Principles Work Group of the American Psychological Association's Board of Educational Affairs (APABEA). (1997). *Learner-centered psychological principles: A framework for school reform and redesign.* Washington, DC: American Psychological Association.

LEARN. (2005). *Portfolio process: On-line resources for teachers*. Retrieved from http://www.learnquebec.ca/en/content/pedagogy/portfolio/general/practice.html

Learning First Alliance. (2000) *Every child reading: A professional development guide.* Baltimore: Learning First Alliance.

Lou, Y., Abrami, P. C., & d'Apollonia, S. (2001). Small group and individual learning with technology: A meta-analysis. *Review of Educational Research*, *71*(3), 449–521.

MacIsaac, D., & Jackson, L. (1994). Assessment processes and outcomes: Portfolio construction. *New Directions for Adult and Continuing Education*, *62*, 63–72.

Mandl, H., & Lesgold, A. (Eds.). (1988). *Learning issues for intelligent tutoring systems.* New York: Springer-Verlag.

Metsala, J. L., & Ehri, L. C. (1998). *Word recognition in beginning literacy*. Hillsdale, NJ: Lawrence Erlbaum.

Mills-Courts, K., & Amiran, M. R. (1991). Metacognition and the use of portfolios. In P. Belanoff & M. Dickson (Eds.), *Portfolios process and product.* Portsmouth, NH: Boynton/Cook Publishers Heinemann.

Mitchell, P. D., & Grogono, P. D. (1993). Modelling techniques for tutoring systems. *Computers in Education*, *20*(1), 55–61.

NRP [National Reading Panel]. (2000). *Teaching children to read: Reports of the subgroups*. Retrieved from http://www.nichd.nih.gov/publications/nrp/report.htm

O'Shaughnessy, T. E., & Swanson, H. L. (2000). A comparison of two reading interventions for children with reading disabilities. *Journal of Learning Disabilities*, *33*(3), 257–277.

Organisation for Economic Co-operation and Development. (2000). *Literacy in the information age: The final report of the international adult literacy survey*. Paris: OECD.

Perry, N. E. (1998). Young children's self-regulated learning and contexts that support it. *Journal of Educational Psychology*, *90*, 715–729.

Pressley, M. (1998). *Reading instruction that works*. New York: Guilford Press.

Pressley, M., Wharton-McDonald, R., Allington, R., Block, C. C., Morrow, L., Tracey, D., et al. (2001). A study of effective first-grade literacy instruction. *Scientific Studies of Reading*, *5*(1), 35–58.

Rack, J. P., Snowling, M. J., & Olson, R. K. (1992). The nonword reading deficit in developmental dyslexia: A review. *Reading Research Quarterly*, *27*, 29–53.

Randi, J., & Corno, L. (2000). Teacher innovations in self-regulated learning. In M. Boekaerts, P. R. Pintrich, & M. Zeidner (Eds.), *Handbook of self-regulation* (pp. 651–685). Orlando, FL: Academic Press.

Reynolds, S. (2001). *Evidence-based practice*. Paper presented to the British Psychological Society Centenary Conference. Glasgow.

Russell, T. L. (1999). *The no significant difference phenomenon*. Raleigh, NC: North Carolina State University Press.

Ryan, R. M., & Connell, J. P. (1989). Perceived locus of causality and internalization: Examining reasons for acting in two domains. *Journal of Personality and Social Psychology, 57*, 749–761.

Savage, R. S. (2006). Effective early reading instruction and inclusion: Reflections on mutual independence. *International Journal of Inclusive Education 10*, 347–361.

Savage, R. S., & Carless, S. (2005). Phoneme manipulation but not onset-rime manipulation is a unique predictor of early reading. *Journal of Child Psychology and Psychiatry and Allied Disciplines, 46*(12), 1297–1308.

Savage, R. S., Carless, S., & Stuart, M. (2003). The effects of rime- and phoneme-based teaching delivered by learning support assistants. *Journal of Research in Reading, 26*(3), 211–233.

Scardamalia, M., & Bereiter, C. (1996). Computer support for knowledge-building communities. In T. Koschmann (Ed.), *CSCL: Theory and practice of an emerging paradigm*. Mahwah, NJ: Erbaum.

Schacter, J. (1999). *The impact of education technology on student achievement: What the most current research has to say*. Milken Exchange on Education Technolog. Retrieved from http://www.mff.org/pubs/ME161.pdf

Schmid, R. F., Tucker, B., Jorgensen, A., Abrami, P. C., Lacroix, G., & Nicoladou, N. (2006, April). *Implementation fidelity of computer assisted tutuoring in Success for All*. Paper presented at the annual meeting of the American Educational Research Association, San Francisco.

Sebba, J. (1999). *Priority setting in preparing systematic reviews*. A background paper for the meeting at the School of Public Policy, Ucl. 15/16 July. Retrieved from http://campbell.gse.upenn.edu/index.html

Share, D. L. (1995). Phonological recoding and self-teaching: Sine qua non of reading acquisition. *Cognition 55*(2), 151–218.

Sivin-Kachala, J., & Bialo, E. R. (2000). *2000 research report on the effectiveness of technology in schools*. Washington, DC: Software & Information Industry Association.

Slavin, R. E., & Madden, N. A. (Eds.). (2001). *Success for all: Research and reform in elementary education*. Hillsdale, NJ: Lawrence Erlbaum.

Solity, J., Deavers, R., Kerfoot, S., Crane, G., & Cannon, K. (1999). Raising literacy attainment in the early years: The impact of instructional psychology. *Educational Psychology, 19*(4), 373–397.

Solity, J., Deavers, R., Kerfoot, S., Crane, G., & Cannon, K. (2000). The early reading research: The impact of instructional psychology. *Educational Psychology in Practice, 16*(2), 109–129.

Statistics Canada (Stats Can) & Organisation for Economic Co-operation and

Development (OECD). (2005). *Learning a living: First results of the adult literacy and life skills survey.* Retrieved from http://www.statcan.ca/english/freepub/89-603-XIE/89-603-XIE2005001.htm

Statistics Canada. (2004). *Literacy scores, human capital and growth across 14 OECD countries,* monograph no 11, 89-552MIE. Retrieved from http://www.statscan.ca

Stuart, M. (1999). Getting ready for reading: Early phoneme awareness and phonics teaching improves reading and spelling in inner-city second language learners. *British Journal of Educational Psychology, 69,* 587–605.

Sullivan, H. J., Okada, M., & Niedermeyer, F. D. (1971). Learning and transfer under two methods of word-attack instruction. *American Educational Research Journal, 8,* 227–239.

Sweidel, G. B. (1996). Study strategy portfolio: A project to enhance study skills and time management. *Teaching of Psychology, 23*(4), 246–248.

Taylor, B. M., Pearson, P. D., Clark, K. F., & Walpole, S. (2000). Effective schools and accomplished teachers: Lessons about primary-grade reading instruction in low-income schools. *Elementary Schools Journal, 101,* 121–165.

Torgerson, C., & Zhu, D. (2003). A systematic review and meta-analysis of the effectiveness of ICT on literacy learning in English, 5–16. In *Research Evidence in Education Library.* London: EPPI-Centre, Social Sciences Research Unit Institute of Education.

Troia, G. (1999). Phonological awareness intervention research: A critical review of the experimental methodology. *Reading Research Quarterly, 34,* 28–52.

Ungerleider, C., & Burns, T. (2002). *Information and communication technologies in elementary and secondary education: A state of art review.* Prepared for 2002 Pan-Canadian Education Research Agenda Symposium "Information Technology and Learning," Montreal, Quebec.

Van Izjendoorn, M. H., & Bus, A. G. (1994). Meta-analytic confirmation of the nonword reading deficit in developmental dyslexia. *Reading Research Quarterly, 29,* 267–275.

Vellutino, F. R., Scanlon, D. M., Sipay, E. R., Small, S. G., Pratt, A., Chen, R., et al. (1996). Cognitive profiles of difficult-to-remediate and readily-remediated poor readers: Early intervention as a vehicle for distinguishing between cognitive and experimental deficits as basic causes of specific reading disability. *Journal of Educational Psychology, 88,* 601–638.

Wade, R. C., & Yarbrough, D. B. (1996). Portfolios: A tool for reflective thinking in teacher education. *Teaching and Teacher Education: An International Journal of Research and Studies, 12*(1), 63–79.

Waxman, H. C., Lin, M.-F., & Michko, G. M. (2003, December). *A meta-analysis of the effectiveness of teaching and learning with technology on student outcomes.* Learning Point Associates. Retrieved from http://www.ncrel.org/tech/effects2/index.html

White, T. G., & Cunningham, P. M. (1990, April). *Teaching disadvantaged children to decode by analogy.* Paper presented at the annual meeting of the American Educational Research Association, Boston.

Wild, M. (2000). Designing and evaluating an educational performance support system. *British Journal of Educational Technology*, 13(1), 5–20.

Wise, B. W., Olson, R. K., & Treiman, R. (1990). Subsyllabic units as aids in beginning readers' word learning: Onset-rime versus post-vowel segmentation. *Journal of Experimental Child Psychology*, 49, 1–19.

Wolf, M., & Bowers, P. (1999). The double deficit hypothesis for the developmental dyslexias. *Journal of Educational Psychology*, 91, 1–24.

Wozney, L., Venkatesh, V., & Abrami, P. C. (2006). Implementing computer technologies: Teachers' perceptions and practices. *Journal of Technology and Teacher Education*, 14(1), 173–207.

Chapter 7

Tools for Learning in an Information Society

John C. Nesbit and Philip H. Winne

At the 2005 World Summit on the Information Society, United Nations Secretary-General Kofi Annan unveiled the $100 laptop, a joint project of the MIT Media Lab and the non-profit One Laptop Per Child Society (MIT Techtalk, 2005). If successful in overcoming considerable barriers to widespread distribution (e.g., wireless networking to the Internet and cultural acceptance), the laptop will be used for educational purposes by millions of children living in developing nations. That such a project would be conceived by a prestigious educational institution and promoted at an international meeting attended by world leaders is evidence of widespread belief in the existence and pervasive influence of the information society.

The term *information society* carries considerable force in popular understandings of developed nations' shared culture and economy. It is used variously to describe the emergence of knowledge as a commodity in the final stages of the industrial revolution, the increasing role of knowledge workers in post-industrial economies, and the more recent and continuing penetration of information and communication technologies (ICT), especially the Internet, in virtually all aspects of modern culture (Duff, 2001). Although we emphasize the latter sense, we regard all these aspects of the information society as cogent to our thesis. Specifically, we recognize the fundamental roles for information and information technologies in driving modern economies and cultures; here we consider the educational implications of ubiquitous digital information and technology.

We and others have noted dramatic increases in the speed and convenience of accessing information occasioned by the growth of the Internet, and the effects of these changes on how students and teachers interact (Nesbit & Winne, 2003). When all learners are networked all the time, the implicitly understood models of teaching and learning will be unpredictably and irrevocably altered. But the ICT revolution does not merely provide access to more information, more quickly. Rather, it yields information in a more malleable form and provides tools that can be used to manipulate it. The ongoing transformation into an information society not only introduces more efficient means to acquire knowledge and skills, it also defines new knowledge and skills that demand recognition and accommodation within our education systems. In addition to new approaches to teaching and learning, the knowledge society implies new learning goals and curricula that are collectively referred to as *information literacy*.

What Skills Do Learners Need to Participate Fully in the Information Society?

Whether by coincidence or cause, the accelerating demand for information-literacy curricula (Swan, 2000) is occurring at the same time as the development of educational models for self-regulated learning (SRL—see definition below) that complement and extend the goals of information-literacy education. We believe that improving people's abilities in both SRL and information literacy is prerequisite to evolving a genuine and worthwhile information society.

Self-regulated learning

SRL models rest on the premise that learners regulate, with greater and lesser degrees of success, how they construct knowledge. The models describe how learners exercise agency in analyzing learning tasks, setting goals, identifying and selecting strategies for achieving the goals, enacting tactics that fit the strategies, and adapting learning activities in response to outcomes. Decision-making required in these activities leads students to monitor and evaluate their cognitive processes and outcomes. Students who are effective self-regulators, as shown in their goal setting, strategy selection, and meta-cognitive monitoring, are more likely to sustain effortful learning strategies needed to master difficult skills and acquire complex knowledge (Garavalia and Gredler, 2002; Winne, 2001; Zimmerman, 2000). Moreover, the relevance of SRL has been identified in varied settings, ranging from individual to collaborative learning, and from test preparation to complex problem solving (Nesbit & Winne, 2003).

Information literacy

As print media are gradually replaced by digital media, traditional conceptions of literacy are expanding to include interactions with digital information. Swan (2000) described the goals of information-literacy education as integrating technology across the curriculum, promoting "literate thinking" through interactions with electronic texts, and developing new forms of literate thinking made possible by technology. The United States Panel on Educational Technology, established to advise government policy, emphasized that "particular attention should be given to the potential role of technology in achieving the goals of current educational reform efforts through the use of new pedagogic methods focusing on the development of higher-order reasoning and problem-solving skills" (Panel on Educational Technology, 1997, Executive Summary section, ¶3). In this chapter we describe how new software technologies informed by models of SRL and objectives for information literacy can foster innovative methods of teaching and learning like those anticipated by the advisory panel.

What is non-print literacy and how does it relate to SRL? In defining "non-print literacy performance standards," Swan (2000, p. 92) distinguished three categories of learning goals—basic skills, critical literacies, and construction skills. Her definition of *basic skills* included the ability to operate personal information technologies such as keyboards, digital cameras, graphing calculators, word processors, and search engines; and the ability to construct knowledge by making notes from non-print media, working cooperatively through technology, and correctly using and citing others work. Swan's definition of *critical literacies* included interpreting graphical representations, evaluating accuracy and bias in non-print resources, distinguishing various genres of non-print media, and understanding societal effects of information technologies. Her definition of *construction skills* included using software and non-print resources to construct information products; revise, edit, and update non-print media; collaboratively create complex information over distance; and creatively solve problems and answer questions.

We believe SRL and information literacy are largely co-dependent. At the core of both SRL and information literacy lie the beliefs that knowledge is often complex, that exposing truths often requires effortful struggle, that knowledge is dynamic rather than static, and that authority derives from reason rather than reason from authority. In today's information society, self-regulating and monitoring learning require information literacy-dependent skills such as comparing one's knowledge with that represented in non-print resources, and selecting the most appropriate information tools for reaching a learning goal. Conversely, attaining information literacy at Swan's critical and constructive levels requires SRL-dependent skills such as monitoring one's progress toward solutions, comparing one's knowledge with others' to determine how best to collaborate, and recognizing and acquiring the knowledge needed to build an information product.

Where Will Learners Develop These Skills?

Developing students' information literacy extends far beyond providing schools with computer equipment and conventional software. The emphasis on higher-order skills in critical and constructive information literacy has far-reaching programmatic implications. Rather than a segregated curriculum for information literacy, students need integrated curricula in which information literacy skills are applied across the curriculum (Smith & Oliver, 2005). In schools where this occurs, students may learn by using software tools to interpret, critique, and construct graphs in math class; using advanced features of search engines and concept-mapping tools to write English essays; collaborating through text chat and wiki software to prepare social studies projects; and designing tables displaying key features of data to prepare for debates in science.

Likewise, we believe SRL skills are most effectively taught across the curriculum rather than in a separate course. This is because SRL skills are often tied to specific categories of knowledge and, when practiced, transfer within those categories. Skills such as graphing one's daily problem set performance and using the graphs to set goals, may be highly effective in Grade 3 mathematics (Fuchs, Fuchs, Prentice, Burch, Hamlett, Owen, et al., 2003), but less applicable in other knowledge domains.

Extending learning beyond classroom walls

Especially in secondary and tertiary education, a large portion of student learning in academic subjects occurs outside the classroom. Thus information literacy and SRL are not only practiced across curricula but also beyond classroom walls. Most opportunities for independent and collaborative learning occur as students complete homework assignments and projects. Indeed, modern access to information and communication technologies allows for far more academic collaboration outside the classroom. Further, information literacy and SRL are broadly applicable to non-academic learning and problem solving. Students exercise information literacy when they search for music to download to an MP3 player. They exercise SRL when they record their time and performance in field goal kicking practice. Like teachers who need guidance beyond in-service professional development, students need ongoing support for information literacy and SRL beyond the classroom.

How Software Can Foster SRL and Information Literacy

We claim that software designed to facilitate learning across subject domains is a key element in fostering SRL and higher-order information literacy. Software can serve this role by providing cognitive tools that students can apply as they learn across the curriculum, at school, at home, and wherever they study. Before describing the cognitive tools we have developed with colleagues, we present the tenets, reasons, and caveats that frame this work.

A Premise: Intelligence for Learning Is Distributed

The "know-how" of learning and literacy is not sequestered to any educational role but is shared among teachers, learners, instructional designers, authors, and others. Each role holds a portion of the intelligence necessary to achieve educational goals. And each player's intelligence often overlaps with that held by others (Winne, 1992). In this distributed model of intelligence, students learn by analyzing and internalizing features of interactions they observe among people, and between people and their environment. Importantly, they learn by internalizing self–other and self–environment interactions.

Curriculum authors signal how to learn by features of instructional designs

As students interact with information resources—as they read a text or receive feedback from a test—they are presented with opportunities to better understand structures of knowledge and processes of learning. Beyond conveying the specific idea that information in a text has a certain structure, headings and subheadings signal the more general idea—the learning strategy—that knowledge can be constructed by arranging information in hierarchies. Beyond marking one's performance on a specific test, performance feedback can signal the more general idea that tests generate data for evaluating one's learning strategies. Thus most instructional design decisions—from text heading structure, to frequency of quizzes, to timing of cooperative activities—provide opportunities to enhance SRL.

Learners have senses of "what works" for them

Because they have partial access to their mental states and learning histories, learners are uniquely situated to select learning strategies and tactics. Virtually all learners have notions about which strategies and information technologies they prefer to achieve their learning goals although, as we shall explain, these notions are often founded on inaccurate estimates of their prior knowledge and misconceptions about the context-specific efficacy of strategies. We presume that as learners gain educational experience, and interact with teachers, learning resources and information technologies, they gradually develop more complex learning strategies, and more sophisticated beliefs about those strategies (Winne, 1997).

Specialized software can mediate interactions among authors, teachers, and learners

Software affords special capability for actively mediating interactions among the roles over which learning know-how is distributed. Unlike print, software can adapt an instructional message to match learner characteristics, mediate conversations between teachers and students, report back to authors on how their products are being used, and in general gather and distribute information important to promoting SRL and information literacy. However, software can only effectively fulfill the function of actively mediating learning interaction if it is intentionally designed to do so.

Most software, including much that is used to promote information literacy, was designed to assist users to complete a task rather than learn how to become better at performing the task. For example, most learners using search engines to find raw material for their projects never use advanced search features even though doing so could save much time and effort. In summarizing results from a search engine usability study, the usability expert Jakob Nielsen (2001, ¶7–9) commented that

> Typical users are very poor at query reformulation: If they don't get good results on the first try, later search attempts rarely succeed. In fact, they often give up . . . There is no question that we need to develop methods to help users hone their searches. Probably *the only long-term solution is for the school systems to teach kids strategies for query reformulation.*

Although search engines such as Google may be widely regarded as excellent tools for searching the web, they are demonstrably insufficient for learning search strategies such as query reformulation. In contrast, specialized learning software could offer a host of features that coach and scaffold information-literacy skills such as searching for information. These potential features range from animated characters with prerecorded voices who suggest alternative techniques at appropriate moments, to performance reports that show learners how their performance improves or deteriorates as they try different strategies.

Caveats and Challenges

There are remarkable challenges entailed by an information literacy and SRL program that deploys specialized software, is integrated across the curriculum, and is situated in learners' classrooms, homes, and other places where they study. Certain notable aspects of the human and technical infrastructure required by such a program are both daunting and unavoidable.

Every student in such a program requires frequent access to a computer at school and at home. Indeed, to increase the likelihood of success, each student should have ready access to a computer throughout the school day. A one-to-one student–computer ratio allows computer use by a whole class without the hindering restriction of time-limited visits to a centralized computer lab. There is evidence that when sufficient laptops are provided, students use them intensively, collaboratively, and independently during daily in-class learning activities, and come to view the laptops as their primary writing tool (Russell, Bebell, & Higgins, 2004).

Potentially more expensive than providing one laptop per student is the constant and extensive technical support required to install software, maintain servers and networks, supply printers, and help users resolve technical difficulties. There are also costs in maintaining and enhancing the software students use. Pragmatically, technical support costs cannot be offloaded onto the more technically knowledgeable teachers, and must be accounted for as the program is planned.

Software Can Help Learners Become Action Researchers Investigating the Four Challenges of Learning

We believe that appropriately designed software can assist students to overcome four key challenges entailed by SRL theory. Each of these challenges can be addressed through opportunities for prompts, assessments, and feedback. Students can use software tools which enable these opportunities as instruments for researching their learning processes.

Calibrating prior knowledge

If learners are asked what they know, they typically err in their estimates; that is, they are miscalibrated about knowledge. In general, the correlation between estimated knowledge and actual knowledge hovers at about 0.3 (Dunning, Heath, & Suls, 2004). Learners with more knowledge, as measured by tests or other objective means, commonly are underconfident about what they know. In contrast, learners with less knowledge tend to be overconfident

(Hacker, Bol, Horgan, & Rakow, 2000). Weak calibration of knowledge interferes with productive SRL. Specifically, learners who overestimate their knowledge are led to believe their studying tactics have greater effectiveness than they do, and thus bypass adapting how they learn. Learners who underestimate what they know may be inclined to switch from effective study tactics when they don't need to, and replace these with less effective tactics.

Calibrating study tactics and learning strategies

As with knowledge, learners err in recalling how they study. This area of research is quite new owing to only recently having tools (such as the *gStudy* software we describe later) to record how learners study. In two experiments, learners were observed to be moderately inaccurate in recalling how they had studied (Winne & Jamieson-Noel, 2002; Winne, Jamieson-Noel, & Muis, under review). Typically, correlations between recollections of the frequency with which study tactics were used and traces of study tactics actually used range from near 0.0 to approximately 0.5. When learners are poorly calibrated about how they study, they are in a weak position with respect to knowing what to change. They may unknowingly choose to repeat study tactics that are less effective.

Underdeveloped study tactics and learning strategies

It is easy to demonstrate that learners are not as well equipped with study tactics as they might be. Almost all of the hundreds of studies in which some learners have been taught study tactics or learning strategies while others have not, reported differences in achievement favoring students specifically taught how to learn (Pressley & Harris, 2006). Regrettably, too few learners have access to explicit instruction about these tools for learning (Rosenshine, 1997).

Tracking progress in knowledge and study tactics

Like forming sentences in conversation or tying one's shoes, studying is often on "autopilot" and much of this activity goes unnoticed. In part, this can explain why unproductive SRL may persist. If learners don't attend to enough of what they do as they learn, they not only are miscalibrated but occupy a weak position for modulating learning "on the fly." When they are challenged by compelling evidence that "something is off track," particulars of what was done while studying are inaccessible. We label this the *tracking problem*. Without accurately tracking study tactics, it is very difficult to make effective repairs. The same is true of knowledge. Although learners are generally less accurate in self-monitoring individual test item perform-ance than overall test performance, high performing students are more precise than others in tracking performance at the item level. As Neitfeld, Cao, and Osborne (2005, p. 24) put it, "poor students understand they are poor students but may not know where to target their efforts to improve, whereas better students may tend to be more strategic and aware of where they need to expend their efforts toward improvement."

Software Can Generate Databases for Researchers (and Learners) to Mine

Software can be designed so that, as learners work with it, their interactions are recorded. Each record may identify the information on which the learner acted, the learner's action, the information context in which the action was performed, and the time at which the action was performed. These data trace the cognitive operations with which learners process infor-mation and mediate instructional designs (Winne & Perry, 2000). With a log of trace data, one can reconstruct a time-marked description of the observable actions that reflect *how* a learner studied or solved a problem. This includes the fine-grained activities that constitute learning, expres-sions of motivation, and the strategic patterns of these that constitute active and self-regulated learning. Referring to activity reports generated by soft-ware that analyses trace data, researchers can investigate how learners study and to what effects. Using activity reports, learners can answer a multitude of questions such as: How often do I make notes? What do my searches reveal about my interests? Is there a regular pattern to my studying? How long did it take me to construct a concept map? Did I forget the vocabu-lary words I missed on the test, or did I not study them? Researchers can use activity reports to answer similar questions relevant to instructional theories. Quantitative and qualitative research methods can be applied to characterize patterns of study activities at individual and aggregate levels (Nesbit & Hadwin, 2006; Winne, Gupta, & Nesbit, 1994). It was the potency of log data for researching SRL, and the promise of software tools to assist students in meeting the four challenges of learning, which motivated our participation in the Learning Kit Project.

The Learning Kit Project

The Learning Kit Project is a collaborative enterprise dedicated to building software that simultaneously both gathers data researchers need to advance theory and supports learners in improving their skills for learning. A fundamental premise of the project is that learners are agents who make decisions about how they will learn—that is, about study tactics and learning strategies. Through the project we aim to increase opportunities for learners to explore study tactics, thereby generating information critical to us *and* them in theorizing about how learning unfolds and what forms of learning are more effective than others.

gStudy: A Laboratory for Studying Learning

gStudy (Winne, Nesbit, Kumar, Hadwin, Lajoie, Azevedo, et al., 2006) is a software application for advancing research in the learning sciences. It provides tools for operating on structured multimedia content packaged in hypertext markup language (HTML) as *learning kits*. Learning kits include text, diagrams, photos, charts, tables, and audio and video clips. Learners and researchers who author learning kits use *gStudy's* tools to create *information objects*. Classes of information objects include:

- notes created with pre-designed and learner-designed templates
- glossary entries created with pre-designed and learner-designed templates
- hierarchical (tree-structured) indexes of information objects
- hierarchical labels for cataloguing information objects
- hierarchical entries in a table of contents
- concept maps showing information objects as nodes linked by arcs
- documents created by learners
- records of text chat sessions that learners have with peers and mentors
- archives of websites learners visit in the Internet
- queries that search for information objects and particular information within them.

Every information object a learner or author creates is automatically linked to the location in the document where the object originated. Information objects can be linked to one another to construct a graph of information that models knowledge and beliefs. *gStudy's* tools for creating information objects and linking are designed to (a) reduce extrinsic cognitive load so learners can re-assign cognitive resources to cognition and metacognition, (b) invite metacognitive monitoring of learning, and (c) introduce new study tactics to increase options for adapting learning. These three conditions set the stage for learners to explore and self-regulate learning in the service of becoming more capable, lifelong learners.

Information architecture

Figure 7.1 is a labeled screen shot of *gStudy* showing the major components of its user interface. Because the figure shows *gStudy* with all panels open, it gives the impression of a crowded and complex user interface. However, learners normally have only two or three panels open at one time, and they can open or close any panel by a single mouse click.

An enlarged view of the leftmost panel of the interface is presented in Figure 7.2. It shows a list of the learning kits that the learner has downloaded, icons representing different types of information objects, a table of contents for the current kit, and an item finder for filtering elements in the table of contents. This section of the interface assists the learner to navigate through kits and information objects. The table of contents may show several levels of subheadings which the learner can show (expand) or hide (collapse) by a mouse click. The learner can view a list showing information objects of a particular type by clicking on the icon for that type in the view bar. For example, if the learner clicks on the note icon, a list of all notes in the learning kit will appear in the space occupied in the figure by the table of contents.

Browser. The central panel in Figure 7.1 is a web browser that displays HTML documents located in the learning kit or on the Web. Unlike other browsers, *gStudy* allows the learner to attach notes and other information objects to sections of text, images, or video. Learners can highlight text with colors of their choice, as they might in textbooks and other printed material. The link margins, vertical bands on either side of the browser panel, mark the location of links.

Linked items. The panel in the lower right area in Figure 7.1 is used to find and display information objects linked to the current browser document. It shows a list of linked items and the contents of the selected item (i.e., the glossary entry, Hydrogen).

Search. Learners design a search query by entering search terms, choosing options from lists (e.g., the learning kit to be searched) and specifying conditions (e.g., return only information objects linked to other information objects). Upon executing a search, the query becomes an information object and its results accumulate as successive rows in a search query table. Each result of an executed query is displayed with contextual information and metadata. *gStudy* returns the text in which the result is embedded (in Figure 7.1, the "Matching Context"), the title and type of the information object in which the result is located, dates on which the information object was created and modified, and other attributes. Selecting a particular result displays that result and its context in the browser panel.

Figure 7.1. Information architecture of gStudy.

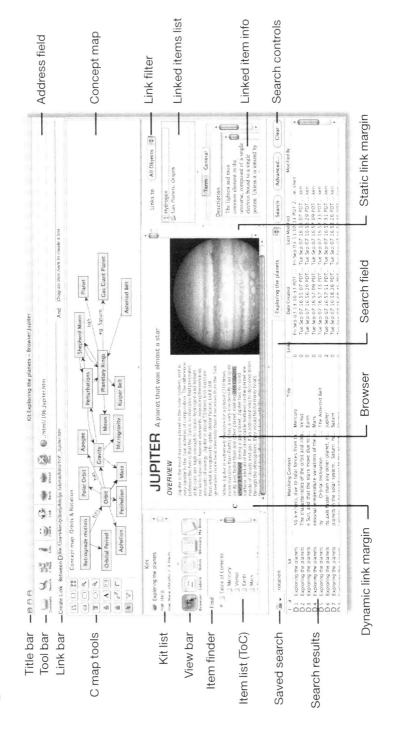

Title bar

Tool bar

Link bar

C map tools

Kit list

View bar

Item finder

Item list (ToC)

Saved search

Search results

Dynamic link margin

Browser

Search field

Static link margin

Address field

Concept map

Link filter

Linked items list

Linked item info

Search controls

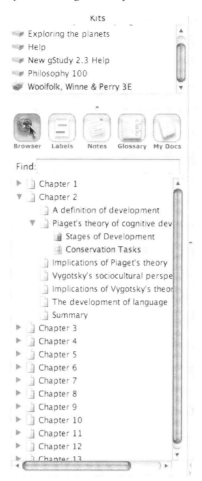

Figure 7.2. The table of contents is a menu that can be extended by the learner.

Coach. The coach is a dual-purpose software agent learners can consult about how to surmount obstacles in learning. One subsystem is a random pattern matcher, which suggests to learners options they may consider for (a) goals, (b) conditions affecting learning tasks, (c) study tactics for advancing toward goals, and (d) content on which to cognitively operate. The second subsystem combines an expert system shell (JESS: Friedman-Hill, 2006) with a model (Kumar, Shakya, & Winne, in press) that operationally defines study tactics, goals, conditions under which a tactic is appropriate, and indices for monitoring how well a tactic is succeeding. This subsystem (a) gathers data about the learner's perceptions of obstacles to learning, (b) diagnoses the learning situation, and (c) recommends a remedy to overcome the learning obstacle(s). Because the two coach subsystems operate through the same chat interface, learners do not recognize them as separate entities.

Collaboration

Collaborative activities are currently supported in three ways. First, learners can communicate synchronously through a text chat tool (Hadwin, Gress, Winne, & Jordanov, 2006). Chat logs are saved for learners to reuse as content in their learning kits. Second, learners can export information objects to a chat partner by dragging-and-dropping the information object into the chat entry field. Third, learners can asynchronously export information objects or entire learning kits for distribution to partners using email or other third-party software.

Few learners ever receive instruction about how to collaborate productively. To guide their synchronous chats and asynchronous collaboration on projects, we build on several strands of research. For example, scripted collaboration has been shown to benefit learning (O'Donnell, 1999). *gStudy*'s chat tool encourages learners to adopt one of several roles (e.g., critic, data analyst) and provides scaffolds in the form of conversational stems matching the adopted role. A concept map depicts the pattern of the participation structure relative to the roles learners adopt. A simple click on a stem copies it to the chat entry field and highlights the function of that conversational act within the pattern shown in the concept map. This design helps learners manage both fine-grained events and overall flow in the chat. The information objects learners create can be shared asynchronously. Before uploading an object so collaborators can access it, learners use templates to catalog each object. This communicates to collaborators what function the data serve in the collaborative enterprise. As with chats, concept maps depict the function of each type of information object relative to other types and the ways in which each object advances progress toward the goals of the collaboration.

Tools for creating information objects

Notes. Using the menu shown in Figure 7.3, learners can link information objects to selections in the browser such as a string of text, a region in a diagram, or a frame in a video clip. Learners can create a note by selecting a note template from a secondary menu. A template is a set of input fields, buttons, and controls customized for a subject domain or learning activity. For example, as shown in Figure 7.4, the debate note template has a six-field structure: issue, position A, evidence for A, position B, evidence for B, and learner's position. Templates provide standards that help learners

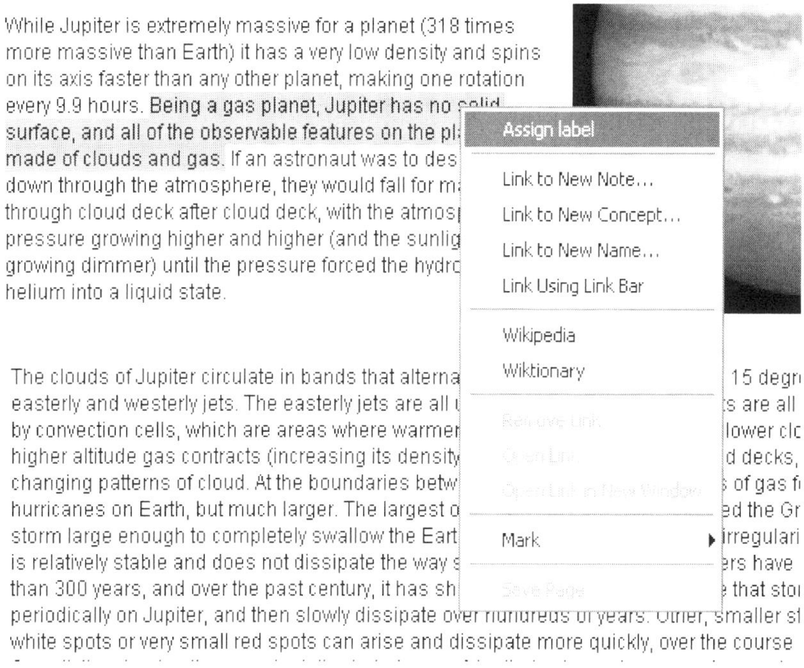

While Jupiter is extremely massive for a planet (318 times more massive than Earth) it has a very low density and spins on its axis faster than any other planet, making one rotation every 9.9 hours. Being a gas planet, Jupiter has no solid surface, and all of the observable features on the pl... made of clouds and gas. If an astronaut was to des... down through the atmosphere, they would fall for m... through cloud deck after cloud deck, with the atmos... pressure growing higher and higher (and the sunlig... growing dimmer) until the pressure forced the hydr... helium into a liquid state.

Assign label

Link to New Note...

Link to New Concept...

Link to New Name...

Link Using Link Bar

Wikipedia

Wiktionary

Remove Link

Open Link

Open Link in New Window

Mark ▸

Save Page

The clouds of Jupiter circulate in bands that altern... 15 degr... easterly and westerly jets. The easterly jets are all ... ts are all by convection cells, which are areas where warmer ... lower clc higher altitude gas contracts (increasing its density ... d decks, changing patterns of cloud. At the boundaries betw... s of gas f... hurricanes on Earth, but much larger. The largest o ... ed the Gr storm large enough to completely swallow the Eart ... irregulari is relatively stable and does not dissipate the way s ... rs have than 300 years, and over the past century, it has sh... that sto... periodically on Jupiter, and then slowly dissipate over hundreds of years. Other, smaller st... white spots or very small red spots can arise and dissipate more quickly, over the course

Figure 7.3. Learners can link a label, note, or other information object to selected text.

to metacognitively monitor comprehension and elaborate information in ways that enhance its retrievability (Bruning, Schraw, Norby, & Ronning, 2004). Learning kits are usually pre-stocked with a set of templates, which learners can expand by defining additional templates of their own.

Labels and indexes. Similar to the way they make notes, learners can assign labels to selections and information objects, or index them. Labels classify information according to types relevant to a subject domain or learning activity (e.g., principle, key experiment). Indexes mark critical items in the discipline being studied. As with notes, *gStudy* links each entry in the list of labels and indexes to the multiple selections or information objects that share attributes of the label. This allows learners, with a single click, to navigate back to the information that was labeled or indexed.

Glossary. Learners can also use the menu shown in Figure 7.3 to add items to the kit glossary. As with notes, glossary entries are created with pre-defined or learner-defined templates.

Concept maps. Concept maps, such as the one shown in Figure 7.5, visually represent concepts and the relationships between them as nodes and arcs. In comparison with text-only conditions, constructing, or studying concept maps can enhance knowledge retention and comprehension

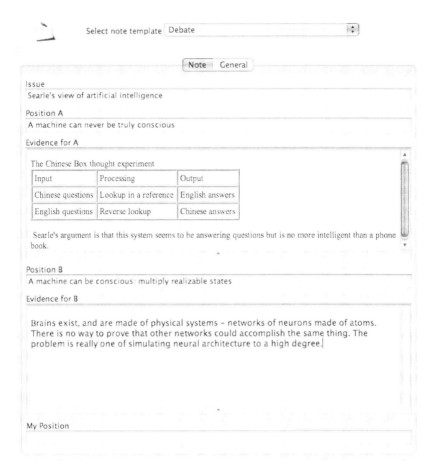

Figure 7.4. Learners can create notes and note templates.

in a broad range of settings (Nesbit & Adesope, 2006). The cognitive advantages of concept maps have been attributed to their capacity for representing information in a simple syntactic structure, showing relatedness of concepts by spatial location, transfering a portion of cognitive load from verbal to visual memory, and clearly representing information macrostructure. All information objects in *gStudy* are automatically included in the concept map of a learning kit. As well, learners can make concept maps from scratch. As they do, they create notes and other information objects which the learner can elaborate later. Concept maps are graphically sortable and filterable using metadata such as author name and date modified.

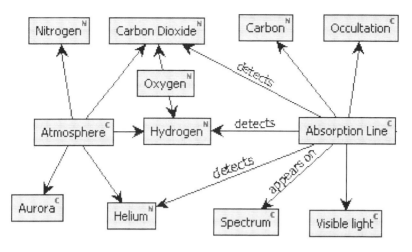

Figure 7.5. A partially completed concept map in *gStudy*.

Scenarios Illustrating How *gStudy* Can Support Learning

Unlike many types of learning software, *gStudy* is designed for use across the curriculum and throughout developmental levels. Its tools are applicable in collaborative or solo learning activities. They can be used to modify and extend pre-existing resources or create new information products. Learners can use *gStudy* in the background to prepare for examinations or assemble essays, or they can use it more conspicuously as the medium in which they present their work or communicate with others. The following two scenarios illustrate the breadth of *gStudy*'s applications.

Writing an essay

The day after her biology instructor announced the essay assignment to her class, Fiona launched *gStudy* to begin planning the essay structure. Although she had already decided to write on the environmental impact of fish farming, Fiona recognized that she needed to define a specific thesis for her essay. Her first step was to find several websites produced by the aquaculture industry, environmental groups, and government departments, and download their content into *gStudy*. Scanning through the materials, she began to label statements related to the environmental safety of fish farms with green highlighting indicating that the statement was a Claim and yellow highlighting indicating that the statement was Evidence. After 30 minutes spent reading and labeling, she reviewed her work by navigating quickly from one labeled segment to the next. She noticed that a significant portion of the claims but little of the evidence related to whether farmed salmon spread parasites, known as sea lice, to nearby wild salmon populations. She decided to define her essay thesis as "Salmon Farming Spreads Sea Lice to Wild Salmon."

Fiona's next step was to create a one-note template named Argument and a second named Counterargument. The Argument template had two text fields: the first for identifying a claim and the second for recording evidence supporting the claim. The Counterargument template had three text fields: one for the claim, one for the evidence, and one for a rebuttal of the claim. Both templates had a 100-point slider to indicate the importance of the argument for the essay. Fiona created either an argument note or a counterargument note for each claim relating to sea lice that she had previously labeled. Any of the scant evidence relating to one of the new notes was also linked to it. To obtain more evidence, she searched for scientific papers on sea lice and salmon, and downloaded three of them into *gStudy*. She linked the evidence she located in these papers to her notes, and summarized it in the evidence fields of her notes.

Realizing with mild surprise that she had already created ten argument notes and six counterargument notes, Fiona turned her attention to assembling these to form the essay itself. After using *gStudy* to view her notes as nodes in a concept map, she began to link the notes together with labeled arcs to indicate their relationships. She used a *subsumes* arc to indicate that an argument (or counterargument) is a generalization of another argument. She used a *precedes* arc to indicate that an argument might effectively prepare the reader for a following argument. While linking the notes, she began spatially assembling them in a presentation order that was consistent with their identified relationships. Finally, Fiona used the resulting concept map as a visual guide to writing her essay. During this final stage, in which she edited text from her notes into polished prose, she discovered that she had too many essay ideas to fit within the space limits set by her instructor. Fiona was able to refer to the importance sliders in each note as she selected which arguments to leave out or merge with other arguments.

Collaborative studying

Ashar and Mark knew that their Grade 9 social studies teacher always had a variety of question types in her exams. She had provided the class with a learning kit containing an entire multimedia textbook on European history. To help them study, the teacher had built into the learning kit note templates which corresponded to each of the question types that would appear on the exam. One template, called *what if*, had two text fields. The first text field was intended to be filled with a hypothetical alteration to history such as: "Because Gutenberg lost his printing press in a game of poker, movable type printing was not developed in Europe until 1600." The second text field, representing a student's response in an exam, was to be filled with a plausible consequence of the alteration along with supporting reasons.

One evening, a week before the final exam, Ashar and Mark logged into *gStudy* for a collaborative study session. Despite living only a block apart, they found it more convenient to collaborate online using *gStudy*'s text chat feature than to meet face-to-face. Their teacher had stocked the text chat tool with question starters that they could use while testing each other. One question starter they used often was "What came first . . ."

Ashar began the session by sending Mark the question "What came first . . . the Council of Trent or the Diet of Worms?" After a quick search on *gStudy*'s search tool, Mark replied "The Diet of Worms came first 'cause it kicked off the Reformation. The Council of Trent was part of the Counter-Reformation."

The two teenagers used the question starters several more times before deciding to change tactics. Over the past few days they had been using their teacher's note templates to create questions they thought likely to appear in the exam. During the remainder of their study session they transmitted these question notes to each other by dragging them into the text chat window. After a question note had been sent, they proposed, discussed, and entered answers. They had learned from previous sessions to link received question notes to relevant information in their own kit, because question notes are easier to review later if they are properly linked.

Perspective on the Future

During the last two years, *gStudy* has been used by over 500 students at Simon Fraser University. In this context, *gStudy* has enabled us to examine the relationship between study tactics and self-reports of goal orientation. Goal orientation is a set of motivational constructs related to self-regulation (Pintrich, 2000). A mastery approach goal, for instance, is indicated by questionnaire items such as "I want to learn as much as possible from this class" (Elliot & McGregor, 2001). Among other outcomes, our research found that students who reported higher mastery goal orientation did less highlighting, a study tactic which is thought to result in shallower understanding than more cognitively engaging tactics such as summarizing (Nesbit, Winne, Jamieson-Noel, Code, Zhou, MacAllister, et al., 2006).

More recently, *gStudy* has been used in high school classes as part of a research project on developing students' argumentation and critical thinking skills. The project is investigating whether predefined note templates can effectively scaffold argumentation elements such as thesis statements, counterarguments, and rebuttals. We expect to further examine the use of *gStudy* in areas such as collaborative problem solving and learning portfolio construction. Through such research, we hope that educational software whose design is informed by SRL will eventually be used by almost every student to strengthen their information literacy, critical thinking, and learning skills across the curriculum.

As barriers to full electronic distribution of learning resources continue to fall—as tablet computers drop in price, monitors become more readable, wireless networks spread through public spaces—competitive pressures will drive publishers to provide their multimedia content in industry-standard formats readable by third-party devices and software. The same pressures will drive content providers to develop efficient distribution models, perhaps similar to Apple's successful iTunes website that allows consumers to make micropayments to download songs onto MP3 devices (von Walter & Hess, 2003). We anticipate that through institutional or open licensing, students in developed nations will be able to browse large online libraries to download high quality multimedia resources onto personal devices. The portable devices that eventually replace the printed textbook will not only allow learners to read information, but will allow them to *operate* on it, and share the results of their operations with others. We imagine that such devices will offer many of the features we have provided in *gStudy*, such as the ability to create links within content as well as links to learner-defined information objects.

Against a backdrop of rapidly changing technologies, the ability to operate on information and transform it into knowledge is a far more transferable and valuable skill than knowing how to operate any specific ICT device. Looking a decade into the future, we imagine that information-literacy education will emphasize the construction skills that Swan (2000) and the Panel on Educational Technology (1997) identified as the highest goal of information-literacy education. To accomplish this goal, learners will use software to operate on information and construct knowledge in ways similar to students using *gStudy*.

Acknowledgments

Support for this research was provided by grants to Philip H. Winne from the Social Sciences and Humanities Research Council of Canada (410-2002-1787 and 512-2003-1012), the Canada Research Chair program, and Simon Fraser University. The authors thank Ken MacAllister for preparing the figures that appear in this chapter.

References

Bruning, R. H., Schraw, G. J., Norby, M. M., & Ronning, R. R. (2004). *Cognitive psychology and instruction*. Upper Saddle River, NJ: Pearson Education.

Duff, A. S. (2001). On the present state of information society studies. *Education for Information*, *19*, 231–244.

Dunning, D., Heath, C., & Suls, J. M. (2004). Flawed self-assessment: Implications for health, education and the workplace. *Psychological Science in the Public Interest*, *5*(3), 69–106.

Elliot, A. J., & McGregor, H. A. (2001). A 2 (2 achievement goal framework. *Journal of Personality and Social Psychology*, *80*, 501–519.

Friedman-Hill, E. J. (2006). Jess®, The rule engine for the Java™ platform. Retrieved from http://www.jessrules.com/jess/docs/70/

Fuchs, L. S., Fuchs, D., Prentice, K., Burch, M., Hamlett, C. L., Owen, R., et al. (2003). Enhancing third-grade students' mathematical problem solving with self-regulated learning strategies. *Journal of Educational Psychology*, *95*, 306–315.

Garavalia, L. S., & Gredler, M. E. (2002). An exploratory study of academic goal setting, achievement calibration, and self-regulated learning. *Journal of Instructional Psychology*, *29*(4), 31–35.

Hacker, D. J., Bol, L., Horgan, D. D., & Rakow, E. A. (2000). Test prediction and performance in a classroom context. *Journal of Educational Psychology*, *92*, 160–170.

Hadwin, A. F., Gress, C., Winne, P. H., & Jordanov, M. (2006). *gChat: A chat interface with scaffolds to enhance collaborative effectiveness* (version 1.0) [computer program]. Burnaby, BC, Canada: Simon Fraser University.

Kumar, V., Shakya, J., & Winne, P. H. (in press). Capturing and disseminating the principles of self-regulated learning in an ontological framework. *International Journal of Metadata, Semantics, and Ontologies*.

MIT Tech Talk (2005). Annan to present prototype $100 laptop at world summit on information society. *MIT Tech Talk*, *50*(9), 4.

Neitfeld, J. L., Cao, L., & Osborne, J. W. (2005). Metacognitive monitoring accuracy and student performance in the postsecondary classroom. *Journal of Experimental Education*, *74*, 7–28.

Nesbit, J. C., & Adesope, O. O. (2006). Learning with concept and knowledge maps: A meta-analysis. *Review of Educational Research*, *76*(30), 413–448.

Nesbit, J. C., & Hadwin, A. F. (2006). Methodological issues in educational psychology. In P. A. Alexander & P. H. Winne (Eds.), *Handbook of Educational Psychology* (2nd ed., pp. 825–847). Mahwah NJ: Lawrence Erlbaum.

Nesbit, J. C., & Winne, P. H. (2003). Self-regulated inquiry with networked resources. *Canadian Journal of Learning and Technology*, *29*(3), 71–91.

Nesbit, J. C., Winne, P. H., Jamieson-Noel, D., Code, J., Zhou, M., MacAllister, K., et al. (2006). Using cognitive tools in *gStudy* to investigate how study activities covary with achievement goals. *Journal of Educational Computing Research*, *35*(4), 339–358.

Nielsen, J. (2001). Search: Visible and simple. Retrieved from http://www.useit.com/alertbox/20010513.html

O'Donnell, A. M. (1999). Structuring dyadic interaction through scripted cooperation. In A. M. O'Donnell & A. King (Eds.), *Cognitive perspectives on peer learning* (pp. 179–196). Mahwah, NJ: Lawrence Erlbaum.

Panel on Educational Technology. (1997). *Report to the President on the use of technology to strengthen K-12 education in the United States.* Washington, DC: President's Committee of Advisors on Science and Technology. Retrieved from http://www.ostp.gov/PCAST/k-12ed.html

Pintrich, P. R. (2000). The role of goal orientation in self-regulated learning. In M. Boekaerts, P. R. Pintrich, & M. Zeidner (Eds.), *Handbook of self-regulation* (pp. 451–502). San Diego, CA: Academic Press.

Pressley, M., & Harris, K. R. (2006). Cognitive strategies instruction: From basic research to classroom instruction. In P. A. Alexander & P. H. Winne (Eds.), *Handbook of educational psychology* (2nd ed., pp. 265–286). Mahwah, NJ: Lawrence Erlbaum.

Rosenshine, B. (1997, March). The case for explicit, teacher-led cognitive strategy instruction. In M. F. Graves (Chair), *What sort of comprehension strategy instruction should schools provide?* Symposium presented at the annual meeting of the American Educational Research Association, Chicago.

Russell, M., Bebell, D., & Higgins, J. (2004). Laptop learning: A comparison of teaching and learning in upper elementary classrooms equipped with shared carts of laptops and permanent 1:1 laptops. *Journal of Educational Computing Research, 30,* 313–330.

Smith, J., & Oliver, M. (2005). Exploring behaviour in the online environment: Student perceptions of information literacy. *ALT-J: Research in Learning Technology, 13*(1), 49–65.

Swan, K. (2000). Nonprint media and technology literacy standards for assessing technology integration. *Journal of Educational Computing Research, 23,* 85–100.

von Walter, B., & Hess, T. (2003). iTunes Music Store—an innovative service to enforce property rights in the Internet. *Wirtschaftsinformatik 45,* 541–546.

Winne, P. H. (1992). State-of-the-art instructional computing systems that afford instruction and bootstrap research. In M. Jones & P. H. Winne (Eds.), *Adaptive learning environments: Foundations and frontiers* (pp. 349–380). Berlin: Springer-Verlag.

Winne, P. H. (1997). Experimenting to bootstrap self-regulated learning. *Journal of Educational Psychology, 89,* 397–410.

Winne, P. H. (2001). Self-regulated learning viewed from models of information processing. In B. J. Zimmerman & D. H. Schunk (Eds.), *Self-regulated learning and academic achievement: Theoretical perspectives* (2nd ed., pp. 153–189). Hillsdale, NJ: Erlbaum.

Winne, P. H., Gupta, L., & Nesbit, J. C. (1994). Exploring individual differences in studying strategies using graph theoretic statistics. *Alberta Journal of Educational Research, 40,* 177–193.

Winne, P. H., & Jamieson-Noel, D. L. (2002). Exploring students' calibration of self-reports about study tactics and achievement. *Contemporary Educational Psychology, 27,* 551–572.

Winne, P. H., Jamieson-Noel, D. L., & Muis, K. R. (under review). *Calibration of self-reports about study tactics and achievement: A replication.* Manuscript submitted for publication.

Winne, P. H., Nesbit, J. C., Kumar, V., Hadwin, A. F., Lajoie, S. P., Azevedo, R., et al. (2006). Supporting self-regulated learning with *gStudy* software: The Learning Kit project. *Technology, Instruction, Cognition, and Learning Journal, 3,* 105–113.

Winne, P. H., & Perry, N. E. (2000). Measuring self-regulated learning. In M. Boekaerts, P. R. Pintrich, & M. Zeidner (Eds.), *Handbook of self-regulation* (pp. 531–566). San Diego, CA: Academic Press.

Zimmerman, B. J. (2000). Attaining self-regulation: A social cognitive perspective. In M. Boekaerts, P. R. Pintrich, & M. Zeidner (Eds.) *Handbook of self-regulation* (pp. 13–39). San Diego, CA: Academic Press.

Chapter 8

Virtual Playgrounds: Children's Multi-User Virtual Environments for Playing and Learning With Science

Yasmin B. Kafai and Michael T. Giang

For the last two decades, digital media have played an increasingly central role in children's play. Videogames, digital books, and robotic toys are just a few examples that have found their place along board games, story books, and dolls (Cross, 1997). More recently, multi-user virtual environments (MUVEs) have become a new genre of popular games among young players (Dede, 2004). Rather than stand-alone play devices, MUVEs present complex online worlds in which players create their online representation, assume new identities, and socialize with other players by chatting or playing online games. There are many examples, such as *Neopets*, *Whyville*, *Habbo Hotel*, and *Puzzle Pirates* that now have over millions of registered users. The number of hours spent in these worlds creating avatars, trading items, chatting, and designing homes are a sure indicator that these environments have something of interest to children that might be repurposed for educational venues.

Historical Context for MUVEs

As one of the first MUVEs researchers, Amy Bruckman (2000) investigated the instructional potential of MUVEs for learning about writing and programming. She found that the social context in her online environment, called *Moose Crossing*, provided incentive and support for players to engage in the programming of objects for others. Chris Dede investigated *Rivercity*, a historical simulation MUVE, and how its collaborative gaming features motivated science inquiry for low performing students (Dede, Nelson, Ketelhut, Clarke, & Bowman, 2004). Sasha Barab designed *Quest Atlantis* to offer a 3D virtual world in which students can participate in collaborative quests to build a community knowledge base (Barab, Thomas, Dodge, Carteaux, & Tuzun, 2005). More recently, some researchers have turned their attention to commercially available MUVEs or MMORPGs (massive multi-player online role-playing games) and examined their potential as learning communities (Gee, 2003). Kurt Squire and Sasha Barab (2004) investigated how *Age of Empires* and *Civilizations* could be used in history classrooms to understand how players develop an interest in history, historical understandings, and school engagement. Benjamin DeVane and Kurt Squire (2006) focused on how game play in *Grand Theft Auto: San Andreas* mediates players' understanding of culture, race, and violence, and the resulting implications for educators. Constance Steinkuehler (2004) examined how participation in *Lineage* created habits of mind traditionally associated with science inquiry. The outcomes in all of these investigations indicated that playing these games is more than just fun and provided evidence of rich opportunities for improving motivation, and learning academic and social skills.

We have chosen to focus on the implications of a MUVE, called Whyville.net, that offered both science play and learning activities in their online world to thousands of players. Unlike *Rivercity* or *Quest Atlantis*, *Whyville* was not designed for a classroom context or a specific instructional purpose. Players come to Whyville on their own volition and time, and have the option, but not the obligation, to engage in a variety of science topics. Access to Whyville is free and open to anybody with an Internet connection. Whyville also differs from many of the existing online science education efforts because it is primarily an informal learning experience. Unlike the occasional museum visit, kids can visit Whyville with greater frequency, at all hours of the day, and stay for hours at a time to engage extensively in topics of their choosing.

Our chapter will present an analysis of different activities available in Whyville, in particular casual, collaborative, and community science-related games, and the potential they hold for science inquiry in informal settings. In our evaluation, we were interested to find out where players spend their time and to what extent they become engaged in Whyville's various science games. We worked with two classes of sixth-grade students aged 10–12 and asked them about their activity preferences in Whyville at different time points during their three months online at school and at home.

Getting around in Whyville

Whyville provides its players, called Whyvillians, with dozens of different places to visit and opportunities to learn about science at the individual to the community level. When a Whyvillian logs onto their account, they immediately arrive at the Welcome Page with links to events for the week, Whyville Times newspaper articles, survival tips, and FAQs. Upon arrival, users can also check their personal email (called ymail), status on their Whyville salary, and whether new mail with clam attachments, called y-grams, have arrived (see Figure 8.1). Whyville has an active community life which elects its own mayor, organizes annual virtual proms, and posts many public petitions that campaign to include or change features of Whyville.

Whyville also allots plenty of opportunities for online social interactions such as chatting, whispering, and sending ymail to others. When they login, Whyvillians may head straight to the sun roof, pool party, and other locales to chat with friends and other users. Some of these locales are connected or next to science activity games. For instance, the sun roof is the top of the sun spot building site, where users can play games related the sun's location, path, and time. Places such as the trading post allow Whyvillians to exchange goods. Others were merely created as social locales to encourage online interactions. Chatting content focuses on topics related to school, friendships, and appearance. While chatting is public (see Figure 8.2), Whyvillians can also whisper to each other, in which case only the designated person gets to see the question and can choose to reply in private or public. Another popular form of socializing is to organize parties at one's online house.

To navigate through the site, each user account has its own personalizable avatar (see Figure 8.3). At the initial sign-up, each player gets assigned an oval with eyes and a mouth but no other distinguishing features. New players can go to Grandma's for donations of free face parts, or purchase them at Akbar's Mall, which lists and sells thousands of different hair parts, lips, eyes, mouths, accessories, and even animated parts. All these parts are created by other Whyvillians who rent design tools and then post their creations at the mall or exchange them at the trading post to cover their costs and as a source of income. To compose your avatar is called "picking your nose," and some Whyvillians are known to change their appearance several times during their login. To pay for the change in appearance of their avatar, Whyvillians have to earn a salary in clams, the virtual monetary unit, by completing an assortment of science-related activities, participating in events, contributing articles to the Whyville Times, and so on. Many articles submitted to Whyville Times are science related, address ways to promote social interaction via science-related games, discuss the Whypox epidemic (a virtual infectious disease, discussed later), among other topics. The bulletin boards along with the Whyville Times provide places for users with similar likes to discuss various (science and non-science-related) topics.

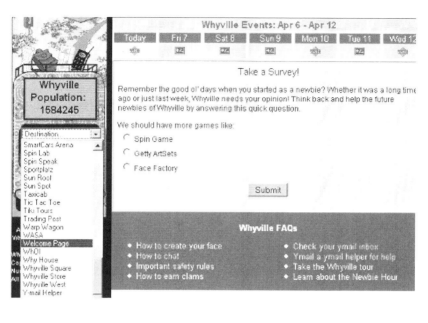

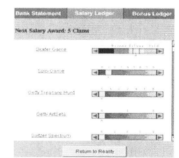

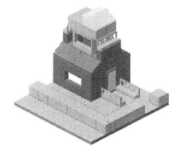

Figure 8.1. Gallery of different Whyville screen shots (clockwise): Welcome screen, Budget ledger, Trading Post, House, and Playground.

Figure 8.2. Screen shot of chatting on the beach in Whyville.

Figure 8.3. Avatar design: picking your nose in Whyville.

Of particular interest to our study are the different types/categories of science games in Whyville, wherein the success at each equates to increases in players' clam salary. At the individual level, most science activities on the site are casual science games. These are one-player games that provide Whyvillians the opportunity to explore different science concepts in the context of a playful activity, or task, with increasing difficulty. For instance, one popular example is the Hot Air Balloon race. In this game, Whyvillians have to navigate a hot air balloon, drop a bean bag over a target on the ground, and safely land the balloon by keeping in mind the burning fuel and releasing hot air (i.e., relationship between temperature and density of gas), speed and wind vectors (i.e., directional forces), and the balloon's position on a coordinate graph. Other casual science games include those from the Spin Lab. Here a player manipulates the position of a skater's arms and legs to make the skater spin as fast as possible, or they manipulate the position and center of rotation of a variety of objects to make each spin faster, thus learning about momentum, rotational velocity, and inertia. Further games include the GeoDig sites where players can learn about different rocks and their origins, and the Rocket Design sites where Whyvillians can learn about velocity, acceleration, and graphing. For all the science games, repeated success at greater difficulty levels equates to an increase in clam salary that is issued at every login to Whyville. See Figure 8.4 for some illustrations of casual science games.

The second category is collaborative science games which have Whyville players sign up in teams to work together on solving a problem. For instance, the Solstice Safari has a group of users working together to collect data about the sunrise and sunset at different locations around the world. This encourages collaboration and social interactions among Whyvillians and teaches them about the earth's position in relations to the sun, notions about time (days, years) and seasons, temperature, and geography (latitude and longitude). A related collaborative game activity is the Sun Spot Alien Rescue in which Whyvillians identify a particular city and its latitude and longitude when given some combinations of clues about an alien's whereabouts (including date, time of sunrise and sunset or number of daylight hours, and geographic information). Players can then use a simulation tool, called the sun tracker, to test visually their solution by representing the path of the sun during daylight, relative to the horizon, for the chosen location and date (Aschbacher, 2003). Other collaborative science games also incorporate casual game components. For instance, in the Smart Cars racing game, Whyvillians design a path of light to navigate their light-sensitive (left and right tires) car to the finish line, and compete with another user who also designs their unique path. The underlying concepts behind this game include the transfer of energy, energy source intensity, and light and

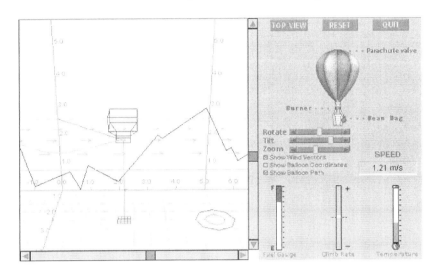

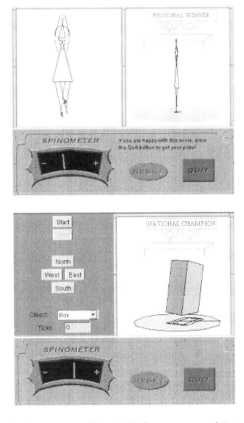

Figure 8.4. Casual science games: Hot Air Balloon game and Spin Lab.

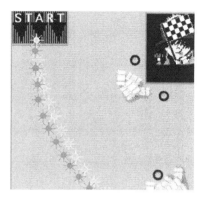

Figure 8.5. Collaborative science games: Smart Cars and the Solstice Safari sign-up locale (Tiki Tours).

mechanical motion. Figure 8.5 illustrates two examples of collaborative science games.

Community science games are the third and perhaps the most unusual category. The most prominent example is the experience of a virtual infectious disease called Whypox that affects the whole community once a year. During an outbreak of Whypox, infected Whyvillians show two symptoms: red pimples appear on their avatars and the ability to chat is interrupted by sneezing (i.e., words are replaced by "achoo"). Whyvillians can become infected in multiple ways—by being close to infected members in the same space, by chatting with others, by throwing projectiles—depending on how the designers of Whyville choose to set the parameters. Unlike adult MUVEs, players' avatars in Whyville do not die or loose power; rather, features central to their community interactions such as chatting and looks are impacted or constrained for a limited time. This approach allows users to draw parallels to real infectious diseases in terms of its spread, symptoms, duration, and cures. Whyville then provides multiple ways for Whyvillians to learn about Whypox and infectious disease (see Figure 8.6). At the individual level, users can learn about Whypox at Whyville's Center for Disease Control (CDC). At the CDC, users can read about past cases, predictions about future outbreaks, and inquiry into cures; they can use tools to simulate the spread of the disease. Contributing to the community and as a source for clam salary, Whyvillians can also write articles about Whypox and post predictions at the CDC based on their readings and the interactions with infected and non-infected others.

When all is well in Whyville, a typical day sees about 14,000 users login for visits that last anywhere from five minutes to more than five hours (average

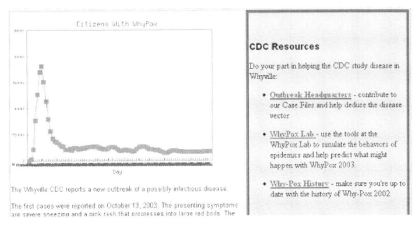

Figure 8.6. Community science games: Whypox graph in CDC and Beach with Whypox infected players.

login length is over 40 minutes) and players participate in over 10,000 science activities on a regular day. We know from a previous study that over 68% of the visitors are girls with an average age of 12.3 years that have computers at home and are interested in science and computers (Aschbacher, 2003; Kafai, in press). In our study, we were particularly interested in students' participation in the various science game activities and the possible integration of these types of science games in the traditional science class-room curriculum.

Playing and Learning with Science Games

In the Fall 2003, we conducted a ten-week study within a laboratory school where Whyville and Whypox were integrated into the classroom curriculum on infectious diseases. Participants were 46 sixth-grade students (age 10–12) from two classrooms taught by the same teacher. Students signed up for an account on Whyville and participated in Whyville online activities in the classroom and at home. As part of their curriculum, students read about a variety of natural infectious diseases and learned about key concepts by preparing individual research reports about a particular disease. Whyville activities were integrated throughout the class sessions, first by having students login from time to time to acquaint themselves with various aspects of Whyville, by participating in several science games, and by tracking the outbreak in their own classroom community. The teacher organized whole-classroom sessions in which students speculated about the causes and cures for Whypox. Students completed their surveys on Whyville participation and infectious disease understanding at the beginning (Time 1), middle (Time 2), and end (Time 3) of the study.

Playing in Whyville

To assess their actions in Whyville, students completed survey items that asked about their general participation and degree of involvement with science and non-science activities there (see Table 8.1). For general participation, students were asked about their frequency for visiting Whyville (1 = less than once a week, 5 = more than once a day) and salary status (1 = 0–25 clams to 5 = 101+ clams) across three time points. Compared to the beginning of the study (M = 3.37), repeated measures analysis of variance across time results showed that students logged onto Whyville with significantly greater frequency at Time 2 (M = 3.75) and Time 3 (M = 3.83). In addition, students had a significantly higher salary at Time 2 (M = 1.52) and Time 3 (M = 1.93) than at the beginning (M = 1.18) of the study. Because salary is often earned through participating in science activities, writing articles for Whyville Times, and other activities, these results suggest that students became more active participants in Whyville over time.

Students were also asked about their involvement with general Whyville science and non-science activities. Given a list of general Whyville activities, such as chatting, science activities, and sending ymail, students were asked

Table 8.1. Frequency of participation in Whyville activities.

Items	Time 1 M (SD)	Time 2 M (SD)	Time 3 M (SD)	Time Main Effect F-value	Contrast F-value T1 v. T2	T1 v. T3
How often do you log onto Whyville?	3.38 (1.13)	3.75 (1.01)	3.83 (1.01)	3.32*	5.87*	4.16*
What is your current salary?	1.18 (0.39)	1.52 (0.85)	1.93 (0.97)	20.85‡	11.06†	31.07‡
Science activities	3.07 (0.91)	3.02 (0.91)	2.84 (0.81)	1.52	0.10	2.66
Reading the Whyville Times	2.00 (1.00)	2.00 (0.98)	1.86 (0.81)	0.79	0.00	0.91
Reading bulletin boards	1.67 (0.97)	1.91 (1.15)	1.65 (0.88)	2.39	3.53	0.04
Signing petitions/parti-cipating in polls	1.38 (0.88)	1.82 (1.00)	2.09 (0.98)	8.80‡	7.11*	16.61‡
Chatting	1.39 (0.94)	2.91 (1.20)	3.09 (0.82)	31.86‡	36.91‡	69.71‡
Ymail	1.34 (0.75)	2.31 (1.28)	2.67 (0.82)	24.88‡	23.89‡	70.54‡
Hanging out	2.07 (0.90)	3.16 (0.94)	2.75 (0.82)	24.31‡	59.83‡	17.57‡
Shopping at Akbar's/Picking your nose	2.12 (1.09)	3.10 (0.88)	2.64 (0.77)	16.56‡	46.91‡	6.75*

* $p < .05$, † $p < .01$, ‡ $p < .001$

"When you are on Whyville, how often do you do the following activities?" For each item, students were given four possible responses that were subsequently scored on a four-point scale: rarely (1), once in a while (2), almost every login (3), and every login (4). Table 8.1 displays all the items, corresponding descriptive statistics, and repeated measures analyses of variance results across time.

For general involvement with Whyville activities, our students showed a shift towards the social rather than science activities with time. That is, repeated measures analyses results showed that students did not differ across time in terms of their involvement with general science activities, reading the Whyville Times, nor reading the bulletin boards. However, students indicated that they were significantly more involved with signing petitions or participating in polls on Whyville at Time 2 and Time 3 than earlier in the study. The social activities in Whyville became more prominent with time. That is, using Time 1 as the baseline, students reported significantly greater involvement with chatting, ymail, and hanging out at social places at Time 2 and Time 3. In addition, these students also indicated that "shopping at Akbar's" or "picking your nose" occurred with significantly greater frequency at Time 2 and Time 3 than at Time 1. Because much of Whyville involves communications through personalizable avatars, and personalization occurs at Akbar's and the "picking your nose" site, these last activities can be consider both personal and social motives.

Playing casual and collaborative science games

For science games, students reported their rate of participation only at the beginning (Time 1) and end (Time 3) of the study. For each science game, students indicated whether they "never tried it," "tried it," "done it," or felt like an "expert." To measure science game experience, these responses were subsequently scored on a four-point scale, with higher scores indicating greater experience. Frequencies and means of science game participation are reported in Table 8.2.

Results showed the majority of students at Time 1 responded that they either never tried or tried most of the science games. The high experience rate for the two Spin Lab games (Skater game and Spin game) and Hot Air Balloon race were caused by the teacher's initial classroom activity and discussion of Whyville. At Time 3, results showed that most students indicated that they "tried it," "done it," or felt like an "expert" on almost all of the science games. The one exception was the Solstice Safari game that required coordination from Whyville users and website designers to organize their occurrence. For this reason, experience in it was generally low. To analyze change in science game experience, paired sample t-tests were conducted for each game (see Table 8.3). Results showed that students' rates of experience were significantly higher at Time 2 for most of the science games. The only non-significant time differences were for the Hot Air Balloon and Solstice Safari games.

Table 8.2. Expertise in playing casual science games.

	Time 1 Frequency (%)		Time 3 Frequency (%)		Time 1 Frequency (%)		Time 3 Frequency (%)	
	GeoGid				**Spin Lab Skater Game**			
Never tried it	32	(.73)	15	(.33)	2	(.04)	0	(.00)
Tried it	8	(.18)	12	(.27)	11	(.24)	1	(.02)
Done it	4	(.09)	7	(.16)	9	(.20)	11	(.24)
Expert	0	(.00)	11	(.24)	23	(.51)	34	(.74)
	Hot Air Ballooning				**Spin Lab Spin Game**			
Never tried it	1	(.02)	2	(.04)	6	(.13)	5	(.11)
Tried it	14	(.32)	11	(.24)	17	(.38)	9	(.20)
Done it	20	(.45)	19	(.42)	11	(.24)	15	(.33)
Expert	9	(.20)	13	(.29)	11	(.24)	17	(.37)
	House of Illusions				**Treasure Hunt**			
Never tried it	22	(.49)	4	(.09)	33	(.75)	11	(.24)
Tried it	9	(.20)	5	(.11)	6	(.14)	10	(.22)
Done It	5	(.11)	10	(.22)	3	(.07)	7	(.15)
Expert	9	(.20)	27	(.59)	2	(.05)	18	(.39)
	Smart Cars				**WASA Rockets**			
Never tried it	25	(.57)	17	(.37)	26	(.59)	16	(.36)
Tried it	12	(.27)	8	(.17)	12	(.27)	8	(.18)
Done it	6	(.14)	8	(.17)	4	(.09)	9	(.20)
Expert	1	(.02)	13	(.28)	2	(.05)	12	(.27)
	Solstice Safari				**WASA Zero Gravity**			
Never tried it	34	(.76)	33	(.73)	19	(.43)	16	(.36)
Tried it	6	(.13)	6	(.13)	21	(.48)	13	(.29)
Done it	5	(.11)	4	(.09)	4	(.09)	9	(.20)
Expert	0	(.00)	2	(.04)	0	(.00)	7	(.16)

Table 8.3. Differences in participation over time in casual science games.

	Time 1 M (SD)	Time 3 M (SD)	t-value
GeoGid	1.34 (0.65)	2.30 (1.17)	−5.41‡
Hot Air Ballooning	2.84 (0.78)	2.98 (0.86)	−1.29
House of Illusions	2.02 (1.20)	3.31 (1.00)	−7.58‡
Smart Cars	1.61 (0.81)	2.34 (1.26)	−4.36‡
Solstice Safari	1.36 (0.69)	1.45 (0.85)	−0.78
Spin Lab Skater Game	3.18 (0.96)	3.73 (0.50)	−3.95‡
Spin Lab Spin Game	2.60 (1.01)	2.98 (1.01)	−2.32*
Treasure Hunt	1.41 (0.82)	2.64 (1.22)	−5.70‡
WASA Rockets	1.58 (0.85)	2.35 (1.23)	−4.29‡
WASA Zero Gravity	1.67 (0.64)	2.14 (1.06)	−3.10†

*p < .05, † p < .01, ‡ p < .001

Playing community science games

The outbreak of Whypox presented an unique opportunity to examine players' participation in a community science game. As part of class activities, students went in teams into the Center for Disease Control's archive to read about past Whypox infections and posted statements about possible explanations. Students also used the simulators to try out different parameter configurations (e.g., number of people infected, days of incubation, run of disease; see Figure 8.7). Students also read about previous Whypox outbreaks pulling articles from the archive of the Whyville Times (see Figure 8.8).

In science classes, students tracked their infection rate on a daily basis and noted the names of those who had been infected by Whypox. Students also checked the population graph in the CDC to compare their class' infection rate with that in the community. The discrepancies in rates gave rise to classroom discussions on why not all students had been infected and what might serve as an explanation for the discrepancies. The excerpts on page 211 illustrate the nature and content of classroom discussions: the first one was taken a few days after the first outbreak, and the other a week later towards the end of the Whypox outbreak.

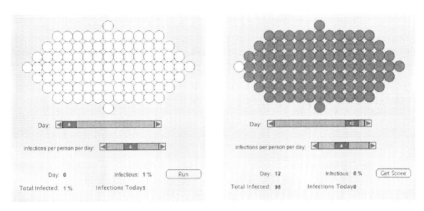

Figure 8.7. Community science games: screen shots of Simulator in CDC.

THE WHYVILLE TIMES

www.whyville.net   Feb 28, 2002   Weekly Issue

Why-Pox No Good?

Hi, it's mewi here and I want to talk about Why-Pox.

mewi
Guest Writer

Why-Pox aren't good! I once wanted them, but not any more – they're infectious and if I get them more people will get them too! So always stay alert and away from people with pox. I'm not saying that you can't talk to your friends on Whyville if they have pox, just stay a fair distance away from them.

Sometimes I wonder, did Whyville's creators just put pox on here for fun or is it a virus or something? Is it on all chat sites or just this one? Who knows??

Also I have heard that if you change your face and also have Why-Pox they will get one step worse until your pox are bright red not just light pink. I have been noticing a large increase of this disease over the past two days. According to my calculations I figure that since in the past few days about 180 people got the virus, it will take about two or three months to reach 10,000 people. So, in a matter of months, almost all Whyvillians will have or have had the pox.

I have taken note of people saying things like you can get pox by someone with pox throwing a projectile at you, sneezing on you, and many other things. Is this real or not? I mean, on Friday I was in the Spin Speak and there were lots of people with pox and I still have none. Does this mean that the pox just comes and goes, or will they never leave your face?

I'm sure everybody knows about the Whyville CDC, so always try to help out by finding information on it and mail it to me so I can try to incorporate a way to get rid of them. Also any information about how to get rid of them or how to get them, mail that to me or Whyville and then we can get it all to stop.

The last thing I want to talk about is a contest I will hold and it will start as soon as this article comes out. I would like to get as much information as possible on whypasses mailed to me so we can get rid of pox. Also another thing that will count as information is how this strange disease got named Why-Pox.

Rules to the contest:
1) Use different information.
2) No cheating; ex: using other people's information.
3) Have fun!
and 4) Have fun!

I will judge the contest by the person who has the most unique information that is true and if a peace of information is on two or more entries it will be eliminated. I hope everyone stays in good shape for the rest of the year and Why-Pox will disappear.

Mewi signing off, *click*

Figure 8.8. Article about Whypox in Whyville Times Archive.

Excerpt of Classroom Discussion at Onset of Whypox Outbreak

> Bert: I was at the beach and I went to someone who had them. Then I moved away.
>
> Teacher: So you got them right away? Do you really think you got them from him? If you are around someone who has a cold and I'm around you right now will by after school I have that cold? No. Why? Because it takes a little
>
> Sam: It takes a little time to go through your body.
>
> Teacher: It's called an incubation period. You're not going to get it immediately.
>
> Susan: I got it immediately
>
> Teacher: So, maybe you didn't get it from him. Just a suggestion.

Sam: I wanted to infect other people so. I went close to them and then I went away and then they got it.

Teacher: We're going to have to talk about Whypox ethics. [She points to the graph on the whiteboard and post-its with names of infected students] So the 17th? 18th? Ok we have Anna, Oscar, Al, and Olivia.

Susan: A lot of people in this class have Whypox.

Teacher: We have a lot more in this class. We need to be visiting (*got cut off*)

Sam: Only those people in the other class have it.

Teacher: Interesting difference huh. Saturday? Sunday?

Susan: I have something to say. Well maybe a lot more people have it in here because Tony said that Theo and Sam got it first and since we're usually on the computers at the same time, maybe that we were together and we were at the same room or something.

Teacher: I'm seeing epidemiologists in all of you. You're already thinking about how did this happen, what could be the reasons, you're analyzing it, you're thinking about it. I want you to continue with that line of thought as you're looking at all of the data. Thinking why, how what. Ok, Garth.

Garth: Well you know how people said it was gone a few weeks ago. I think Theo got it first a long time ago then Theo said it's gone. And it said on the news bulletin, Whypox has gone. But then two weeks later suddenly it's like a giant plague

Susan: It's an epidemic.

Garth: It's the giant plague. It traveled back. It's like a Whyplague. Now it's like everybody is getting it.

Susan: It's an epidemic.

Excerpt of Classroom Discussion at End of Whypox Outbreak (a week later)

Teacher: How many of you had symptoms and have just passed. Ok, eight of you have recovered successfully from Whypox. [She is counting raised hands 1, 2, 3, 4, 5, 6, 7, 8]

Sam: I went to beach and only 1 person out of 20 or 30 had Whypox.

Teacher: 1 person out of 20 or 30 and that was different from last week. What was it like? Allen.

Allen: Everyone was sneezing

Susan: Just the opposite. One person didn't and everyone else had it. This time only one person had it and everyone else didn't. So what do you think happened?

Garth: It's passing.

Teacher: So what do you mean passing? Anna?

Anna: All the Whypox is going away.

In a related study (Neulight, Kafai, Kao, Foley, & Galas, 2007), we examined these classroom discussions for science connections and themes that compared the understanding of Whypox to students' understanding of natural diseases. First, when discussing Whypox, students and teachers often related and included natural disease terminology and concepts (e.g., contagious, exposure, symptoms, infection, incubation period, epidemiologist, epidemic, quarantining, immunity). Second, analogies and comparisons between Whypox and real natural diseases (e.g., SARS, plague, common cold) were often concurrently mentioned. Third, students and teachers were shown to provide a combination of experiential, social, and casual references when describing Whypox. That is, they often provided examples of personal experiences with Whypox, noticed someone who has it, and/or present causal explanations or hypothesis about how someone got it.

To investigate the impact of a community science game on science learning, Neulight et al. (2007) analyzed the pre-post data on the impact of Whypox on students' understanding of natural infectious disease (Au & Romeo, 1999). At the beginning and end of the study, students were given a scenario (about a girl whom became sick the day after visiting a sick friend) and were asked the following open-ended questions: "Why did it take a whole day for her to feel sick after the germs got inside her body?" and "How did the germs make her feel sick in so many parts of her body at the same time?" Responses were then coded as either pre-biological (e.g., got sick because they were in the same room) or biological causal mechanism (e.g., got sick because germs grew, reproduced, or attacked cells). Analyses revealed that students generally responded with more pre-biological answers than biological answers to both questions. However, while the number of pre-biological responses was generally similar across time, the number of biological answers increased twofold.

Neulight et al. (2007) also asked students "In which ways was Whypox like a real infectious disease?" and "How do you think Whypox spread through the community?" Responses to both questions drew many parallels between virtual and natural infectious diseases. For the similarities, the majority of responses mentioned that Whypox was contagious, while other responses included the fact that Whypox had symptoms and was analogous to other specific diseases. For explaining Whypox, students mentioned contact, chat, and sneezing; no student was able to generate more functional explanations of how a computer virus such as Whypox would spread in a virtual community.

Discussion

Our investigations into Whyville as a virtual playground revealed that players are drawn to the social activities that constitute community life in Whyville: chatting, whispering, and sending ymail are preferred and prominent activities of Whyville users. Science-related activities, such as the casual games, are completed because they provide other things to do while online and, most importantly, they provide the salary necessary to finance shopping sprees at the local mall for new face parts or resources to trade or purchase new items. The community-driven science games such as Whypox were more successful in drawing Whyvillians into science activities and learning about infectious disease. The classroom discussions about Whypox indicated that the participation in a virtual epidemic allowed students to train their observations and make connections to their understanding of natural disease.

Our analyses of different science games genres provided us with a new perspective on how science could be integrated within an informal MUVE learning environment. The most promising and interesting ones are the community science games because they immerse the whole community in the science experience. The umbrella of community science games can also include casual and collaborative science games that are specifically targeted towards infectious disease aspects. For instance, the simulators in the Center for Disease Control offer Whyvillians the opportunity to run and test parameters for virtual epidemics on a smaller scale. Just running simulations does not make for a rich instructional experience. In a more recent study (Feldon & Gilmore, 2006), we redesigned the simulators in such a way that they provide feedback about the accuracy of players' predictions. Now Whyvillians can continue to run simulations by setting infection parameters but they are also asked to make predictions about the outcomes and to provide justifications. The completed simulations inform players about the accuracy of their predictions and thus provide feedback for parameter changes. We are currently analyzing whether Whyvillians take advantage of these new features to improve their simulation results as a possible indicator for science engagement and learning.

We have also examined other ways to enhance the immersive aspect of the community science game Whypox by tying it more closely to economic interactions prominent in Whyville. We noted that many Whyvillians, including the students in our study, always check their salary ledgers and income when logging in and spend much time at Akbar's buying avatar improvements. The trading post in Whyville is a popular space for finding avatar parts no longer available for sale, for exchanging face parts, or for selling off a not-needed inventory of face parts to generate additional income. We used the recent flu vaccine shortage as an inspiration to create a tighter connection between Whypox and economic interactions (Kafai, 2006). Before an outbreak of the epidemic, one dose of a vaccine against Whypox was distributed to one third of the active Whyville population. All Whyvillians were informed that they needed two additional doses of vaccine to achieve immunity before the outbreak, which they could get via donations or the trading post. As part of our research, we documented baseline data of Whyville's economic activity and the trading volume, interactions, and conversations around vaccine sales and exchanges at the trading post (Kafai, 2006).

The findings from the present study provided us with ample food for thought on what and how to study MUVEs such as Whyville in future studies. It is clear that we need multiple ways to document the complexity of interactions in Whyville—self-reports and observations are a first stepping stone and need to be complemented by automatic data collection tools that track a Whyvillian's pathway through the community. But we also need to investigate Whyville's use in different contexts—classrooms and homes are possible but not the only settings. Many afterschool places are public venues that resemble Internet cafes popular in other parts of the world (Lin, 2005). Afterschool places allow for communal game play when dozens of children are logged into Whyville while being concurrently in a shared physical space of a computer club or community technology center. Kafai (2006) included afterschool programs in different community settings.

Our findings are constrained by some methodological issues. For one, we had to rely on students' self-reports of Whyville use at different time points throughout the project. It is quite possible that students overstated or underestimated their actual participation in Whyville activities. The assessments provided by students thus present at best summaries or compilation of events. Future research will collect behavioral data about students' visits to different places in Whyville and report the time spent on each activity and chatting among participants. Such data would allow us to track students' pathways through the MUVE and establish possible connections between science activities.

We are also aware that the use of Whyville at school and home is not representative of the large number of Whyvillians who join the site on their own leisure time. The inclusion of classrooms allowed us to examine the feasibility of integrating MUVEs in regular instructional science activities. It is not at all obvious how open-ended MUVEs such as Whyville compare to more instruction-driven MUVEs such as *Rivercity*. In *Rivercity*, the occurrence of infectious disease drives students' exploration of the environment but in a different manner: Lab books provide structured activities that direct members to collect data probes at different environmental places to examine the sanitary conditions. *Rivercity* is also a closed environment where students interact with artificial avatars and other class members but no outside visitors. Students who participated in this Whyville study also used *Rivercity* and revealed in comparison that they preferred the social nature of Whyville but felt more focused on science in *Rivercity* (Kao, Galas, & Kafai, 2005).

Conclusions

Our analyses have shown that MUVEs such as *Whyville* offer a promising informal place for children to learn and play with science in multiple ways. The categorization of different science game genres helped us to identify Whypox as a distinct feature of MUVEs because it facilitated the immersion of the whole community rather than individual players. It is clear that these immersive features in MUVEs deserve further design efforts and study in how they can lead to greater engagement in science and technology that possibly might lead to improved understanding of science and technology ideas.

Acknowledgments

The writing of this chapter is supported by a grant of the National Science Foundation (NSF-0411814) to Yasmin Kafai. The views expressed are those of the author and do not necessarily represent the views of NSF or the University of California.

We wish to thank Linda Kao, Brian Foley, and Cathleen Galas who participated in the implementation of the pilot study.

References

Aschbacher, P. (2003). *Gender differences in the perception and use of an informal science learning website.* Grant-funded by National Science Foundation, PGE-0086338. Arlington, VA.

Au, T. K., & Romeo, L. F. (1999). Mechanical causality in children's "folkbiology." In D. Medin & S. Atran (Eds.), *Folkbiology.* Cambridge, MA: The MIT Press.

Barab, S. A., Thomas, M., Dodge, T., Carteaux, R., & Tuzun, H. (2005). Making learning fun: Quest Atlantis, a game without guns. *Educational Technology Research & Development, 53*(1), 86–107.

Bruckman, A. (2000). Situated support for learning: Storm's weekend with Rachael. *Journal of the Learning Sciences, 9*(3), 329–372.

Cross, G. (1997). *Kids' stuff: Toys and the changing world of American childhood.* Cambridge, MA: Harvard University Press.

Dede, C. (2004). Enabling distributed-learning communities via emerging technologies. In *Proceedings of the 2004 Conference of the Society for Information*

Technology in Teacher Education (SITE) (pp. 3–12). Charlottesville, VA: American Association for Computers in Education.

Dede, C., Nelson, B., Ketelhut, D. J., Clarke, J., & Bowman, C. (2004). Design-based research strategies for studying situated learning in a multi-user virtual environment. In Y. B. Kafai, W. A. Sandoval, N. Enyedy, A. S. Nixon, & F. Herrera (Eds.), *Proceedings of the Sixth International Conference of the Learning Sciences.* Mahwah, NJ: Lawrence Erlbaum.

DeVane, B. M., & Squire, K. (2006). *Learning about race, culture, and gender from "Grand Theft Auto: San Andreas."* Paper presented at annual meeting of American Educational Research Association in San Francisco, CA.

Feldon, D., & Gilmore, J. (2006, June). *Patterns in children's online scientific problem-solving and explanation behaviors: Using a large-N approach for a microgenetic study.* Paper presented to the EARLI SIM workshop in Leuven, Belgium.

Gee, J. P. (2003). *What videogames have to teach us about learning and literacy.* New York: Palgrave Macmillan.

Kafai, Y. B. (2006, June). *The value of looks over health: Observations of chidren's economic interactions during a virtual epidemic.* Paper presented to the Games, Learning, & Society Conference in Madison, WI.

Kafai, Y. B. (in press). Synthetic play: Teen gaming together and apart in virtual worlds. In Y. B. Kafai, C. Heeter, J. Denner, & J. Sun (Eds.), *Beyond Barbie and Mortal Kombat: New Perspectives on Gender and Games.* Cambridge, MA: MIT Press.

Kao, L., Galas, C., & Kafai, Y. B. (2005). *"A totally different world": Playing and learning in multi-user virtual environments.* Paper presented at the DIGRA conference in Vancouver, CA.

Lin, H. (2005). *(Gendered) gaming experience in different social environments: From home to cyber cafés.* Paper presented at the DIGRA conference in Vancouver, CA.

Neulight, N., Kafai, Y. B., Kao, L., Foley, B., & Galas, C. (2007). Children's participation in a virtual epidemic in the science classroom: Making connections to natural infectious diseases. *Journal of Science Education and Technology, 16*(1), 47–53.

Squire, K., & Barab, S. A. (2004). Replaying history: Engaging urban underserved students in learning world history through computer simulation games. In Y. B. Kafai, W. Sandoval, N. Eneydy, A. Nixon, & F. Hernandez (Eds.), *Proceedings of the Sixth International Conference of the Learning Sciences.* Mahwah, NJ: Lawrence Erlbaum.

Steinkhuehler, C. (2004). Learning in MMORPGs. In Y. B. Kafai, W. Sandoval, N. Eneydy, A. Nixon, & F. Hernandez (Eds.), *Proceedings of the Sixth International Conference of the Learning Sciences.* Mahwah, NJ: Lawrence Erlbaum.

Chapter 9

Can Students Re-Invent Fundamental Scientific Principles? Evaluating the Promise of New-Media Literacies

Andrea A. diSessa

Introduction

This chapter combines two rather different intellectual lines. The first line involves considering several cases of students re-inventing fundamental ideas in science and mathematics, such as Newton's laws and the idea of Cartesian graphs. I take up the question of how it is possible and in what ways is it a legitimate learning activity for students to accomplish such apparently prodigious feats. In answering those questions, the main (although only partial) answer has to do with the power of representations, in particular computational "new media" representations. The fact of intellectual power in the use of computational representations constitutes an empirically tractable aspect of the second main intellectual line of this chapter: How can we conceptualize and actually test promised riches in new-media literacies? The main goal here is to provide a more sharply focused and better-grounded view—separating hype from legitimate hope—of some of the best intellectual possibilities offered by new media. I begin by considering how we can most productively think about the promise of new-media literacies.

Perspectives on literacy

New-media literacies are touted as opening fantastic vistas for future intellectual and expressive power. I have my own version of that story, a part of which will unfold here. However, an equally exciting prospect (exciting for very different reasons) is to test and extend existing theories of literacy in the face of developing possibilities. My conviction is that past theories of literacy have implicitly assumed properties of the medium to be just like text, that central prototype for possible literacies. But, new media are not just like text, in small and large ways. Looking at nascent forms of new-media literacies—and, more importantly, anticipating and fostering the best possible literacies—will require a more general framing than that which may suffice for textual literacy. I sketch here just enough of my views on a revised theory of literacy to serve as an introduction to some of the important focuses in this chapter.

Oversimplifying, the modern theory of literacy has gone through two broad phases. The earlier phase (although it extends essentially to the present), involving researchers such as Goody (1977) and Ong (1982), might be characterized as cognitive and in some measure techno-centric. Phase I was cognitive in positing that the power of literacy came from attributes of transformed thinking fostered by literacy. People became more logical, capable of abstract thinking, "distanced," dispassionate, critical, and so on, in virtue of the discovery of alphabetic text as a way of encoding verbal language. The phase has been uncharitably characterized as embracing an "autonomous" view of literacy (Street, 1995), assuming that the effect of literacy arises from the very fact of using the textual representational system. I prefer the more generic and descriptive term "techno-centric" to capture a central focus on properties of the "technology," the medium, in providing "enhanced thinking powers."[1]

The second phase has been described by adherents as "ideological" (Street, 1995) or "new literacy studies" (Gee, 1996). This phase has a characteristic focus on the multiple social functions of literacy, such as identifying members of social groups and multiple roles in, for example, producing and reproducing social strata and in allocation of social goods. In this view, there is no homogeneity in the effects of literacy—hence it is more natural to think of "literacies"—and certainly no technological determinism, as might have been attributed to the earlier work. Studies by Scribner and Cole (1981) and others pointed out that the effects of literacy depend on the social practices (e.g., forms of schooling) in which it is embedded. In the early to mid-1990s, Phase II literacy studies seldom made any reference at all to representational forms. Of course, with the increasing visibility of new media in literacy studies, a focus on the medium, however vague, has returned to a greater prominence.

My own perspective can be drawn out of this abbreviated discussion, and it is largely synthetic of the two phases.

1 Both social and cognitive perspectives are necessary for a deep understanding of the nature of literacies.
2 As emphasized much more in Phase I of literacy studies, representational forms and their properties are heavily involved in creating at least some of the powers of literacy. However, representational form is far from determining; techno-centricity must be moderated. Most "powers" of literacy must be seen as emergent in a joint material/cognitive/social system.

3 While the social viability and social functioning of literacies depend on more things than individual intellectual power, my personal interest here is, in fact, specifically in intellectual powers that might emerge from new-media literacies. I am most interested in transformations of the way science and mathematics are taught—indeed, in the way they are conceptualized—that may come about from use of new media (diSessa, in press). I do not deny more characteristically social functions, but I claim that a focus on intellectual power is legitimate.

4 Unlike the primary emphasis of Phase I studies, I believe that some of the most important intellectual powers conveyed by new-media literacies might manifest only in episodes of person-plus-medium or group-plus-medium activity. While I do not deny power in "intellectual residue" conveyed to people not in the presence of media, I also think analysis of media-plus-people systems might be more systematically productive.

5 While I focus on intellectual powers, as do Phase I theorists, times have changed with respect to theoretical and empirical accountability for the reality and efficacy of claimed powers. Most of the general powers named in Phase I literacy studies seem underspecified, undemonstrated, and even implausible given modern standards, especially with respect to empirical validation.

Statement of goals

Bridging toward the analyses that I show here:

1 I look toward specific empirical accountability in validating the powers I attribute to literacies, intending to do better in this regard than older Phase I studies could manage, and probably more than much Phase II research as well. (However, this review chapter will, at best, point to the kinds of data and argument that validate claims; I cannot afford the space to draw out important empirical details in the several cases discussed.)

2 I look specifically into human–material "cooperation" (that is, thinking in the context of representations) rather than at purely intellectual residues of literacy.

3 While I look, somewhat in passing, at social considerations in the form of human–human collaborative patterns (mediated by representational forms), I will not reach essentially large-scale social issues involved in the creation of new-media literacies. For some of that, consult diSessa (2000).

"Re-inventing" fundamental science and mathematics

This chapter is driven by a series of empirical results over years of work in my research group. In each of the studies cited, students ended by reproducing, in some approximation, fundamental scientific or mathematical results, from Cartesian graphing to Newton's laws of motion. Of course, they did not construct these in the fullest sense, reproducing historical genius. However, we have maintained the legitimacy and importance of what students accomplished. A main part of my task here will be to expose just a little more than the barest bones of the process and results of these re-inventions.

That students can reproduce (even partially) results of the greatest geniuses in the history of science is a challenging claim. To many researchers, it is immediately implausible and, possibly, dismissible. For example, I quote two highly respected and high profile contributors to mathematics and science education.[2]

> "Models [laws] are things that scientists make and students use."

> "It is neither reasonable nor efficient to expect students to invent for themselves the content of . . . disciplines."

A main part of my task is to take some of the mystery out of student re-invention (but not all of the mystery—I hope that students' work will remain impressive!). In this regard, many other researchers have participated in advocacy and explanation of "re-inventing" basic mathematics and science. For example, the Dutch realistic mathematics work (e.g., Gravemeijer, 1994) speaks of scaffolded reconstruction as a core instructional method. Several other people, mainly specialists in the learning of mathematics (e.g., Bamberger, 2006; Hughes, 1986; Nemirovsky & Tierney, 2001), have explored students' abilities to design representations, which topic will figure prominently here.

Principles

To help unify and focus later discussion of student re-inventing, I produce here a general set of principles by which I believe re-inventing became possible. The set is grouped into three subsets. The first principle (a singleton set) is special in that it does not concern power emerging from new-media representations. Instead, it provides an important perspective on what I believe to be a likely fundamental characteristic of new-media literacies.

The second set includes specific ways in which representations might be helpful in these re-inventing activities. We have data, at various levels of convincingness, on all of these principles. The third set consists of non-representational principles. These are token in illustrating a larger set of non-representational principles that must also be invoked to explain success in our re-inventing activities. They also seem salient enough in our data that it would be unfair to omit them.

The meta-representational principle

1   Modern students—even elementary school students—come to class with a lot of exposure to representations in many forms. A large literature shows that students come to know basic things about, for example, pictures. They learn that pictures are usually or always made by people, that they refer to a non-present reality, and that they are intended to convey or display something to an "audience" (Freeman, 1985). Our own work documents extensive creative capacities that seem commonplace in even sixth-graders (diSessa, 2004). One special case of this principle is the mere idea of mathematizing the world with the expectation of understanding it better for having done so. This is such a commonplace in the modern world, which includes clocks, thermometers, scales, and numbers like "miles per gallon" at every turn, that it would be easy to miss the fact that this is a culture-specific experience, not a universal inclination. Before Galileo's time, for example, it cannot have been true that ordinary people, much less children, would spontaneously mathematize in expectation of using thus exposed regularities in order to understand better. We see this instinctive mathematizing in our data.

Representational principles

2   *The power of abstract, well-adapted representations:* Much of modern science relies, near its core, on representations such as algebra, calculus (which is both a conceptual and representational accomplishment), differential equations, etc. A particular representation can pick the "right" level of abstraction, and thus constrain the search for valid and comprehensible laws and models. Certain (mainly) representational entities, such as vectors, are perspicuously adequate to encode exactly what the history of science has found out about certain domains, notably many aspects of physics. Thus, providing a representational form can also provide important hints and constraints in "re-inventing" basic science. Of course it is critical that students understand those representations enough to use them creatively. This is precisely a key advance of new

media, extending traditional scientific representations with ones that are as expressively powerful but much easier to learn. A big and perhaps surprising lesson here is that writing simple programs turns out to be much easier than writing, for example, algebraic expressions for important science, and it is arguably as or more expressive of the important underlying ideas (see the discussion in diSessa, 2000, and Sherin, 2001).

3 *Representational task tuning; conceptual/representational pump-priming:* Many of our re-invention tasks are framed in representationally partially formed terms. For example, we often provided a template that gives a hint or starting place for inquiry, helping students by putting the focus on a key conceptual point, or by providing an organization of the task. A related strategy, pump-priming, involves prior exploration or instruction in related tasks, or in a task that is a sub-task of the full re-invention task. This can take the form of an inquiry that results in a model that is related to or part of the target re-invention. Considerations in formulating a starting template or in designing a prior exploration can tune tasks to an appropriate level of difficulty.[3]

4 *Dynamic representations:* Paper and pencil, algebraic, and similar representations lack a pair of characteristics that are an important part of the story for new media: dynamics and interactivity. These have implications both for expressiveness and for learning. With respect to expressiveness, laws of nature expressed as simple programs can be run, and students can see the effects of the laws, for example in actual motion of objects. In developing their own versions of laws, students can see, consider, and react to their symbolic hypotheses. This is more than supporting feedback loops; it also invokes intuitive and perceptual knowledge that might otherwise be locked out of student work.[4]

5 *Support for social collaboration:* External, perceptually shared representations support good collaboration. Of course, the representation needs to be properly expressive of the ideas at issue. Thus adaptation to both science's best ideas (item 2 above), and to student ideas (in item 4 above) is important. A positive evaluation of a representational form depends on how the medium meets these requirements. Support for collaboration has at least the following aspects:

a *"Reading" student ideas*—Words are notoriously vague, and in many cases new-media and computational representations provide a better expressive language for students to display, and teachers to "read," student ideas.

b *Goal and hypothesis clarity*—Creating computational representations has an evident end-state in many cases: A program runs and shows adequate behavior. Contrast this to "producing a theory" or even creating an equation, which has uncertain implications. At earlier stages, students can express hypotheses often in terms of particular, unambiguous expressions.

c *Summary representation*—Like famous equations that litter the history of science, from Newton's $F = ma$ to Einstein's $E = mc^2$, computational representations can provide compact and precise summaries of key ideas. This compactness and precision are often in sharp contrast to natural language or pictures. Many who extol the virtues of new media completely ignore the fundamental and transformative power of symbolic formulations.

e *A focus for teacher intervention*—We have seen teachers use external computational representations in many ways to help students along productive intellectual pathways (conceptual support) and, more broadly, to provide practical and discussion/organizational guidance (pragmatic support). For example, a teacher can focus attention on a particular part of a program, or, more strongly, suggest a possible direction of pursuit (either a known-to-be-productive direction, or one chosen for interesting contrast) in concrete, representational terms.

Non-representational principles

6 *Building on productive intuitive ideas:* Our project has been strongly committed to understanding and building on students' "naïve" intuitive resources. This, of course, is scarcely unique to our project, but it has been important, in our judgment, in the success we have had.

7 *Designing a good task framing and setting a proper task context*: I will mention some particulars in examples, but, in general, we feel that task design and teachers' skills in supporting student accomplishment are always important.

8 *Knowing it is possible:* It is highly non-trivial support to ask students to accomplish achievable tasks, framed in ways we know can succeed. This contrasts with the task that faced the first scientists in discovering fundamental science: they formulated the tasks themselves. I will say no more about this evident principle.

Examples

This section presents a series of mostly successful examples of students' re-inventing or re-designing fundamental mathematics and science. I sketch the tasks as framed and the contexts in which the students worked, including some of the pump-priming we did. I also describe outcomes, including variation and limitations we have discovered. These examples make a prima facie case that students' re-invention of fundamental mathematics and science is possible, and show some of the "how" and "why."

The main new-media point of these examples is partial validation of intellectual powers granted by the use of new media in these "exceptional" accomplishments. "Exceptional" is quoted because our attitude is that these accomplishments are surprising mainly in that they are much more difficult—if they are possible at all—without new-media support. We take them to be examples of what can become everyday accomplishments in the future. Consistent both with our general statement of goals and with each of the relevant principles, we are concerned with powers and advantages conveyed by representations when they are partners in thinking by individuals and groups, not with respect to any residue in changed thought in the absence of the representations (contra Phase I modal claims). Finally, while some social features of representational use are highlighted, these remain at the classroom level. Essential large-scale issues concerning new literacies are simply not addressed, owing to the nature of the empirical work described here.

"Inventing graphing"

Task	Students are given the task of creating paper-and-pencil depictions that are "as simple as possible" to show various concrete motions. The initial motion-to-be-depicted was called the "desert motion": a car drives through a desert, but the driver stops to get a drink from a cactus, and then he slowly speeds up and drives away.
Mode	Students engage in iterative design, where individuals or small groups propose or refine representations, alternating with full-class critique sessions. The teacher prompts consolidation of representations, group-consensus criteria, and proposes new motion problems with greater difficulties, such as reversed motion.
Outcome	Students in our first edition produced a plethora of representations, gradually moving toward more abstract and scientific representations. In the end, their favorite representation was in essence Cartesian graphing. Students were exceptionally motivated and engaged.

Replications   We have done about a half dozen replications. All showed substantial competence to design and critique representations, and substantial further development of that competence in students from sixth grade into high school. Each replication revealed new kinds of representations. A related series of studies asked students to design representations of "landscapes," which, while not as rich, generally converged on approximations of topographical maps (Azevedo, 2000).

The first example of students' re-invention, which we call "inventing graphing," is exceptional in that it relates in a very different way to new literacies compared to the examples that follow. In essence, we discovered that students have remarkable meta-representational competences (MRC). That is, they know much more about representations in general than most would expect. In particular, (a) they know how to generate a wide range of new representations; (b) they can effectively critique particular representations as adequate, or not, for particular uses. Although not highlighted here, (c) students also are surprisingly articulate about representation (much intuitive knowledge is more tacit and implicit); (d) they know a significant amount about how representations work; and (e) they can quickly learn some classes of representations with little instruction. These five aspects of representation form the core of our definition of MRC.

The first edition of inventing graphing (diSessa, Hammer, Sherin, & Kolpakowski, 1991) took place in a sixth-grade class over four-and-a-half 45-minute periods (roughly a week of "math class"). What attracted us to do analysis of this sequence of classes was the exceptionally high level of engagement shown by the students. But what emerged from analysis was an impressive competence to design and critique representations. diSessa (2004) reviews the extended research program that evolved from the original episode.

Figure 9.1 suggests some of the richness of MRC shown by students, selected from our first edition of "inventing graphing." It also unpacks some of the steps that, in this case, led to Cartesian graphing. Figure 9.1a is a fairly typical "concrete" early representation. Figure 9.1b shows a representation that responded to a teacher's challenge to represent the length of a stop. Here, the horizontal line represents the speed of the object, and the vertical line represents "how long it was going at that speed." The sequence of discrete icons is a typical and important early phase of representation. Figure 9.1c was a brilliant innovation; speed is represented by the slope of the line, freeing up length to represent another aspect, such as duration or distance. Figures 9.1d and 9.1e represent follow-up innovations of, first, connecting the slanted

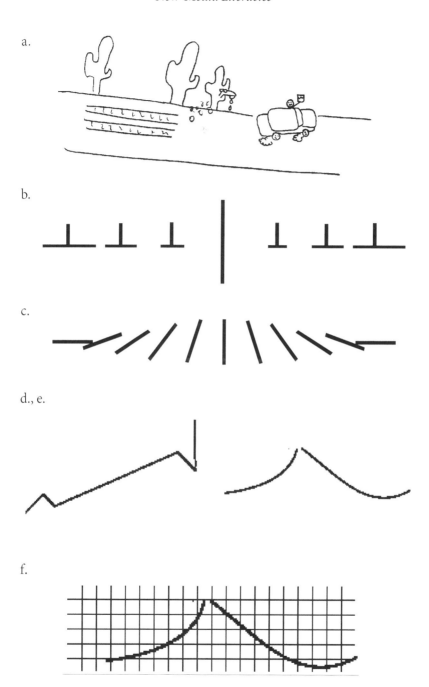

Figure 9.1. A sequence of student-designed representations of motion.

lines, and then representing continuously changing speeds. Finally, a student suggested adding a grid so that different aspects (speed and time or distance) could be read off numerically.

We do not question the fact that these students likely had seen graphing before (although not, as far as we could determine, in their mathematics classes). But the main point is not whether they reproduced graphing per se and by themselves. The really important point is that they were building on and developing a flexible, well-articulated meta-representational expertise in these activities. The students explored many alternatives to graphing, and they explicitly considered multiple criteria for evaluating them, such as clarity, simplicity, completeness, and so on. (See, for example, diSessa, 2002.) Other classes that never re-invented graphing per se worked just as well in this regard. In complementary manner, when students introduced graphing as a way of representing motion without critical reflection of its advantages and disadvantages with respect to alternatives, the meta-representational agenda might have been only marginally advanced, if at all.

Our take, from the extended research we have done in this area, is that the main reason for students' excellent accomplishment is a culturally well-prepared MRC, a nearly invisible current literacy. This parallels our finding and building on sometimes invisible competences (principle 6) in some of the other examples, below. In the intellectual line of remarkable "re-inventing," the work here stands without need for elaboration. In the line of new literacies, the connection is indirect and somewhat speculative. However, we believe the existence of MRC provides a fundamental insight into possible new literacies.

To reach this insight, one must consider the fact that, unlike text, new media, especially in the service of mathematics and science, do not provide just one or a few new representational forms. Instead, they provide a basis for hundreds of new representations crafted to special purposes. Exploratory statistical displays, image processing for astronomical analysis, Internet-available displays of economic growth, and so on, all make the following point: Learning representations one at a time (such as graphs, algebra, tables, etc.) is no longer a tenable approach, if it ever was. Instead, new-media literacies in the techno-scientific niche (at least) will be permeated with meta-representational capacities to understand and control myriad representations. That is, new-media literacies will have a far larger component of meta-representational competence than is necessary now, with conventional literacy. Inventing graphing shows that we have opulent student resources to build on, and that the newly necessary MRC is a plausible target of instruction in future literacies.

Designing Newton's laws

Task	Students are given a sketchy template for a program that simulates the motion of a rocket ship in outer space. The ship is controlled by an engine that provides individual bursts of thrust in a direction that is controllable by the captain of the ship.
Mode	Students engage in full-class cooperative design of the program, guided by the teacher.
Outcome	The students produced a program that is the programming equivalent of Newton's laws, algebraically represented as $F = ma$. In particular, the thrust of the space ship (F) adds to the existing velocity of the ship (in precisely the way that an acceleration [a, determined by F] defines the amount of change to existing velocity). See later discussion and Appendix A.
Replication	None

This and the following examples all involve an unusual representational form that has often been completely neglected in new-media studies. We examine the power of simple computer programs to enhance the learning and understanding of science.[5] Here I do not make any special point about the particular language used, which is called Boxer (www.PyxiSystems. com; diSessa, 2000). Indeed, I consider this only an early-stage example of the programmability of new media, some versions of which may be more graphical and less explicit (e.g., "programming by example"). However, two larger points are important to mention. First, it is the explicit and analytic nature of programming that here provides its power to extend algebra (Sherin, 2001), which is one of the core old-media representations in science and mathematics. Intuitions concerning very different, possibly easier-to-approach new media must be tested against their genuine capability to provide intellectual power. In the case of programming, we have data that assures learnability at much earlier ages than algebra, and that suggests at least as much intellectual power, compared to a difficult-to-challenge forebear, algebra.

The second point comes from considering whether new-media literacies will be truly democratic and empowering *two-way literacies*, where everyone gets to both read *and* write. Or will they be *one-way literacies*, where production is limited to an elite class (say, "media companies"), and "the masses" are, at best, consumers? I cannot take the time for an extended discussion. However, I can state my position. One-way literacies are intellectually and politically suspect; some version of programming is the only way that members of a wider society can enter into the production side of dynamic and interactive representations, which hold a key ground in the promise of intellectual power in (at least some) important new-media literacies (diSessa, 2000). Programming may change its form in the future, but the function of designing dynamic and interactive representations is, in my view, not negotiable.

Figure 9.2 shows the template that we provided an experimental class of eight high school students. The graphic at top shows the (circular) space ship and the aimable rocket engine. The "top level" program *go* simply repeats over and over *tick* (*tick* names what is executed at each "tick of the clock") and checks the control buttons that execute *kick, right-turn*, and *left-turn*, according to which buttons are pressed.

Figure 9.3 (left part) is a normative model of Newton's laws. The *tick* procedure represents Newton's first law. In the absence of thrust (force), an object merely continues moving in a straight line at a constant speed: On each *tick* of the clock, the object is commanded to *move* in the direction of the *velocity* vector, and a distance proportional to the velocity's length. The *kick* program contains the essence of Newton's third law, which specifies what forces do to existing velocity. In short, a bit of acceleration (technically *impulse*), which is by $F = ma$ proportional to force, is added to the existing velocity each instant while the force is acting. (*Change* is the generic Boxer command to change a variable, here *velocity*, to a new result. In general, square-corner boxes represent procedures, things that are run, and rounded-corner boxes represent variables, namely data.) Appendix A is an extended discussion of how this program represents Newton's laws. The appendix also discusses some of the more important conceptual issues in understanding Newton, and how representational systems relate to them.

The right part of Figure 9.3 shows the isomorphic program produced by the students. Of course, the important issue is whether the work of the students was legitimate and powerful, and how the representational form contributed their work. Sherin, diSessa, and Hammer (1994) and diSessa (1995) show the details of the empirical analysis, of which we report an abbreviated version organized by our representational principles (pages 222–224). See these papers and, for example, Sherin (2001) for a justification of the legitimacy of the programming version of Newton's laws. While this work has not been replicated—so its generality is uncertain—its importance is in specific, data-based analyses that show each of the principles in action.

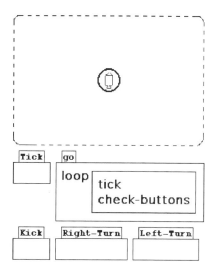

Figure 9.2. A template for the rocket ship program.

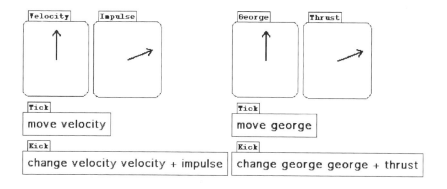

Figure 9.3. Left, A normative programming model, equivalent to $F = ma$ (suppressing the role of m). *Right,* The relevant part of the spaceship program, developed by students.

1 *The power of abstract, well-adapted representations:* We trace much of the success of this activity to the fact that we framed the task in terms of programming. In particular, students had learned about vectors, which therefore constituted a ready language in which to express problems of motion. Vectors are precisely the right level of abstraction for expressing Newton's laws, although traditionally algebra and calculus are used in

place of programming constructs. In this activity, students spontaneously introduced vectors into the program, although they named them whimsically (e.g., *George* as the name of the velocity vector). An important remark is that learning vectors and some relations to motion was remarkably easy. Students had seen simple programs that moved objects with a vector velocity. The meaning of vector velocity became intuitively clear in dragging the tip of the velocity vector around, showing that the object moved always in the direction of the vector, with a speed proportional to its length. Vectors, in fact, were also easily learned in this way (according to principle 4, of dynamic representations) by much younger (sixth grade) students. They became very popular as user interface controls in game programs. While another prerequisite to this task, vector addition, might be deemed an abstract principle in traditional instruction, its meaning was easily visible and important in manipulating motion in the context of such games.

A productive level of abstractness is one hint that a representation can provide. Programming representations have another advantage, mathematical precision, which we saw working to students' advantage. For example, in a preliminary activity a few days before, students discussed the effect of a "hit" (an impulse) on a moving object. In that natural language context, students accepted as adequate a simple statement that the hit "combined with" previous motion. In the context of formulating a program, however, the idea of combination was just the start of an extended inquiry into exactly how impulse and velocity should combine and be situated in the overall program.

An absolutely critical point in all of these examples is whether the students understand their accomplishment, or whether the representational (and other support) they are given led them on an un-illuminating garden path, however correct we might view the result. In this case, I report, too briefly, that students struggled substantially with the main conceptual element here, how thrust combines with existing velocity. Several proposals were tried and eventually rejected. Even after the idea of vector addition was introduced as a possibility, how it should be used in this case was unclear. Finally, one student tentatively proposed that *thrust* combined by adding with existing velocity (*George*) to create the new, self-perpetuating velocity. Several students immediately reacted with enthusiasm at the proposed solution, and this generated the final form of the program. Consult Sherin, diSessa, and Hammer (1994) and diSessa (1995) for details.

2 *Representational task tuning; conceptual/representational pump-priming:*
   It should be clear that we prepared the way for students' work by intro-

ducing vectors as a way to describe motion, and also by introducing them to vector addition. In fact, they had used and experimented with vector addition as a way to represent combined, simultaneously present motions, such as the motion of a boat in the current of a river. Students introduced the idea of vector addition in the spaceship context by explicitly invoking the boat-and-river-current model. But they still had more work to do to adapt it to this problem. In particular, they had to understand how the *transient thrust* becomes permanently incorporated into motion (via vector addition).

The template we provided, Figure 9.3, scaffolded focus on the key conceptual parts. The *tick* procedure represents Newton's first law. The *kick* procedure is the locus of Newton's second law. As the group seemed just at the limit of its competence in accomplishing this task, we feel the activity would likely have failed without this simple but effective partitioning of concerns.

3 *Dynamic representations:* I have already mentioned the effectiveness that we felt dynamic representation had in conveying an understanding of vectors in simple programs that controlled the real-time motion of objects. In developing their version of Newton's laws, the students often ran the program in their imagination to evaluate hypotheses for filling in slots in the template. In addition, once the program was complete, students played with it to solidify its meaning and to develop an intuitive fluency with its implications.

4 *Support for social collaboration:* As a full-class exercise, managing student–student and student–teacher collaboration is a critical need. In this case, a single, hour-long episode that targeted a particular result depended in important measure on how the members of the class coordinated their efforts. Here, I mention a few examples of the types of coordination that we listed under the general topic of collaboration.

   a *"Reading" student ideas*—The evident currency for the discussion was "programming code." While perhaps as ambiguous as words at first mention, code fragments can be disambiguated by imagining or actually running the program. While nuances of student intuition were not necessarily captured directly in code, it constituted a public, stable, and precise backdrop on which the more subtle job of physical reasoning and judgment could be played out. In this activity students seemed to participate with a feeling that code fragments could stand for their ideas. For example, students pointed to code when referring to "my idea" or to the ideas of colleagues.

   b *Goal and hypothesis clarity*—How does one know when one has a theory of motion? On the other hand, the concrete goal of this exercise was to produce a complete, working, and sensible program. Although "sensible" may be an important topic for debate, the completeness of the program for accomplishing the given task, and the fact of its "working," are easily observed by the whole community.

In managing the discussion, the teacher often asked for clarification concerning what students meant in terms of code. He asked, "what does that mean for our program?" "What does that say about what's in *kick*?"

c *Summary representation*—The end-state of this design was a simple, memorable program, similar in function to mnemonic recitation of equations like $F = ma$. We know students could easily reproduce these little templates; for example, the river-and-boat code fragment that introduced vector addition into this problem came in as an easily re-produced code fragment. Of course, mnemonic symbol sequences are not the same as understanding. But they are a part of it. Scientists sometimes think by drawing in equations when appropriate and manipulating them. Student understanding of Newton's laws works, in some measure, as a person-plus-symbol-system interaction, which is, as mentioned, my prototype for the very meaning of literacy.

d *A focus for intervention*—Conducting this discussion was a challenging task, even for the talented (graduate student) instructor involved in designing Newton's laws. In our analysis, we saw him using focus on the representational form of the problem to bring students together, and to move the discussion forward. He often asked students to focus on a particular place in the program, or how their ideas related to particular expressions and places. He sometimes intervened in suggesting more mnemonic terms for elements in the program. *Thrust*, for example, emerged from a negotiation with students. (*George* would be renamed in later work, following this activity.) As a last resort, teachers can suggest particular expressions, which can then be examined for their meaning and sensibility. In this case, the instructor did not provide any substantial suggestions about what should be in the program. In general, teachers' competence at these skillful interventions would be an important part of *their* new literacy.

With respect to non-representational principles, the success of this case seemed to us most sensitive to the framing of the task (principle 7). We believe the semi-concrete but also non-earthly context provided enough remove from familiar contexts to allow consideration of some of the non-intuitive aspects of Newton's law—for example, the idea that motion would continue forever without a thrust. At the same time, students evaluated the resulting motion in terms of productive "earthly" intuitions (principle 6). See Sherin, diSessa, and Hammer (1993) for details.

Galileo's model of a falling body

Task Students are given a simple but defective program that simulates the motion of a dropped ball. The students are asked to improve it.

Mode This exercise has been run in many variations, usually in a few iterations of small-group design, interspersed by sharing and discussion in the full class.

Outcome Students (and even teachers, performing the task as a part of professional development) engage in a fairly regular development involving (a) recognition of increasing velocity in a fall, (b) recognizing the regularity of the motion, (c) almost always producing the two models that were discussed by Galileo.

Replication This task has been replicated in many classrooms, from late elementary school through high school, including being run by teachers new to the idea of teaching motion, and new to the use of programming representations. Results generally validate similar developments and outcomes. However, none of the replications has undergone the kind of detailed analysis we reported above for "designing Newton's laws." Of all our re-inventing activities, this one has had the most work in "real" classrooms, with "real" teachers.

Figure 9.4 shows the initial faulty program. Figure 9.5 shows a normative model. In our experience, almost all editions have exposed a diversity of ideas and a fairly extended development, but almost always two competing models have emerged. One is the "additive" model, shown in Figure 9.5, and the other is the "multiplicative" model, shown in Figure 9.6. Students produce many variations in form and syntax that are identical to these, but we will not display them here.

The multiplicative model is highly attractive. It has many intuitively plausible qualities, and the fall is dramatic in its speedup. The "correct" model is less dramatic. Galileo proved that the multiplicative model (which is equivalent to falling at a speed proportional to distance fallen) is impossible. His strategy was to show that, according to the multiplicative model, a fall of twice as far would take the *same time*, an impossible condition. An "easier"

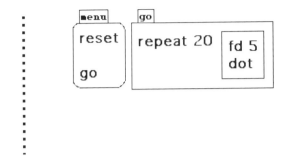

Figure 9.4. The starting "prompt" program with its visual result at left. *Fd* means "move forward" (downward), and *dot* means "draw a dot." *Reset* and *go* (in the *menu*) are clicked on to reset and activate the simulation.

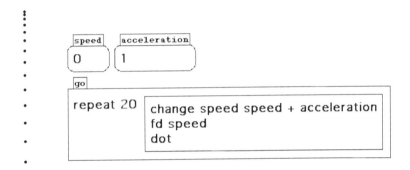

Figure 9.5. The normative model (Galileo's model); a constant amount (acceleration) is added to speed each tick of the clock. Speed is thus proportional to time.

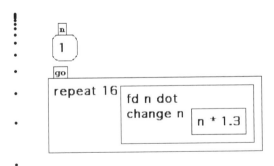

Figure 9.6. The multiplicative model of a fall.

counter to the multiplicative fall is that the model can't get started: Distance, and therefore speed, are zero at the start, so the falling object can't move at all. Another counter is more subtle. Reversing the model to make a toss, the multiplicative model becomes a dividing model, which never gets to the peak of the toss. However, our experience has been that these arguments are too subtle to regularly work with students, even high school students with a fair amount of scaffolding. So, we have come to be happy with convergence to these two models, using other work (such as taking data and matching to the models) to settle the issue.

Steps along the way are informative of the work students actually do in constructing these models. For example, for elementary school students, the very fact of falling at an increasing speed is often problematic, and it takes some time to work through. Here, augmenting the task by "feeling" the impact of objects falling from different heights is usually convincing. Galileo also suggested that experiment. Another interesting development among students is toward an assumption of uniformity in the fall. Figure 9.7 shows the initial models produced by a high school student. I return in a moment to his first model, *go*, but notice that in both *go* and *ho*, the incremental (decremental) distances are non-uniform; they switch between an increment (decrement) of 1 and one of 2 half way through the motion. In our experience, almost all classes produce such non-uniform models (or "step-wise" models, where the object falls a constant distance for some number of steps, and then a new, greater constant distance for the same number of steps). Group discussion of the simplicity of a uniform model, or of a smoother one, have systematically won out in student discussion. Uniformity is an aesthetic consideration that Galileo emphasized, and it seems that groups of students can regularly come to appreciate its attractiveness in teacher-scaffolded discussion. Here we see important commonalty between scientists and students, not in the models that they have or produce, but in the aesthetics displayed in ultimate choice of model.

Younger students sometimes include a phase of slowing down at the end of their falls. The rationale is surprisingly strong. If the ball stops at the bottom, surely it must slow down before it stops! Indeed, the ball does slow down, but only after it contacts the ground. That can be the subject of a good discussion of why and when a ball actually slows down in a drop.

Representational considerations often arise in this modeling activity. The first model in Figure 9.7, *go*, shows a surprisingly common issue. When the program is run, the ball noticeably slows down at the bottom! However, the first time we saw this in a sixth-grade classroom, one of the pair of boys who produced it explained that it was intended to show speeding up. He said, essentially, "we didn't want to show the ball speeding up, we wanted to show *that it sped up*." The problem in our interpretation was that, like many other

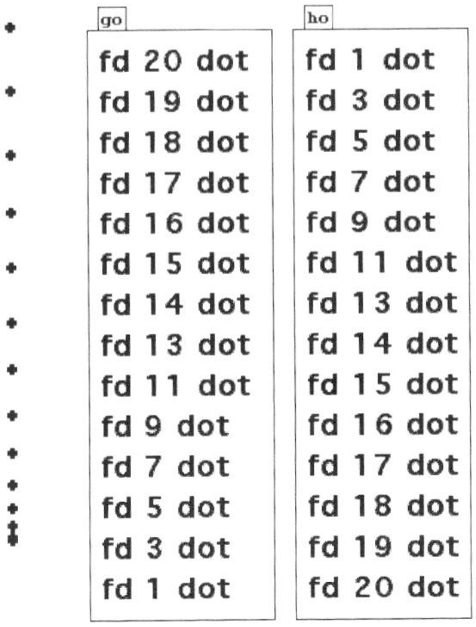

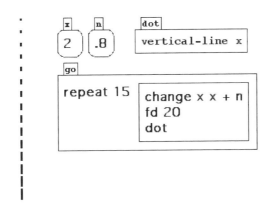

go	ho
fd 20 dot	fd 1 dot
fd 19 dot	fd 3 dot
fd 18 dot	fd 5 dot
fd 17 dot	fd 7 dot
fd 16 dot	fd 9 dot
fd 15 dot	fd 11 dot
fd 14 dot	fd 13 dot
fd 13 dot	fd 14 dot
fd 11 dot	fd 15 dot
fd 9 dot	fd 16 dot
fd 7 dot	fd 17 dot
fd 5 dot	fd 18 dot
fd 3 dot	fd 19 dot
fd 1 dot	fd 20 dot

Figure 9.7. Two models by a high school student. The trace at left is of the first (*go*) model.

x	n	dot
2	.8	vertical-line x

go	
repeat 15	change x x + n fd 20 dot

Figure 9.8. A student model showing speed proportional to distance in the fall.

students, and also some adults, students may choose to display increasing speed as increasing numbers (density) of dots. This is non-conventional, but not wrong in any sense. We can summarize by saying that these students intended the program to produce a representation, not a simulation (!), and that they used an unusual but not wrong convention (greater density of dots represents more speed).

Another representational issue is shown in Figure 9.8. Here the student is showing increased speed not by using the distance between dots but by using the length of the dots. He re-defined *dot* to draw a line, and then systematically changed the length of the line, which he called *x*. As mentioned, this is identical, but not transparently so, to the multiplicative model.

In summary, scaffolded development of models of a dropped object regularly converge to two plausible scientific models. Along the way, student models open up excellent discussions of possibilities and plausibilities. A lot of development toward the two models arises naturally and by near consensus, but not instantly, out of discussion. Obviously, the richness and productivity of the discussion depends substantially on teacher preparation (for what s/he will see in the students' ideas and programs; and for more technical competence, for example in recognizing programs with identical outcomes but different forms), and on negotiating the variations produced in a particular class. (Again, these examples forecast new-media literacy for teachers, as well as students.) There is no need to invoke magic in these students' accomplishments. The convergence is the work of (a) good student intuitions, which, however, need cultivating, articulating, and considering, and (b) the use of an apt representational form that allows the expression of intuitive student ideas at the same time that it can carry the development to a respectable and precise normative model.

Temperature equilibration

Task	Students are asked to think about how a glass of cold milk warms up when it is taken out of the refrigerator and placed on the kitchen table. Later, students take data, and then collectively try to produce a program, from a sketchy template, to reproduce the data.
Mode	The initial discussion is run by the teacher in full-class mode. Small groups of students take data, and then the teacher scaffolds the full class in making a model that can reproduce the data.
Outcome	Students seem regularly to produce a model that is correct, but not in a normative form. Students seem sensitive to the advantages of the normative model.
Replication	We have run two instances of this activity with high school students in small classes (6–8).

We report our final case briefly, as it is still in formative stages; detailed results have not been published (but see diSessa, in press). The power of representational scaffolding seemed very evident in the introductory discussion of the heating of a cold glass of milk. Open discussion brings out many hypotheses about how and why the milk warms, some of them quite fanciful, and usually with no emerging consensus. When students are coaxed to use (old-media!) graphs, however, we see the typical constraint representational forms can productively apply; predictions of how heating occurs converge to a few possibilities.

In one edition, one student suggested that the temperature followed a simple pattern, with increases of 1, 2, 4, 8, 16, . . . degrees. This reflects the simplification that mathematization can convey, but also the lack of feedback that simply numerical or algebraic representations are prone to. We are confident that if this student produced a program that "warmed up" according to his pattern, he would have judged it implausible. (All students in our three classes seemed convinced that the rate of heating slows down, if not in the beginning, then at least toward the end of the heating. Numbers on a page do not seem to be instinctively interpreted in a process-oriented way.)

Both of our experimental classes converged on the model at left in Figure 9.9. A normative model is shown for contrast at right. The positive outcome is that the student-generated model is very similar to the normative model. In fact, although it is not evident, the two models produce identical outputs, and can perfectly match (within experimental error) the data students took. Even more promising, students in both groups voiced advantages of the normative model over the student-generated model when the normative model was shown to them. For example, the normative model shows the ambient temperature, a measurable parameter, explicitly. In addition, the role of ambient temperature in "driving" temperature change is transparent. (Consult the *change t-change* line in the normative model on the right in Figure 9.9.) In the student model, the ultimate temperature, ambience, is a complex function of *both* the constant *k and* the initial *t-change*. (In the normative model, *t-change* is computed, not externally set, even for the first step.)

A significant failure of this re-invention of the law of heating/cooling became evident in the second class. When the students were introduced to the task, they quickly converged on the model at left. The next week, when we engaged them in discussion, they seemed at first not even to remember creating the model. But, within a few minutes, they created it again by virtually the same set of steps they had used the week before![6] In retrospect, we believe that the students were following a representational garden path of trial and error. In contrast to all of the other re-invention tasks, it seems the representation and template make this one too easy, cutting away so many possibilities that essential conceptual discussion is short-circuited. This, of course, is an expected possibility, at least in some cases. Computational representations cannot always produce exactly the right level of scaffolding to

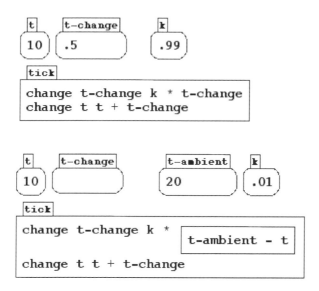

Figure 9.9. Above, The student-generated model of temperature equilibration. *Below,* The normative model (Newton's law of heating).

make the task of re-invention possible but appropriately challenging conceptually. Here, at least as we proposed the task, the representational scaffolding is too strong. Undoubtedly there are cases to be discovered where scaffolding is too weak.

Our judgment is that we can relatively easily fix the problem here by enriching and "complexifying" the task. That, however, remains to be demonstrated. The meta-lesson is, again, that there is little magic in these re-inventions. They depend on a good choice of representation and apt task design. They depend on teacher scaffolding and on a helpful diversity in student ideas. Use of a computational representation does not guarantee, certainly not by itself, that students will engage in important conceptual work and converge on acceptable scientific principles. On the other hand, all of the re-inventions we described provided exceptional contexts in which to engage and develop students' scientific competencies.

Summary and Future Research

It is natural to be enthusiastic about new-media literacies. Beyond doubt, new possibilities are in the offing. It is exciting to see widespread, grassroots use of new media in, for example, blogging as a new medium for news and commentary, MySpace and even simple web pages as expressions of self and new social possibilities, computer games as an emerging part of common culture or as a promising basis for future learning, and video as a widespread new critical and artistic medium. But in calling new-media uses "literacies," we must carefully separate fads or even more permanent changes in fashion from civilization-changing possibilities. In this chapter, I have applied a high threshold of validation in considering *empirically supported analyses* that show consequences in terms of things that have nearly *incontestable social value*: science and mathematics learning. The work discussed here suggests that students can learn mathematics and science effectively at much younger ages and with much more agency and pleasure than previously. We have seen that students, with support from new-media representations, can accomplish tasks such as re-inventing fundamental mathematics and science. Just as important, I believe that the ways these remarkable accomplishments are achieved can be pinned on properties of the new-media representations used—not to ignore the roles of good task design, good collaborative patterns, and student-sensitive teaching. To sum up, a cornerstone of this chapter is a high level of empirical accountability for the actual impact of the representation or literacy in producing results we understand and value as important.

The perspective on literacy that frames this work draws equally from early and newer theories of it. From early "cognitive" work, we insist that all representations—the technology of literacies—are not equal, and that the specifics of the representations have strong consequences in the powers we realize from literacies. For example, I do not believe multimodality (Kress, 2003) per se explains the success of programming in the re-inventings discussed here.[7] But we reject technological determinism. We also focus not on general intellectual powers that are supposed to result from literacies but on specific, cogently formulated and falsifiable consequences of thinking-and-collaborating-in-the-presence-of-external-representations.

From newer theories of literacy I accept the importance of studying particular literacies in particular social practices. One must recognize that powers are conveyed in particular uses, not in the mere presence of a technology. However, socially oriented literacy studies have backgrounded or even dismissed the contributions of the props of literacy, its technology. With the intellectual powers for students that we discuss here, this seems a foolish slight, in need of redress.

This work motivates future research at several levels. Proximally, the practical and theoretical possibilities of re-invention as an important mode of mathematics and science learning are open. Study of the micro-structure of learning with dynamic and interactive representations, both by individuals and in groups, has barely begun.

At a mid-level, of course, changing representational infrastructure should be as relevant to other learning focuses, from other topics in mathematics and science to history and social studies. I hope our work focuses attention on specific issues, such as the expressiveness of particular representations for particular ideas, and the exact nature of scaffolding that they can supply. Over the longer term, multiple representations and literacies will come to equilibrium with each other. For example, I forecast that computational representations will not replace algebra or calculus. However, patterns in schooling[8] and in professional use will change dramatically. How will different representations feed into or complement each other's learning and use? To my knowledge, there is yet no research specifically on this issue.

Larger-scaled especially social issues concerning the new literacy possibilities explored here remain unaddressed. Can "programming" come to be seen by society at large as a masterable and powerful tool? In this regard, it is illuminating to remember that algebra and even text were both historically regarded as the province of technical experts, and certainly of no value to ordinary folk. How long will it take for schools to realize the promise of new literacy possibilities, *especially* in core high-stakes learning where conservatism is likely to be strongest, such as mathematics and science? How do intellectual powers, such as competence in mathematics and science, interact with social functions of literacy, especially destructive ones, such as social class divisions and preservation of privilege and power? No one has good answers to those important questions. In coming to address them, we will need better and more refined theories of literacy that take into account (a) the nature of humans as knowers, learners, and actors, (b) the extensions in thinking and doing made possible by particular new media, and (c) the social embedding of new literacies, including the dynamics that might bring them into existence.

Acknowledgments

The studies cited were accomplished by and with the help of many members of the Boxer Research Group at the University of California, Berkeley. Authors of cited papers were primary contributors. Current members of the group who contributed to the temperature equilibration modeling work include Jeanne Bamberger, Lauren Barth-Cohen, Janet Casperson, Karen Chang, Michael Leitch, Katie Lewis, Orit Parnafes, and Jed Stamas. Jeanne Bamberger provided helpful comments on an earlier draft.

This work was supported, in part, by a grant from the Spencer Foundation to Andrea A. diSessa. The conclusions and interpretations drawn here are those of the author, and not necessarily those of the Foundation. The author has a financial interest in PyxiSystems LLC, which is the owner of the Boxer software in which simulations and models were produced for this work.

References

Azevedo, F. S. (2000). Designing representations of terrain: A study in meta-representational competence. *Journal of Mathematical Behavior*, *19*(4), 443–480.

Bamberger, J. (2006). Restructuring conceptual intuitions through invented notations: From path-making to map-making. In E. Teubal, J. Dockrell, & L. Tolchinsky (Eds.), *Notational knowledge: Historical and developmental perspectives*. Rotterdam/Taipei: Sense Publishers.

diSessa, A. A. (1993). Toward an epistemology of physics. *Cognition and Instruction*, *10*(2–3), 105–225.

diSessa, A. A. (1995). Designing Newton's laws: Patterns of social and representational feedback in a learning task. In R.-J. Beun, M. Baker, & M. Reiner (Eds.), *Dialogue and interaction: Modeling interaction in intelligent tutoring systems* (pp. 105–122). Berlin: Springer-Verlag.

diSessa, A. A. (2000). *Changing minds: Computers, learning, and literacy*. Cambridge, MA: MIT Press.

diSessa, A. A. (2002). Students' criteria for representational adequacy. In K. Gravemeijer, R. Lehrer, B. van Oers, & L. Verschaffel (Eds.), *Symbolizing, modeling and tool use in mathematics education* (pp. 105–129). Dortrecht: Kluwer.

diSessa, A. A. (2004). Meta-representation: Native competence and targets for instruction. *Cognition and Instruction*, *22*(3), 293–331.

diSessa, A. A. (2007). Systemics of learning for a revised pedagogical agenda. In R. Lesh, E. Hamilton, & J. J. Kaput (Eds.), *Foundations for the future in mathematics education*. Mahwah, NJ: Lawrence Erlbaum.

diSessa, A. A., Hammer, D., Sherin, B., & Kolpakowski, T. (1991). Inventing graphing: Meta-representational expertise in children. *Journal of Mathematical Behavior*, *10*(2), 117–160.

Freeman, N. H. (1995). The emergence of a framework theory for pictorial reasoning. In C. Lange-Kuttner & G. V. Thomas (Eds.), *Drawing and looking: Theoretical approaches to pictorial representation in children*. New York and London: Harvester Wheatsheaf.

Gee, J. P. (1996). *Social linguistics and literacies: Ideology in discourses* (2nd ed.). London: Taylor & Francis.

Goody, J. (1977). *The domestication of the savage mind*. Cambridge, UK: Cambridge University Press.

Gravemeijer, K. P. E. (1994). *Developing realistic mathematics education*. Utrecht: CD-ß Press / Freudenthal Institute.

Hughes, M. (1986). *Children and number: Difficulties in learning mathematics*. Oxford, UK and New York: Blackwell.

Kress, G. (2003). *Literacy in the new media age*. London and New York: Routledge.

Nemirovsky, R., & Tierney, C. (2001). Children creating ways to represent changing situations: On the development of homogeneous spaces. *Educational Studies of Mathematics*, *45*, 67–102.

Ong, W. J. (1982). *Orality and literacy: The technologizing of the word*. New York: Routledge.

Scribner, S., & Cole, M. (1981). *The psychology of literacy.* Cambridge, MA: Harvard University Press.

Sherin, B. (2001). A comparison of programming languages and algebraic notation as expressive languages for physics. *International Journal for Computers and Mathematical Learning, 6,* 1–61.

Sherin, B., diSessa, A. A., & Hammer, D. M. (1993). Dynaturtle revisited: Learning physics through collaborative design of a computer model. *Interactive Learning Environments, 3*(2), 91–118.

Street, B. V. (1995). *Social literacies.* London and New York: Longman.

Appendix A: How Programming Representations Relate to Algebraic Ones

I aim here to show how the programming representation for Newton's laws relates to the usual, algebraic representation. It is intended to help those less comfortable with the physics. In addition, I want to expose and talk more about how particular representation does, or does not, alter the conceptual landscape. In general, the footnotes in this appendix are for physics experts.

Start with the conventional representation of Newton's laws:

$$F = ma$$

First, we drop the m (or, equivalently, set it to one). Mass (m) is just simply another thing to learn about. In fact, mass is not important in terms of the main conceptual problems students have with Newton's laws. Hence:

$$F = a$$

We can use the definition of acceleration as the rate of change of velocity, the ratio of the change of velocity to the change in time:

$$F = \frac{\Delta v}{\Delta t}$$

In traditional physics, this ratio is taken *in the limit*, as Δt approaches zero. (If Δt is large, this formula give the *average* force.) But, in the programming world, time is not continuous; it jumps, one tick of the clock (one iteration of the program's "loop") at a time.[9] The best we can do for small times is to take the smallest Δt possible, one tick.[10] Furthermore, for convenience, we can choose units of time so that Δt is just 1—one tick of the clock.[11] So we have:

$F = \Delta v$

Force is precisely the change in velocity (of the object to which the force is applied) for each tick of the clock. If force is an impulse, which occurs in brief (one-tick) bursts like the rocket engine proposed in our designing Newton's laws task, one gets a change in velocity equal to the magnitude of the force during a tick precisely when the rocket fires, and none otherwise. The programming form for a thrust is thus:

change v $v + F$; that is, "change v to the old velocity, v, + F"

This is precisely the *kick* part of the program spaceship program. If the force persists, this command would be executed each tick of the clock.

Conceptual Issues

One consequence of this program fragment is that, if there is no force, velocity never changes. This is called Newton's first law, and it is counterintuitive. In everyone's experience, (earthly) motion always dies away. The representation makes no difference as far as this existence of the issue is concerned.

A second typical problem is that, like Aristotle, many students feel the speed (magnitude of the velocity) of an object should be proportional to the force that you apply to it. A bigger engine makes a car go faster; in order to run faster, you have to "do more work." But this would correspond to a law where velocity, not change in velocity, is proportional to force, *change v F*, rather than *change v $v + F$*. Again, the conceptual problem remains.

For these two conceptual problems, the programming representation strips away a lot of complications, including units and limits (calculus), so that the core conceptual problems are exposed. For engaging those problems, students have the advantage of seeing exactly how different laws ($F = v$ or $F = \Delta v$) correspond to different behaviors. They can make a simple edit to the program, and can see (or, perhaps better, run in their imagination to infer) the consequences. In net, the programming representation does not finesse the conceptual problems, it "purifies" so as to expose them more clearly, and it embeds them in a richer analytical/empirical set of experiences (which are, of course, dependent on the social practices engendered in the classroom).

One sees the same pattern in learning again when forces and velocities become vectors. A principal conceptual problem is that when force is perpendicular to velocity, the speed (magnitude or length of velocity) does not change at all, but the velocity vector rotates. This is how it can be that objects orbit in a circle (roughly like the moon around the earth) at a constant speed, even as gravity is "accelerating them" toward the center of their orbit (accelerating the moon downward, toward the earth). Students in high school or freshman physics classes memorize "in circular motion, the acceleration is toward the center of the circle," but they seldom understand it. The computational representation allows students to see exactly what happens to the vectors, one step at a time. With standard representations, seeing the consequences of a given force law involves a technically advanced task, solving a differential equation. Furthermore, with a simple program, students can play with the phenomenology. They can see how a force not-quite perpendicular to velocity speeds the object up or slows it down, while still re-aiming it (rotating the velocity). At the other extreme, a force aligned with velocity increases or decreases speed, but there is no change in direction. Forces not-quite aligned with velocity rotate it a little, in addition to changing speed. All together, these different experiences lend a fabric of sensibility to the initially counterintuitive fact that a force perpendicular to a velocity maintains speed, but rotates the velocity. Here, the contribution of the representational form is that simple experiments can be transparently notated, conceptualized (in seeing each step in the program), and experienced.

Notes

1 I want to make clear that I do not consider these fair and complete characterizations of Phase I researchers. They are rather homogenizing descriptions, closer to caricatures by critics. For my purposes, they are intended as backdrop oversimplifications that nonetheless provide a ground on which to position the points that follow.

2 I do not cite the individuals because I have reason to believe that both have moderated or changed their views since they spoke these words.

3 Surprisingly, however, many of our tasks seem to work as well for sixth- or seventh-grade students as for advanced high schoolers.

4 diSessa (1993) describes the nature of some intuitive knowledge that is virtually perceptual in form. A fair amount of work in experimental psychology has shown that modality of presentation (text, pictures, moving pictures) makes a difference in conceptualization.

5 The role of such representations in professional science is a critical complementary study. In short, we believe new media of exactly this type are revolutionizing science. That is, however, not a topic for this chapter.

6 This set of steps were reported to us by the teacher. Unfortunately, we did not video the first session.

7 For example, multimodality does not necessarily entail the level of abstraction, the precision, the degree of explicitness, the grain-size of articulation, the "fit"

to relevant ideas, or the compactness of final description that programming offered.

8 For example, I think we will generally be able to teach with computational representations long before one can use traditional representations, like algebra.

9 People often complain that the world is not discrete, so students still have to learn limits. However, the Newtonian world, as usually represented, is an idealization, too. In addition, are you really so sure there is no quantum of time, much smaller than a second? In fact, no everyday happenings would be different if time were discrete with a tiny quantum! All science is idealization. Programming-represented Newton's laws are just a different idealization.

10 In a discrete world, the finite (one tick) ratio is not *approximately* the acceleration, it is the *definition* of acceleration.

11 In a world with no obvious, fundamental "yardsticks," it makes sense to write formulae so that they do not depend on the units you chose. But, in a programming world, it is so obvious to measure time by counting ticks, that writing in unit-independent terms is an unnecessary burden. In advanced physics, one often takes the speed of light to be 1, which is a similar simplifying move. In our physics curriculum, the boring stuff of units is an advanced topic. Students get to understand and use Newton's laws long before they can finesse units.

Chapter 10

Domain Knowledge and Learning From the Internet

Malinda Desjarlais, Teena Willoughby, and Eileen Wood

The Internet is a widely used resource for finding and retrieving information, particularly among high school and university students (Dryburgh, 2001; Environics Research Group, 2001; Jones, 2002; Lenhart, Rainie, & Lewis, 2001; Rainie & Packel, 2001). In a survey of 25,090 Canadians, 90% of adolescents between the ages of 15 and 19 reported using the Internet during the year 2000 (Dryburgh, 2001). Similarly, almost three-quarters of American adolescents between the ages of 12 and 17 reported using the Internet that same year (Rainie & Packel, 2001). One of the most common uses of the Internet among school-age children has been to complete school-related tasks. In fact, over a third of youth in Grades 4 through 11 across Canada who rely on the Internet to retrieve information have used this source at least once a week to complete homework (Environics Research Group, 2001). Indeed, the Internet tends to be the first source for information that they turn to when doing school work. Similarly, the majority of American adolescents aged 12 to 17 access the Internet to complete school-related research (Lenhart et al., 2001). Prevalence of Internet use, however, does not necessarily mean that it is an effective learning tool. Just having information available does not necessarily translate into learners being able to effectively retrieve or use information. A significant constraint on its effectiveness may be when learners are searching for information on the Internet corresponding to a low knowledge domain.

Researchers have consistently demonstrated that existing domain knowledge enhances performance on memory tasks (Chi, 1978; Fincher-Kiefer, Post, Greene, & Voss, 1988; Schneider, Korkel, & Weinert, 1989; Spilich, Vesonder, Chejese, & Voss, 1979). Domain knowledge not only facilitates how much learners remember but also what information they recall (Marchionini, 1995; Schneider, Korkel, & Weinert, 1990; Spilich et al., 1979). For example, third-grade soccer experts (in terms of their domain knowledge) recalled significantly more novel information about this sport than novices in their own grade and even older novice children in Grades 5 and 7 (Schneider et al., 1989). Adults with a rich knowledge base for baseball not only recalled more information from textual passages detailing a base-ball game but also recalled more relevant information in comparison to less knowledgeable peers (Spilich et al., 1979). The positive effect of existing domain knowledge, however, does not extend beyond the specific domain. For example, although children chess experts were able to more accurately recall chess configurations than adult novices, the children's ability to recall digit spans was inferior compared to the adults (Chi, 1978). Therefore, there is not an overall increase in the capacity of working memory as domain knowledge increases, but rather information processing is more efficient when the assigned task corresponds to a high knowledge domain (Bjork-lund & Schneider, 1996; Chi, 1978).

According to cognitive schema theory, learners' knowledge about con-cepts is stored within interrelated networks of more general information (Anderson & Pearson, 1984). As knowledge increases, the complexity and validity of these networks are enhanced (Bjorklund & Schneider, 1996; Chi, 1978). Thus connections between concepts are being created and strength-ened which increases the probability of the concept being activated at a later time (Rumelhart, Hinton, & McClelland, 1986). As a result, when knowl-edgeable learners encounter novel domain-related information, they often create meaningful associations in order to connect the material to an exist-ing knowledge base (Chase & Simon, 1973; Stein, Morris, & Bransford, 1978). This elaborate processing of information is often automatic. Moreover, indi-viduals with higher domain knowledge typically have more effective search strategies to find and extract information from text (Symons, MacLatchy-Gaudet, Stone, & Reynolds, 2001; Symons & Pressley, 1993) or closed archival information systems (e.g., PsycINFO; Downing, Moore, & Brown, 2005). If the knowledge base is high enough, however, knowledge can over-ride the need for strategies altogether (Schneider et al., 1990). Indeed, Moos and Azevedo (2006) demonstrated that undergraduate students used fewer learning strategies as their existing knowledge for a domain increased.

Automatic processing and lack of required strategy use reduce cognitive load. This is valuable since working memory has a fixed limited capacity (Baddeley & Hitch, 1974; Miller, 1956). Cognitive resources are typically allocated, for example, to holding material in working memory, interpret-ing the information at hand, integrating novel information with existing knowledge and employing learning strategies. When one of these aspects do not need to be carried out or can be carried out automatically, cognitive resources may be reallocated to working memory's remaining functions. Therefore, the cognitive demands associated with the learning task will be unlikely to exceed working memory capacity.

In contrast, novices experience greater challenges allocating working memory resources. When domain knowledge is low, schemas are typically insufficiently developed and thus the process of creating connections is more challenging, less efficient, and less automatic (Fincher-Kiefer et al., 1988; Willoughby, Anderson, Wood, Mueller, & Ross, under review). Not only do individuals tend to interpret content inaccurately or less extensively when they have less knowledge related to the domain (Fincher-Kiefer et al., 1988), but they also tend to expend a great deal of mental effort in interpreting and integrating the information (Mayer, 2001). Consequently, there is a shortage of cognitive resources available for the sophisticated processing of novel material. Ultimately, less knowledgeable learners may be overwhelmed when faced with a challenging task. Interacting with the Internet may be an example of a challenging task, and therefore such learners may exhibit little or no learning when using this resource.

There is a lack of empirical research, however, that examines the role existing domain knowledge plays when using the Internet. Instead, researchers have investigated learners' interaction with closed hypermedia. Unlike open-ended hypermedia such as the Internet, closed hypermedia are comprised of a fixed amount of reliable information, usually available in the form of educational computer software (e.g., Encarta) or electronic databases (e.g., PsycINFO or online library catalogs). Although we are uncertain as to whether the results from closed hypermedia research extend to the Internet, this area of research may provide valuable insight into the importance of domain knowledge. This chapter, therefore, examines the role of domain knowledge when using the Internet in particular, building on what we know from closed hypermedia research. Specifically, we address the importance of domain knowledge when searching for information, when websites are poorly designed, and when learning from the Internet. The chapter ends with a discussion on whether low domain knowledge can be compensated for when using the Internet.

The Role of Existing Domain Knowledge When Searching for Information on the Internet

As a type of hypermedia, the Internet is a computerized presentation of text, illustrations, video, and/or audio files. Typically, hypermedia are viewed as offering advantages to the learner compared to traditional learning contexts. For example, learners typically select the content to read, the order in which they wish to read it, and control the pace of their learning (Curry, Haderlie, Ku, Lawless, Lemon, & Wood, 1999; Eveland & Dunwoody, 2002; Large, 1996). Moreover, learners are able to access an infinite amount of information on a wide variety of topics at any time and from almost any-where (Eveland & Dunwoody, 2000). Despite these advantages, however, learners with little domain knowledge may experience challenges when conducting their searches, identifying relevant information, and/or integrating information within and across individual websites. These in turn may negatively impact learning outcomes.

Challenges with searching for information

Information on the Internet can be accessed in a variety of ways. For example, three methods of retrieving information include clicking on a topic presented in an index (i.e., browsing), going directly to the desired website by entering its URL or web address (e.g., http://www.msn.com), or clicking on a link within the website which would take learners either to a page within the current website or to a different website entirely (Kuiper, Volman, & Terwel, 2005). The majority of Internet users, however, frequently rely on one of the many search engines available, such as Google or Yahoo, to retrieve information corresponding to a topic (Lorenzen, 2001). Learners input keywords related to their search topic into the search engine and are provided with a list of websites containing the specified term(s), also known as hits, which may or may not be relevant to the desired topic. This list typically contains hundreds of thousands or even millions of websites, which not only vary depending upon the search engine used, but also may change daily when using the same search engine owing to the constant changes, deletions, or additions of websites.

Existing domain knowledge may facilitate the use of superior search strategies. For example, experts have a greater awareness of major concepts and vocabulary within their domain (Marchionini, 1995); therefore, they may be able to generate more appropriate keywords, resulting in a greater amount of relevant information. In addition, Marchionini (1995) suggests that experts become experienced searching for information in their domain. They become familiar with solving typical problems and with searching for answers within various resources devoted to their domain. Consequently, when using the Internet, highly knowledgeable learners may also be aware of where to find the desired information and be able to quickly identify high quality websites from the hits list.

Allen (1991), for example, investigated the relation between the quality of search terms and existing domain knowledge. University students' level of existing knowledge for planetary exploration was determined by scores on a pretest. Using a median split, half the students were classified as high knowledge and the other half as low knowledge. After reading an article on Voyager 2's encounter with Neptune and completing an interpolation task, participants were instructed to search an online library catalog. Their task was to create a list of books that they would want to use to write a detailed article on Voyager 2's encounter with Neptune.

The quality of their searches was assessed by how many citations on the participants' list matched the 50 books that two expert reference librarians would request if they completed the task. Surprisingly, learners were able to identify the same amount of relevant books regardless of existing domain knowledge. In fact, less knowledgeable learners conducted searches as effectively as highly knowledgeable students; in other words, experts and novices used similar search terms when using an online library catalog (Allen, 1991). Allen suggested that the task may have been too easy. Simply by inputting the terms "Project Voyager" in the search engine over half of the books on the librarians' list resulted. One may question, however, whether or not novices would have used these search terms if they were not exposed to information directly related to the topic immediately prior to their searches. In fact, using specific and technical language to formulate queries has been characteristic of more knowledgeable learners when using closed hypermedia (Marchionini, Dwiggins, Katz, & Lin, 1993; Marchionini, Meadow, Dwiggins, Lin, Wang, & Yuan, 1991). When searching for a less familiar topic, on the other hand, learners often have difficulty generating synonyms and tend to rely on "common sense" and familiar terms to further searches (Marchionini et al., 1993).

To investigate the relation between domain knowledge and search quality when using the Internet, Willoughby and colleagues (under review) recorded learners' searches for information on the Internet pertaining to two experimenter-assigned essay topics. One topic was directly related to individuals' major or discipline and the other was unrelated to their discipline. Willoughby and colleagues (under review) also compared the quality of the essays between those who were exposed to the Internet and a control group who completed the essays based solely on their existing knowledge. Learners did not demonstrate any major differences in the search strategies they used to retrieve information, or any differences in the relevancy of the websites that they accessed, as a function of domain knowledge. In other words, students used similar search strategies whether they were searching for information corresponding to the high or the low knowledge topic. In addition, they accessed the same number of relevant websites for both essays. Despite these similarities, however, students who were exposed to the Internet did not perform any better on the low domain knowledge essay than a control group who had no access to the Internet prior to writing the essay. As expected, students generated better essays when they wrote on the topic for which they had high domain knowledge. Willoughby et al. (under review) suggested that search engines today generate a relevant array of sites from which to search, and therefore even those with little background information may be able to conduct valuable searches. However, these learners still are faced with the problem of identifying and understanding relevant information.

Challenges with identifying relevant information

There is a lack of empirical research investigating learners' ability to identify relevant information when using the Internet specifically. However, students' interaction with more traditional learning environments such as closed information systems (e.g., CD-ROM programs, online databases) or print materials provides insight into the role of domain knowledge for judging relevancy. For example, college students majoring in biology or business searched for articles in a closed archival information system (e.g., PsycINFO) that corresponded to two biology-related topics, and two business-related topics (Downing et al., 2005). Therefore, the individuals conducted queries corresponding to a domain in which they had high knowledge as well as a domain in which they had little knowledge. For each of the four questions, participants were provided with five minutes to search for, retrieve, and print off articles they believed would contain relevant information to answer the question. Not surprisingly, experts took less time to retrieve the first relevant article and printed off more relevant articles in total compared to less knowledgeable learners (Downing et al., 2005). In a similar study, expert fifth-grade children also found more relevant books when using an online library catalog than their less knowledgeable peers (Hirsch, 1997). When asked to search for books that they would use to write a school paper that focused on a science topic, students who had higher marks in science identified more relevant books than those with lower grades.

Although novice learners may be able to identify sources that likely contain relevant information, conclusions cannot be drawn from Downing et al. (2005) and Hirsch's (1997) studies regarding a novice's ability to actually distinguish between relevant and irrelevant information. There is no doubt that experts are able to make accurate judgments regarding relevancy when searching full-text databases (Marchionini et al., 1993), but it is of more interest whether novices are able to make successful judgments. Spilich and colleagues (1979), for example, directly examined the proportion of relevant and irrelevant information recalled from a description of a baseball game. Novices often recalled more irrelevant information after reading the passage in comparison to experts. Similarly, Symons and Pressley (1993) also instructed novices and experts to search printed text materials for relevant information. Learners with high domain knowledge identified the target information more often than those lacking domain knowledge, even though the novices scanned the pages that contained the relevant information.

Not only do novices have difficulty identifying relevant information, but they also tend to use inferior techniques when trying to do so. Although Marchionini et al. (1993) only examined the search strategies of eight participants using an online database, they did find that less knowledgeable adults had a tendency to judge relevancy of full-text articles based on the type and date of the article, the nationality of the author, the comprehensiveness of the title and whether the title contained key terms. On the other hand, experts used more appropriate strategies such as judging whether or not the information addressed the question at hand (Marchionini et al., 1993). Therefore, the lack of learning when using the Internet that Willoughby and colleagues (under review) observed likely is not a result of an inability to retrieve relevant material but rather may be attributable to a deficiency in distinguishing between relevant and irrelevant information. Empirical support that directly examines the relation between domain knowledge and relevancy judgments when using the Internet, rather than closed hypermedia, is necessary to qualify this claim. Another possibility, however, may be that novices were unable to understand or successfully integrate the information they accessed.

Challenges with integrating information

When using the Internet, learners decide the order in which they wish to access information. Closed hypermedia researchers have compared the learning for less knowledgeable learners who were either forced to adhere to the presentation order as set by the programmer (i.e., program-controlled) or were able to decide for themselves what information they would view as well as the presentation sequence (i.e., learner-controlled). Program-controlled presentations often only provide learners with the options of moving forward or backward within the hypermedia. In contrast, in a learner-controlled setting the constant presence of links connecting students to any section within the presentation permits students to jump from section to section, skipping sections of information entirely.

Gay (1986), for example, identified that undergraduate students with little conceptual understanding for an assigned topic performed worse on retention and recall tests after studying from a learner-controlled multimedia presentation in comparison to a program-controlled version. However, students with high conceptual understanding performed equally well regardless of whether or not they could direct their own learning session (Gay, 1986). Shin, Schallert, and Savenye (1994) examined whether this pattern was consistent for the learning of children. Second-grade students with computer experience were randomly assigned to one of the two following conditions. Learners either navigated through the material in the closed hypermedia freely or they had to adhere to a predetermined sequence by simply clicking "next page" to view the information. Consistent with Gay (1986), learner control significantly hindered novices' comprehension of the material whereas this format did not impact learning for their more knowledgeable peers. Therefore, having to decide what information to access and in which order has negative results for learning when existing domain knowledge is low for students of all ages (see also Alexander, Kulikowich, & Jetton, 1994; Dillon & Gabbard, 1998; Fry, 1972; Gall & Hannafin, 1994). According to Shyu and Brown (1995) and Fry (1972), domain knowledge not only promotes understanding of the information but also enables learners to make decisions about their learning progress, and whether additional instruction is needed. Similarly, Lawless and Brown (1997) suggested that learners are able to identify what information is necessary to be successful and can seek out such information in a nonlinear presentation.

When learners are not provided with directions to efficiently navigate through the presentation, they are left to their own resources to figure out the relation among the material they access, both within and across individual websites. To determine the impact that this lack of organization and structure has on learning for novices, closed hypermedia researchers have compared learning outcomes in cases where learners are exposed to nonlinear presentations either with or without an overview of the content. For instance, McDonald and Stevenson (1998) examined whether the inclusion of a spatial map would facilitate the recall of information for learners with little domain knowledge. The spatial map was classified as a navigational aid such that it provided learners with an overview of the structure of the content and thus illustrated the relation among the information within the closed hypermedia.

University students who were majoring either in the related discipline (i.e., high knowledge) or another discipline (i.e., low knowledge) were exposed to closed hypermedia either with or without a spatial map. Individuals searched through the nonlinear computerized document to answer ten questions. The inclusion of the spatial map acted as an enhancer for less knowledgeable learners, such that these learners performed just as well as their highly knowledgeable peers when provided with an overview (McDonald & Stevenson, 1998). Therefore, the spatial map may have clarified the relation among the information, and in turn facilitated a deeper understanding. McDonald and Stevenson (1998) suggested that when hypermedia excluded navigational aids, less knowledgeable learners were not aware of what information was available or what information they needed to read. Structure and organization, therefore, may be important aspects to facilitate learning when the material corresponds to a low knowledge domain.

The structure and organization placed on the information, however, may need to match the learners' intentions in order for it to be beneficial. In other words, if the material is organized according to one theme, but the learner wants to identify commonalities across a different theme, then learning may still suffer. In fact, Shapiro (1999) investigated just this hypothesis. Undergraduate students with little ecology knowledge were presented with one of two versions of a closed hypermedia program containing information on the biology and ecology of fictitious animals. Half the students received a version that categorized the information by animal family (i.e., birds, herders, reptiles, or rodents) and included an interactive overview that clearly identified the animals belonging to each family. The remaining participants studied from another version which organized the information by ecosystem (i.e., forest, desert, or mountains) and included an interactive overview that clearly identified the animals that belonged to each ecosystem. All learners were instructed to study the relation among animals in each ecosystem for as long as they desired. Shapiro compared learning for the two groups by using a short-answer post-test. In comparison to the ecosystem overview group, those provided with the animal family overview were less able to identify commonalities and differences across ecosystems even though they studied the information with this goal in mind. Although the animal family closed hypermedia version was organized very well, the structure did not match the learning goals of the students. Therefore, although structure and organization facilitate learning, to be effective the information must be organized and structured in a way that is consistent with students' learning goals.

The Internet, unfortunately, rarely structures or hierarchically organizes information (i.e., from most critical to least critical or from general to specific points; Willoughby et al., under review), and even when information is organized, there is little chance of this organization being consistent with novices' learning goals. As a result, novices may learn very little when interacting with the Internet. Researchers, however, have not explicitly examined the interaction between existing knowledge and organization when using the Internet specifically.

The challenges faced by learners with differing levels of knowledge do not end here. Learners must not only attempt to manage cognitive demands associated with the Internet as a whole, but also each individual website. Since anyone may post information on the Internet, there are no set formats for presenting the material. In fact, presenting information in certain ways increases the cognitive load associated with learning the presented information.

The Role of Existing Domain Knowledge When a Website Is Poorly Designed

The Internet is comprised of an infinite amount of web pages that vary in their combination of text, illustrations, animation, and narration, and as such may be considered a collection of individual multimedia presentations. Mayer and colleagues have identified that some types of multimedia formats (redundancy, extraneous material, and placement of information) increase the cognitive load required to learn the material contained within the presentation (e.g., Mayer & Anderson, 1991; Mayer, Heiser, & Lonn, 2001; Moreno & Mayer, 1999: Moreno & Mayer, 2002). In studies conducted by Mayer and colleagues, the multimedia presentations used were typically short in duration (e.g., 30 or 180 seconds) and program-controlled; thus, they did not provide learners with the opportunity to read the information at their own pace or to review self-selected information (e.g., Mayer, Mathias, & Wetzell, 2002; Moreno & Mayer, 1999). This poses a problem when generalizing the findings to naturalistic learning situations available when learners use the Internet, because being able to control one's learning is characteristic of the Internet. Therefore, Mayer et al.'s conclusions that learners may experience cognitive overload when reading information on a web page once may not be true when learning from the Internet, because learners can review the material multiple times (Mayer et al., 2001, 2002; Mayer & Moreno, 2002).

In support of these conclusions, however, researchers have observed that students with limited domain knowledge rarely reread sections of text when interacting with a closed hypermedia environment (Lawless, Brown, Mills, & Mayall, 2003). Therefore, there is the possibility that learners may interact with individual web pages in the same way as they interact with a single multimedia presentation. Moreover, since learner control is a disadvantage for less knowledgeable learners (Shin et al., 1994), it is likely that such learners would perform most poorly when interacting with the Internet. Therefore, factors such as redundancy, extraneous material, and placement of information may not only influence learning for viewers of multimedia but also for viewers of websites. However, until researchers directly examine the impact of these factors when learners with limited domain knowledge use the Internet, we cannot be certain whether the negative learning outcomes are generally true of this resource.

Redundant information

An example of a poorly designed multimedia presentation is one that includes redundant information. Mayer, Heiser, and Lonn (2001), for instance, investigated whether the performance of college students with low domain knowledge would be negatively impacted when multimedia contained redundant information. Novices were exposed to one of two 140-second multimedia presentations. One group was shown how lightning works by using animation and narration only. The remainder of the participants viewed the same presentation but with the inclusion of on-screen text, a duplication of the narration. Performance on both recall and problem-solving transfer tests were superior when the on-screen text was not included. This same pattern of results was found when the multimedia presentation's length was increased twofold (Moreno & Mayer, 2002). As knowledge increases, however, performance differences due to formatting tend to disappear (Kalyuga, Chandler, & Sweller, 2000). Specifically, trade apprentices performed the same on recognition tests regardless of whether they were exposed to the material using illustration-text-and-narration, illustration-and-text, illustration-and-narration, or illustration only (Kalyuga et al., 2000). When knowledge becomes high, however, experts tend to do better when provided with the illustration only in comparison to the illustration-and-narration. Kalyuga and colleagues (2000) claim that for experts the narration provides the same information as the illustration and thus is classified as redundant information. In effect, the narration, if attended to, increases the cognitive load for these learners. Mayer et al. (2001) suggested that the detrimental effects associated with redundant information is attributable to the allocation of cognitive resources to processing both the narration and the on-screen text as separate sections of information. This may require more cognitive resources than is available; learners, therefore, especially novices, may quickly experience cognitive overload. Highly knowledgeable learners, on the other hand, may be able to recognize and ignore repetitive information, allowing them to efficiently process the material.

Extraneous information

The inclusion of extraneous material also has presented problems for less knowledgeable students when using closed hypermedia. Although extraneous material is related to but irrelevant for understanding the multimedia presentation topic, it is often included in an attempt to increase learners' interest and, therefore, their performance on learning measures (Mayer, Heiser, & Lonn, 2001). Mayer and colleagues (2001) presented college students who lacked knowledge for meteorology with a multimedia presentation detailing how lightning works, which either did or did not incorporate unnecessary video clips of lightning storms. Both presentations contained identical relevant animations and narrations. Results indicated that the extraneous material hindered learners' ability to transfer relevant information to novel problem-solving situations. These researchers also found the same effect when video clips were substituted for verbalizations of interesting but irrelevant facts associated with lightning storms (Mayer et al., 2001). Mayer and colleagues suggested that the learners may have focused unsuccessfully on trying to relate the extraneous material to the relevant information in the multimedia presentation; as a result, they were unable to form a deep understanding for the material.

It is possible that learners would avoid exposure to extraneous material if given the chance. Typically, as children get older their ability to ignore distractions or irrelevant responses increases (Dempster, 1981). Lawless and colleagues (2003) examined the relation between the amount of time that learners spent with extraneous material in a closed hypermedia environment and their level of domain knowledge. College students were instructed to navigate through a nonlinear and non-hierarchical hypermedia program to learn as much as they could about the topic. Although the program presented information primarily by using text, participants were given the option of accessing narration, animation, and video—some of which were extraneous. Not only did less knowledgeable students spend more time with extraneous material in comparison to their highly knowledgeable peers, but they often viewed the irrelevant video clips multiple times (Lawless et al., 2003). Therefore, learners with little domain knowledge may not be able to distinguish between relevant and irrelevant information, in turn creating challenges for allocating cognitive resources.

Temporal and spatial considerations

Challenges associated with processing information not only arise because of *what* information is included in multimedia presentation but also *how* the information is organized. For example, Mayer and Anderson (1991) exposed college students to either a 45-second successive (animation then narration) or 30-second simultaneous multimedia presentation of the same animation and narration. Novice learners were able to create a greater proportion of solutions on the problem-solving transfer task when the information was presented at the same time rather than viewing the entire animation and then listening to the narration. The superior test performance associated with simultaneous presentation of material persisted even when learners viewed the successive presentation three times (Mayer & Anderson, 1992). Learners' understanding of the material may be affected by the proximity between textual descriptions and their respective illustrations or animations.

Moreno and Mayer (1999) tested whether proximity between text and animation was critical. Novice college students were presented with animation and corresponding textual descriptions. Those who were exposed to descriptions physically close to the animation provided more accurate solutions on the problem-solving transfer test than those who were presented with descriptions far away on-screen from the animation. Therefore, the separation of information either by order of presentation or physical proximity impacts the formation of deeper understanding. Mayer and colleagues suggest that during the successive presentations, the learners were required to hold information they extracted from the animation in working memory, while either listening to the narration or searching for the corresponding description (Mayer & Anderson, 1991; Mayer & Anderson, 1992; Moreno & Mayer, 1999). Holding information in working memory requires cognitive resources; in such instances, therefore, less knowledgeable learners may no longer have sufficient resources to efficiently process the material, resulting in inferior learning.

Although experts may be able to use their knowledge to compensate for a poorly designed multimedia presentation (Mayer, 2001), it is clear that less knowledgeable learners are challenged by poor presentations. Recall that these findings are based on research conducted in closed hypermedia environments. The Internet presents additional challenges that may exacerbate the limitations faced by less knowledgeable learners. For example, learners with limited domain knowledge may experience difficulty when using the Internet in selecting quality information from the vast amount of information available, or in identifying relevant information on the Internet (Symons & Pressley, 1993). Consequently, researchers have begun to investigate the learning outcomes of less knowledgeable learners after searching and retrieving information from the Internet in particular.

The Role of Existing Domain Knowledge When Learning From the Internet

Given that existing knowledge is a critical prerequisite for organizing, extracting, encoding, and retrieving information (e.g., Schneider & Weinert, 1990), it is logical to assume that individuals gathering information from the Internet would perform better in high knowledge domains in comparison to low knowledge domains. In fact, this has been reflected in children's interactions with closed hypermedia (Shin et al., 1994). Researchers have investigated the role of existing domain knowledge when learning from the Internet by examining students' interaction with either a single website or the entire World Wide Web.

For example, Lawless, Schrader, and Mayall (2006) restricted students to a single website that consisted of 100 pages of information which collectively comprised 11 topic areas both relevant and irrelevant to the topic students were instructed to study. Undergraduate and graduate students completed a pretest measure of existing knowledge, searched the website for 30 minutes, and then completed an immediate post-test of topic knowledge identical to the pretest. Half the participants, however, read a 500-word paper-based article that globally outlined the major topics in human genetics, the assigned subject matter, prior to their Internet navigation. The other half did not receive exposure to pre-reading material. The groups did not differ in their level of existing domain knowledge, which was relatively low (approximately 45% correct on the pretest). Even after statistically accounting for the pretest scores, results indicated that pre-reading facilitated students learning, such that their post-test knowledge scores were greater than those who were not exposed to the pre-reading material. In fact, there was no change from pre- to post-test scores for the control group. Lawless and colleagues (2006) suggested that the pre-reading material provided students with "an overall schema for the domain into which new knowledge could be integrated" (p. 13), and therefore, facilitated the integration of information across individual pages in the website. More importantly, without this scaffolding university students were unable to create coherent mental models of the accessed information and thus increases in knowledge did not occur.

One major limitation in Lawless and colleagues' (2006) research was that they did not include a control group who were exposed only to the pre-reading material. Without comparing the learning gains of the pre-reading group to a control group, we cannot determine how much learning can be credited to the Internet exposure over and above the pre-reading content. A second limitation is the use of a pretest to measure domain knowledge. A pretest would encourage students with high domain knowledge in particular to access their existing knowledge prior to interacting with the material. This would not be true for their less knowledgeable peers.

Although Willoughby and colleagues (under review) also explored how domain knowledge interacts with performance, they examined learning outcomes after learners searched for and retrieved information from the Internet as a whole. Undergraduate students majoring in environmental studies or biology were randomly assigned to either an Internet or control condition, such that each condition was comprised of half environmental studies students and half biology students. Each participant completed the same two essays, one corresponding to an environmental studies topic and the other to a biology topic. Therefore, one topic represented an area for which they had high domain knowledge and the other topic represented an area for which they had low domain knowledge. Those in the Internet condition were asked to search and retrieve information corresponding to the essay topic for 30 minutes prior to writing the essay. The control group, on the other hand, relied purely on their existing knowledge to answer each question, permitting researchers to determine the relative contribution of existing knowledge.

Essay performance was represented by the frequency of correct facts. As expected, students had superior performance on the essay corresponding to their area of expertise than to the unfamiliar topic, regardless of condition. However, most importantly, learners who searched the Internet for information pertaining to the topic in which they lacked existing knowledge wrote essays similar in quality to the control group (Willoughby et al., under review). On the other hand, when learners had high domain knowledge, being able to search the Internet resulted in superior performance in comparison to the control group. For example, the environmental studies students received higher scores on the environmental studies essay when they conducted Internet searches than those in the control condition. In contrast, environmental studies students who conducted Internet searches for the biology essay did not differ from their peers who did not use the Internet. The results were reverse for the biology students. The researchers concluded that studying from the Internet may benefit only those with existing knowledge, and that simply having access to information does not automatically translate to acquiring more knowledge. The Internet, therefore, may only be a valuable resource when learners have a rich knowledge base in the topic area (Willoughby et al., under review).

Can Low Domain Knowledge Be Compensated for When Using the Internet?

Existing domain knowledge has been shown to be essential to learn from the Internet. However, this does not necessarily mean that less knowledgeable learners should not use the Internet, but rather that they may need assistance to be able to learn successfully. Learners may receive the help they need either prior to or during their interaction with the Internet.

Assistance prior to using the Internet

Instructors may be able to provide learners with necessary skills and abilities prior to navigating the Internet that will make the learning process less challenging for novice learners. One way is to provide learners with a list of appropriate websites (Kafai & Bates, 1997). This would enable students to be exposed to quality information prior to their independent searches. If novices are not forced to make decisions regarding the information they will initially study, then they may be able to develop a knowledge base to successfully guide subsequent searches. Secondly, learners may benefit from instruction prior to Internet use. Mayer, Mathias, and Wetzell (2002) as well as Lawless, Schrader, and Mayall (2006), for example, demonstrated that learning may be enhanced if students develop an overview schema of the information prior to interacting with closed hypermedia. Mayer and colleagues (2002) provided half the participants with a diagram of a braking system with the components labeled prior to observing a multimedia presentation detailing how brakes work. The other half of the undergraduate students studied the multimedia presentation without viewing the pre-training material. In comparison to novices who were not exposed to the pre-training, learners with little domain knowledge performed significantly better on post-test measures of learning. Mayer et al. (2002) suggested that the pre-training decreased the cognitive load associated with processing information in the multimedia presentation and thus allowed learners to obtain a deeper understanding of the material.

Similarly, Lawless et al. (2006) assigned a group of undergraduate students with relatively low levels of domain knowledge to read a paper-based passage outlining the major topics in human genetics immediately before studying related information from a single website. The remaining participants were not provided with prior scaffolding. Learning outcomes were greatest for those who were exposed to the pre-training material before navigating the website. Lawless and colleagues (2006) claimed that the passage increased learners' knowledge about how the domain-related content on the Internet fit together; as a result, learners were more capable of managing the complexity of the environment. Thus, prior exposure to quality material, even at a basic level, Internetmay facilitate learning when using the Internet.

It is not always feasible, however, for instructors to determine learners' level of domain knowledge prior to each assignment, especially in college or university settings. Therefore, researchers have examined the impact of electronic and human assistance while learners are navigating the Internet.

Assistance while using the Internet

Less knowledgeable learners also may demonstrate learning benefits if they work with peers while interacting with the Internet. Lazonder (2005) found that college students who searched for and retrieved information from the Internet were able to answer a greater number of the assigned questions successfully, as well as correct wrong answers more often, when they completed the searches with a partner rather than alone. According to Lazonder (2005), when working in pairs, students must come to a consensus regarding the relevance of the material found on the Internet for answering the question at hand. It might be expected that less knowledgeable learners would exhibit the best results when they have the assistance of more knowledgeable peers to find the correct answer on the Internet. In this study, however, this hypothesis was not explicitly tested.

Winters, Azevedo and Levin (2004) investigated the learning gains of heterogeneous ability pairs. High school students with little domain knowledge were partnered with more knowledgeable peers to solve three science problems by retrieving information from a closed hypermedia program. Identical pre- and post-test measures of knowledge were compared for learning gains. More knowledgeable students did not experience any differences in their level of knowledge following the task. However, less knowledgeable students did exhibit significant improved scores on the post-test. By primarily questioning their partner about the material, the novice learners were able to increase their understanding (Winters et al., 2004). Such results are not surprising considering that scaffolding has led to knowledge acquisition after navigating closed hypermedia for students of all ages with little domain knowledge (Azevedo, Cromley, & Siebert, 2004; Azevedo, Cromley, Thomas, Seibert, & Tron, 2003; Azevedo, Cromley, Winters, Moos, Levin, & Fried, 2004). Therefore, peer collaboration may compensate for low domain knowledge when initially using the Internet, and thus is another research area in need of empirical support.

Assistance during the learning process not only can be provided through human interaction, but also may be supported with computer software. *Artemis* and *gStudy* are two examples of software which provide organizational support for learners. *Artemis* is an online library designed for middle and high school students that contains a collection of quality science-related websites pre-selected by librarians (http://artemis.goknow.com/artemis/index.adp). Unlike many electronic databases, *Artemis* provides learners with a workspace where they can organize past search results, and attach notes to the information they retrieve (Lumpe & Butler, 2002). When using *Artemis*, Lumpe and Butler found not only that high school students frequently use these organizational features but also that such use enhanced learning outcomes. Additional research is necessary to determine whether organizational scaffolding is enough to decrease the cognitive load experienced when using the Internet such that learning improves for novices.

The software program *gStudy* is currently being examined for its potential to enhance learners' strategy use and self-monitoring when interacting with multimedia (Nesbit & Winne, 2008). However, this software application includes features which may be especially useful when using the Internet to learn about a topic corresponding to a less knowledgeable domain. For a full description of the software's applications and example scenarios of how the program can facilitate learning, see chapter 3 in this book.

Similar to *Artemis*, *gStudy* also provides learners with the ability to efficiently organize information they retrieved from various hypermedia, including the Internet. For example, students first search the Internet for information pertaining to the topic at hand; information they believe addresses the topic is then downloaded into *gStudy*. Students are then able to highlight segments of information they deem as important or relevant, and then provide each segment with a label such as principal or key experiment (Nesbit & Winne, 2008). An index, one of *gStudy*'s many features, arranges the segments according to their labels. Therefore, students are able to review all of the notes pertaining to a single label, such as key experiments, with a single click of the mouse. Learners, however, are also able to organize their own notes by using one of the many note-taking templates offered or by creating one of their own templates. For example, the debate template enables learners to input the issue and positions of A and B and then organize their highlighted segments according to the evidence for A, evidence for B, and their own position (Nesbit & Winne, 2008). The index and note-taking templates keep related information together which may decrease cognitive load and facilitate the integration of information, in turn leading to a deeper understanding of the topic at hand. Moreover, if students are having difficulties understanding the information, they may use *gStudy*'s chat tool to communicate with their peers—including those more knowledgeable—to seek clarification.

One limitation with software applications such as *gStudy* is that students are still forced to make decisions regarding the relevancy of the information on the Internet. While the software may promote effective strategy use and self-monitoring as well as decreasing the cognitive load associated with integrating information, students with little domain knowledge may still either download irrelevant information into the program or highlight irrelevant segments. However, if learners recognize such difficulties they could ask their peers for help by using the chat feature. *gStudy*, therefore, shows great potential to facilitate learning when students with little domain knowledge use the Internet.

Conclusion and Future Directions

Students often perceive the Internet as a valuable source for information (Ng & Gunstone, 2002), mainly because they can potentially access information on any topic at their convenience (Eveland & Dunwoody, 2000; Fidel, Davies, Douglass, Holder, Hopkins, Kushner, et al., 1999). It is not surprising, then, that the Internet is increasingly being used as a tool for information gathering and learning. Simply providing access to the Internet, however, may not be enough to facilitate learning. Indeed, having a rich knowledge base and/or providing supports to accommodate learners with a low knowledge base are essential for learners to acquire knowledge when using the Internet (Lawless et al., 2006; Willoughby et al., under review).

Unfortunately, the majority of hypermedia research investigating the effect of domain knowledge has included undergraduate students as participants. Therefore, there is limited research on children's learning with the Internet. The predominant focus on young adults is important as there are improvements in how much information can be held in working memory across development. For example, adult learners are able to recall a greater span of digits (Chi, 1978) and to-be-learned passages (Schneider, Korkel, & Weinert, 1989) in comparison to younger children. Throughout childhood and adolescence, there also is an increase in the ability to ignore distractions (Dempster, 1981), and in the ability to use memory strategies efficiently (Bjorklund & Schneider, 1996). Increases in these abilities may alleviate the cognitive demands associated with processing information, which then enables adult learners to attend to more information simultaneously or with less cognitive effort than younger learners (Schneider, 2000). In addition, language skills and writing competence increase dramatically over the early school years, which enable older children to approach the Internet with more tools to search and evaluate online information. As a result, younger children may interact with the Internet differently or even less efficiently than older learners. Therefore, different or additional learning challenges may surface if researchers take a developmental perspective.

In conclusion, it is important that researchers investigate the relation between cognitive processes and domain knowledge for both adults and children when using the Internet. In addition, this needs to be done with the Internet instead of closed hypermedia (e.g., online library catalogs or single websites). Only after we fully understand the cognitive demands of the Internet, particularly for novices, can we create appropriate scaffolding to enhance their learning.

Acknowledgments

Support for this research was provided by a grant to Teena Willoughby from the Social Sciences and Humanities Research Council of Canada and a grant to Teena Willoughby and Eileen Wood from the Canadian Language and Literacy Research Network.

References

Allen, B. (1991). Topic knowledge and online catalog search formulation. *Library Quarterly, 61*, 188–213.

Alexander, P. A., Kulikowich, J. M., & Jetton, T. L. (1994). The role of subject-matter knowledge and interest in the processing of linear and nonlinear texts. *Review of Educational Research, 64*, 201–252.

Anderson, R. C., & Pearson, P. D. (1984). A schema-theoretic view of basic processes in reading. In P. D. Pearson (Ed.), *Handbook of reading research.* New York: Longman.

Azevedo, R., Cromley, J. G., & Seibert, D. (2004). Does adaptive scaffolding facilitate students' ability to regulate their learning with hypermedia? *Contemporary Educational Psychology, 29*, 344–370.

Azevedo, R., Cromley, J. G., Thomas, L., Seibert, D., & Tron, M. (2003). *Online process scaffolding and students' self-regulated learning with hypermedia.* Paper presented at the annual meeting of the American Educational Research Association, Chicago.

Azevedo, R., Cromley, J. G., Winters, F. I., Moos, D. C., Levin, D. M., & Fried, D. (2004, April). *Adaptive scaffolding and self-regulated learning from hypermedia: A developmental study.* Paper presented at the annual meeting of the American Educational Research Association, San Diego, CA.

Baddeley, A. D., & Hitch, G. (1974). Working memory. In G. H. Bower (Ed.), *The psychology of learning and motivation* (vol. 8, pp. 47–89). New York: Academic Press.

Bjorklund, D. F., & Schneider, W. (1996). The interaction of knowledge, aptitude, and strategies in children's memory performance. In H. W. Reese (Ed.), *Advances in child development and behavior* (vol. 26., pp. 59–89). San Diego, CA: Academic Press.

Chase, W. G., & Simon, H. A. (1973). The mind's eye in chess. In W. G. Chase (Ed.), *Visual information processing.* New York: Academic Press.

Chi, M. T. H. (1978). Children's thinking: What develops? In R. S. Siegler (Ed.), *Knowledge structures and memory development* (pp. 73–96). Hillsdale, NJ: Lawrence Erlbaum.

Curry, J., Haderlie, S., Ku, T., Lawless, K. A., Lemon, M., & Wood, R. (1999). Specified learning goals and their effect on learners' representations of a hypertext reading environment. *International Journal of Instructional Media, 26*, 43–52.

Dempster, F. N. (1981). Memory span: Sources of individual and developmental differences. *Psychological Bulletin, 89*, 63–100.

Dillon, A., & Gabbard, R. (1998). Hypermedia as an educational technology: A review of the quantitative research literature on learner comprehension, control, and style. *Review of Educational Research, 68*, 322–349.

Downing, R. E., Moore, J. L., & Brown, S. W. (2005). The effects and interaction of spatial visualization and domain expertise on information seeking. *Computers in Human Behavior, 21*, 195–209.

Dryburgh, H. (2001). *Changing our ways: Why and how Canadians use the Internet.* Retrieved from http://www.statcan.ca/cgi-bin/downpub/listpub.cgi?catno=56F0006XIE2000001

Environics Research Group. (2001, November). *Young Canadians in a wired world: Phase 2.* Retrieved from http://www.media-awareness.ca/english/research/YCWW/phaseII/students.cfm

Eveland, W. P. Jr., & Dunwoody, S. (2000). Examining information processing on the world wide web using think aloud protocols. *Media Psychology*, *2*, 219–244.

Eveland, W. P. Jr., & Dunwoody, S. (2002). An investigation of elaboration and selective scanning as mediators of learning from the web versus print. *Journal of Broadcasting & Electronic Media*, *46*, 34–53.

Fidel, R., Davies, R. K., Douglass, M. H., Holder, J. K., Hopkins, C. J., Kushner, E., et al. (1999). A visit to the information mall: Web searching behavior of high school students. *Journal of the American Society for Information Science*, *50*, 24–37.

Fincher-Kiefer, R., Post, T. A., Greene, T. R., & Voss, J. F. (1988). On the role of prior knowledge and task demands in the processing of text. *Journal of Memory and Language*, *27*, 416–428.

Fry, J. P. (1972). Interactive relationship between inquisitiveness and student control of instruction. *Journal of Educational Psychology*, *63*, 459–465.

Gall, J. E., & Hannafin, M. J. (1994). A framework for the study of hypertext. *Instructional Science*, *22*, 207–232.

Gay, G. (1986). Interaction of learner control and prior understanding in computer-assisted video instruction. *Journal of Educational Psychology*, *78*, 225–227.

Hirsch, S. G. (1997). How do children find information on different types of tasks? Children's use of the science library catalog. *Library Trends*, *45*, 725–745.

Jones, S. (2002). *The Internet goes to college: How students are living in the future with today's technology*. Retrieved from http://www.pewInternet.org/PPF/r/71/report_display.asp

Kafai, Y., & Bates, M. J. (1997). Internet web-searching instruction in the elementary classroom: Building a foundation for information literacy. *School Library Media Quarterly*, *25*, 103–111.

Kalyuga, S., Chandler, P., & Sweller, J. (2000). Incorporating learner experience into the design of multimedia instruction. *Journal of Educational Psychology*, *92*, 126–136.

Kuiper, E., Volman, M., & Terwel, J. (2005). The web as an information resource in K-12 education: Strategies for supporting students in searching and processing information. *Review of Educational Research*, *75*, 285–328.

Large, A. (1996). Hypertext instructional programs and learner control: A research review. *Education for Information*, *14*, 95–106.

Lawless, K. A., & Brown, S. W. (1997). Multimedia learning environments: Issues of learner control and navigation. *Instructional Science*, *25*, 117–131.

Lawless, K. A., Brown, S. W., Mills, R., & Mayall, H. J. (2003). Knowledge, interest, recall and navigation: A look at hypertext processing. *Journal of Literacy Research*, *35*, 911–934.

Lawless, K. A., Schrader, P. G., & Mayall, H. J. (2006, April). *The impact of domain knowledge and navigation on learning online*. Paper presented at the annual meeting of the American Educational Research Association, San Francisco, CA.

Lazonder, A. W. (2005). Do two heads search better than one? Effects of student collaboration on web search behaviour and search outcomes. *British Journal of Educational Technology*, *36*, 465–475.

Lenhart, A., Rainie, L., & Lewis, O. (2001). *Teenage life online: The rise of the instant-message generation and the Internet's impact on friendships and family relationships.* Retrieved from http://www.pewInternet.org/PPF/r/36/report_display.asp

Lorenzen, M. (2001). The land of confusion? High school students and their use of the world wide web for research. *Research Strategies, 18,* 151–163.

Lumpe, A. T., & Butler, K. (2002). The information seeking strategies of high school science students. *Research in Science Education, 32,* 549–566.

Marchionini, G. (1995). *Information seeking in electronic environments.* New York: Cambridge University Press.

Marchionini, G., Dwiggins, S., Katz, A., & Lin, X. (1993). Information seeking in full-text end-user-oriented search systems: The roles of domain and search expertise. *Library and Information Science Research, 15,* 35–69.

Marchionini, G., Meadow, C., Dwiggins, S., Lin, X., Wang, J., & Yuan, W. (1991). A study of user interaction with information retrieval interfaces: Progress report. *Canadian Journal of Information Science, 16,* 42–59.

Mayer, R. E. (2001). *Multimedia learning.* New York: Cambridge University Press.

Mayer, R. E., & Anderson, R. B. (1991). Animations need narrations: An experimental test of a dual-coding hypothesis. *Journal of Educational Psychology, 83,* 484–490.

Mayer, R. E., & Anderson, R. B. (1992). The instructive animation: Helping students build connections between words and pictures in multimedia learning. *Journal of Educational Psychology, 84,* 444–452.

Mayer, R. E., Heiser, J., & Lonn, S. (2001). Cognitive constraints on multimedia learning: When presenting more material results in less understanding. *Journal of Educational Psychology, 93,* 187–198.

Mayer, R. E., Mathias, A., & Wetzell, K. (2002). Fostering understanding of multimedia messages through pre-training: Evidence for a two-stage theory of mental model construction. *Journal of Educational Psychology, 8,* 147–154.

McDonald, S., & Stevenson, R. J. (1998). Navigation in hyperspace: An evaluation of the effects of navigational tools and subject matter expertise on browsing and information retrieval in hypertext. *Interacting with Computers, 10,* 129–142.

Miller, G. A. (1956). The magical number seven, plus or minus two: Some limits on our capacity for processing information. *The Psychological Review, 63,* 81–97.

Moos, D. C., & Azevedo, R. (2006, April). *Self-regulated learning with hypermedia: The role of prior domain knowledge.* Paper presented at the annual meeting of the American Educational Research Association, San Francisco, CA.

Moreno, R., & Mayer, R. E. (1999). Cognitive principles of multimedia learning: The role of modality and contiguity. *Journal of Educational Psychology, 91,* 358–368.

Moreno, R., & Mayer, R. E. (2002). Verbal redundancy in multimedia learning: When reading helps listening. *Journal of Educational Psychology, 94,* 156–163.

Nesbit, J. C., & Winne, P. H. (2008). Tools for learning in an information society. In T. Willoughby & E. Wood (Eds.), *Children's Learning in a Digital World.* Oxford, UK: Blackwell.

Ng, W., & Gunstone, R. (2002). Students' perceptions of the effectiveness of the World Wide Web as a research and teaching tool in science learning. *Research in Science Education, 32,* 489–510.

Rainie, L., & Packel, D. (2001). *More online, doing more: 16 million newcomers gain Internet access in the last half of 2000 as women, minorities, and families with modest incomes continue to surge online*. Retrieved from http://www.pewInternet.org/PPF/r/30/report_display.asp

Rumelhart, D. E., Hinton, G., & McClelland, J. L. (1986). *Parallel distributed processing, Vol. 1*. Cambridge, MA: MIT Press.

Schneider, W. (2000). Research on memory development: Historical trends and current themes. *International Journal of Behavioral Development, 24*, 407–420.

Schneider, W., Korkel, J., & Weinert, F. E. (1989). Domain-specific knowledge and memory performance: A comparison of high- and low-aptitude children. *Journal of Educational Psychology, 81*, 306–312.

Schneider, W., Korkel, J., & Weinert, F. (1990). Expert knowledge, general abilities, and text processing. In W. Schneider & F. Weinert (Eds.), *Interactions among aptitudes, strategies, and knowledge in cognitive performance* (pp. 235–250). New York: Springer-Verlag.

Schneider, W., & Weinert, F. (1990). The role of knowledge, strategies, and aptitudes in cognitive performance: Concluding comments. In W. Schneider & F. Weinert (Eds.), *Interactions among aptitudes, strategies, and knowledge in cognitive performance* (pp. 286–302). New York: Springer-Verlag.

Shapiro, A. (1999). The relationship between prior knowledge and interactive overviews during hypermedia-aided learning. *Journal of Educational Computing Research, 20*, 143–167.

Shin, E. C., Schallert, D. L., & Savenye, W. C. (1994). Effects of learner control, advisement, and prior knowledge on young students' learning in a hypertext environment. *Educational Technology, Research and Development, 42*, 33–46.

Shyu, H., & Brown, S. W. (1995). Learner-control: The effects on learning a procedural task during computer-based videodisc instruction. *International Journal of Instructional Media, 22*, 217–231.

Spilich, G. J., Vesonder, G. T., Chejese, H. L., & Voss, J. F. (1979). Text processing of domain-related information for individuals with high and low domain knowledge. *Journal of Verbal Learning and Learning Behavior, 18*, 275–290.

Stein, B. S., Morris, C. D., & Bransford, J. D. (1978). Constraints on effective elaboration. *Journal of Verbal Learning & Verbal Behavior, 17*, 707–714.

Symons, S., MacLatchy-Gaudet, H., Stone, T. D., & Reynolds, P. L. (2001). Strategy instruction for elementary students searching informational text. *Scientific Studies of Reading, 5*, 1–33.

Symons, S., & Pressley, M. (1993). Prior knowledge affects text search success and extraction of information. *Reading Research Quarterly, 28*, 251–261.

Willoughby, T., Anderson, A. S., Wood, E., Mueller, J., & Ross, C. (under review). The role of prior knowedge when learning from the Internet. Article submitted for publication.

Winters, F. I., Azevedo, R., & Levin, D. M. (2004, April). *How do highschool students regulate their learning when using a computer-based environment to collaboratively engage in inquiry?* Paper presented at the annual meeting of the American Educational Research Association, San Diego, CA.

Chapter 11

The Integration of Computer Technology in the Classroom

Julie Mueller, Eileen Wood, and Teena Willoughby

In this chapter we explore the impact of technology from the perspective of the educator. Given that the school environment often serves as the one level playing field in allowing children of diverse backgrounds access to technology, educators can play a critical role in exposing children to computer technology and demonstrating how to use technology effectively for learning. Educators then, have the challenge of acquiring skill with the technology and utilizing it effectively as part of their instruction. This chapter explores the educators' experiences both in formal schooling contexts (elementary and secondary classrooms) and in less formal contexts such as early childcare contexts (daycare, preschool, etc.).

Part I Elementary and Secondary School Classrooms

The past several decades have produced rapid advances in computer technology and increased access to that technology within schools. For example, national and international statistics show that schools around the world are becoming increasingly well-equipped with computer hardware (Collis, Knezek, Lai, Miyashita, Pelgrum, Plomp, et al., 1996; Ertl & Plante, 2004; Pelgrum, 1992) and access to the Internet (Greene, 2000; Riel & Becker, 2000). Simply reporting descriptive statistics regarding Internet connections and pupil–computer ratios, however, tells us little about the quantity and quality of student and educator interaction with computers.

Despite widespread access to computers and possible learning advantages with introducing computer technology, researchers suggest that computers continue to be underutilized in many schools. For example, in an early study, Rosen and Weil (1995) reported that although computers were available in every school they investigated, only half of the educators used them. Similarly, Cuban, Kirkpatrick, and Peck (2001) reported that only 4 of the

13 educators in their case studies had modified their classroom teaching in major ways to accommodate the introduction of technology. This was true even among schools designated as having high access to computers. Further, according to 78% of the principals in a Canada-wide study, computers were used primarily for word processing, with only 34% using the Internet/ intranet to disseminate information (Ertl & Plante, 2004). International research paints a similar picture. Work conducted in the United Kingdom, Thailand, Greece, and the Netherlands suggest that computers are still under-used in terms of quantity and quality of use (Conlon & Simpson, 2003; Demetriadis, Barbas, Molohides, Palaigeorgiou, Psillos, Vlahovas, et al., 2003; Pelgrum, 2001; Wilson, Notar, & Yunker, 2003; Wooley, 1998). Hence, the potential of computer technology is not being realized (Abrami, 2001; Cuban, 2001; Muir-Herzig, 2004; Sutherland, Armstrong, Barnes, Broawn, Breeze, Gall, et al., 2004). The impetus for researchers, then, is to understand why computers are underutilized even when they are available.

Understanding the integration of computer technology

Early research in the field of educational technology examined barriers to integration and identified "computer anxiety" as a roadblock to computer use. Following a meta-analysis of studies in this area, Rosen and Maguire (1990) concluded that computer experience was negatively correlated with computer anxiety. That is, fear and apprehension of the computer itself were thought to be responsible for the limited use of computers in the early years of implementation (Anderson, 1996; Lian Chua, Chen, & Wong, 1999; Rosen & Weil, 1995). Another alternative is that educators may have been fearful of the innovation that would be required in their teaching resulting from the introduction of computers.

If lack of familiarity and experience with computers were the sole factors accounting for the limited use of computers in schools, we should expect to see high levels of use now that computers are no longer new. This is not the case. The prevalence of technology has not eliminated the underutilization of computers in the clasroom (e.g., Wood, Mueller, Willoughby, Specht, & DeYoung, 2005). Robust integration of computers in the curriculum has not been achieved, and appears to be much more complex than the simple provision of equipment.

Several researchers have suggested that integration of any new technology or innovation proceeds in stages or phases (e.g., Sandholtz, Ringstaff, & Dwyer, 1997; Steinberg, 1991; Valdez, McNabb, Foertsch, Anderson, Hawkes, & Raack, 2005). Computers may present a uniquely challenging medium to integrate because the technology changes at a rapid pace. Educators constantly need to update their technological knowledge. In addition, these technological advances can affect the potential learning environment, as was seen when the Internet became available in schools. Constant changes in the technology may inhibit its smooth acquisition and adoption. Understanding the trajectory from acquisition through to integration is reviewed below.

Steinberg (1991) outlined a three-phase process of acquisition. Initially, consumers are resistant to change. Early in the integration process educators see technology as "merely a different or more convenient tool to accomplish old tasks" (p. 4). Tasks are transferred directly to the new technology with little difference from how things were taught before (Hokanson & Hooper, 2000). For example, traditional worksheets are merely transferred to the computer which is used as a word processor. The transfer of traditional methods is done with no added benefits.

The next phase of technology integration is more than the application of past experience—it is an add-on to it. Educators may be aware of distinctive features of the new technology but do not consider that the interactions of the new characteristics with the old might warrant modification of traditional methods. For example, educators may understand that they can individualize children's instructional contexts through the many options available with computer-assisted instruction, but fail to do so (Steinberg, 1991).

In the third phase of integration, the value of past teaching experience is identified and maintained as the exploration of the new technology increases. There is a synthesis and integration of old and new methods for the most effective applications of the technology. Relevant information from old technologies is kept, but attention is also paid to the limitations of the old technology and the potentials of the new.

Another model of learning was proposed by Sandholtz, Ringstaff, and Dwyer (1997). They identified a five-stage process for technology integration that followed from their intervention study (i.e., The Apple Classroom of Tomorrow), which provided educators with support and training as well as up-to-date technology in classrooms across the United States. They suggested that educators went through the following stages:

1 *Entry*: At this stage, anxiety was an issue; required time and effort was a barrier; often educators quit at this stage. Computer activities looked similar to traditional tasks.
2 *Adoption*: Assimilation began but there were still few changes in practice. For instance, in writing class, students typed a story from a written draft; standard worksheets were done using a word processor.
3 *Adaptation*: Adaptation occurred when computer technology was thoroughly integrated. Educators saw the benefits of integration and students

began to create using the computer. For example, students gathered data in a spreadsheet, created a bar graph, compared charts with other groups and made conclusions. In writing, students used software to plan writing, create an outline and draft a paper on computer.

4 *Appropriation:* At this stage, educators integrated computer technology into their own planning and instruction. Educators used the computer for research in preparation of classes, for email communication, collaboration with other classes, and computerized assessment and evaluation. Educators used a laptop or desktop in the classroom as an everyday tool.

5 *Invention:* Educators who reached this level of integration were leaders in writing curriculum that included technology. They tended to be expert educators within the school, often serving as a catalyst for integration by other educators.

Most recently, Valdez and colleagues (2005) organized the development of computer-based technology integration into three phases. The phases move through steps of integration similar to the adoption stages described by Sandholtz et al. (1997), but are focused more specifically on the tasks of the students or the relationship of the technology to instructional design. One unique feature is that the rate at which these stages or phases of integration progress can differ across individual educators, schools, and technologies.

Phase One: Print automation: Similar to the previous two models, the initial phase of integration proposed by Valdez and colleagues (2005) suggests that very little has changed with regard to traditional instruction. Students use technology to automate print-based practices. Learning objectives are focused on skills and inert knowledge with little conceptual integration; there is limited exchange of ideas; vision is focused on obtaining hardware and software; there are few efforts to involve parents and community in terms of technology. Later in this phase, technology is seen as a cognitive tool. Educators begin to question how students know what they know. The emphasis in technology implementation moves to the development of higher-order thinking skills. Learning with technology becomes the development of logic, problem-solving skills, and knowledge construction (Abrami, 2001; Saettler, 1990).

Phase Two: Expansion of learning opportunities: During the second phase of technology integration, the focus moves to learning-centered experiences. Users of technology provide information in interactive hypertext and hypermedia formats. Students use technology to organize and report, and educators use it to gather information, model problem solving, and provide greater understanding of how technology is used in the workforce. Although the learning approach is still directed at the individual, outcomes are often shared within the classroom. The focus is on finding and presenting information but connections to the real world are superficial and forced. Vision is focused on increasing learning opportunities and strategies to succeed better in an information-rich world.

Phase Three: Data-driven virtual learning: In the third phase of technology, the pace of technological development is a focal point. For example, the introduction of the Internet leads to an increased capacity to address data-driven issues and opportunities. Students use technology to explore diverse information resources inside and outside school, and to produce information for real-world tasks. Educators use technology to guide and engage students in self-directed learning activities, model problem solving, and focus on areas that are difficult to teach. Learning is a seen as a developmental process, enhanced by others inside and outside the classroom. Students have opportunities to link to experts in real-world contexts and other authentic tasks. Technology use at this point is aligned with national standards. Conceptual integrity is important and a variety of resources and strategies are linked to integrated concepts.

In summary, all three of the models outlined above depict a similar learning acquisition and adoption trajectory. The evolution starts with mapping computers onto existing repertoires of instruction and ends with changing instruction to map onto the learning opportunities afforded by computer technology.

What are the instructional possibilities afforded by computer technology?

The development of computer technology, and the identification of new possibilities for learning throughout the integration process, point to differences between traditional instruction and computer-assisted instruction (CAI). Differences can be classified in terms of mode of communication, instructor–learner interaction, and environmental factors (Steinberg, 1991).

Modes of communication: Traditional instruction uses several modes of communication—verbal, physical actions, written text, and diagrams. CAI has a verbal emphasis requiring a high degree of literacy (Poynton, 2005). Advances in technology have added visual and oral components (Mayer & Moreno, 2002; Moreno & Mayer, 2002). The learner in traditional classrooms produces information through speech, writing, and drawing. Learners using a computer have options including touch screens, point and click with a mouse, keyboard response, and (more recently) speech options in some software (e.g., *Dragon Naturally Speaking* by Scansoft).

Instructor–learner interaction: In traditional classrooms, students are generally encouraged to "think" of their answers and one student responds. The educator observes behavior to judge progress. CAI, on the other hand, requires overt responses from each user. Traditional instruction is generally group-paced and educator led while CAI can be individually paced and the flow can be controlled by the computer, the learner, the educator, or a combination.

Environmental factors: These also differ between traditional teaching and CAI. Progress in traditional tasks is usually self-evident in terms of how much is left to be done and how the learner compares to others. Students have an established framework for in-class lessons, whereas CAI may still be relatively novel and different with each lesson. The "give and take" of the traditional classroom may not be so innate in a computer-assisted environment. However, CAI can easily be individualized and progress can be recorded (e.g., Chambers, Abrami, McWhaw, & Therrien, 2001).

Many of the differences between traditional and CAI are consistent with growing changes in pedagogy and instructional approaches. Educational reform has changed the view of the learner from a passive receptor of information in a world where knowledge is considered to exist outside the learner, to a learner who is an active participant in the construction of knowledge (Abrami, 2001; Hokanson & Hooper, 2000; Scott, Cole, & Engel, 1992; Staub & Stern, 2002; Vygotsky, 1978).

Constructivist pedagogy generally involves the following characteristics:

1 attention to the individual and respect for the students' background and developing understandings of and beliefs about elements of the domain (this could also be described as student-centered);
2 facilitation of group dialogue that explores an element of the domain with the purpose of leading to the creation and shared understanding of a topic;
3 planned and often unplanned introduction of formal domain knowledge into the conversation through direct instruction, reference to text, exploration of a website, or some other means.
4 provision of opportunities for students to determine, challenge, change, or add to existing beliefs and understandings through engagement in tasks that are structured for this purpose; and
5 development of students' meta-awareness of their own understandings and learning processes. (Richardson, 2003, p. 1626)

The potential of computer technology and the vast database of immediately available information via the Internet provide increasing support for constructivist pedagogy. A constructivist philosophy encourages integration of computers as a cognitive tool, and changes in teaching philosophy may also be a consequence of computer integration (Schofield, 1995). Web-based instruction allows learners to construct meaning, engage in social interaction, and problem-solve in a real-world context (Abbey, 2003). Technology can be used to build knowledge through simulations, database searches, manipulation and display of content, analysis, problem solving, exhibits, collaboration, collection and manipulation of data, design, programming, interactive hypertext, and communication. All of these activities help to support the learner in the active construction of knowledge while collaborating with others and presenting work to an audience.

What is the role of the educator in an instructional model that integrates computer technology?

To use computers as a cognitive tool in knowledge construction, educators must play a major role. They must acknowledge the computer as a learning tool and be able to incorporate it into the classroom. The educator is the key to the implementation of educational reform (Schofield, 1997). Educators' knowledge, skill, and philosophy determine their instructional methods (Staub & Stern, 2002) and have significant effects on the students that they teach (Brophy & Good, 1986). Educators ultimately determine whether and how computers will be used (Mercer & Fischer, 1992; Sanders & Horn, 1994).

Becker (1994) compared American educators who were either exemplary or non-exemplary in their use of computers for instruction. Becker assessed goals for computer use, student use of computers, and the role of computers in the classroom. In comparison to those educators that did not fit the exemplary category, the exemplary educators spent twice as many hours non-class time on school computers, had more formal training in computers, had more teaching experience, more postgraduate education, and were more likely to have majored in math, science, social science, or humanities rather than education. Clearly, individual training and experience play an important role in predicting who is most likely to become an exemplary educator in the use of technology.

Successful integration depends on the appropriate matching of educator's pedagogical beliefs (Flowerday & Schraw, 2000), content knowledge, technology expertise, and learning objectives (Valdez et al., 2005). Educators' beliefs about their efficacy with computers are also related to adoption of innovative practices, such that stronger beliefs are correlated with a willingness to experiment with the innovation and with the eventual adoption of the practice (Evers, Brouwers, & Tomic, 2002; Fuchs, Fuchs, & Bishop, 1992). In a recent examination of the relative impact of these individual characteristics on Canadian educators, Mueller and Wood (2006) confirmed the importance of computer use at home, comfort with computers, and beliefs related to the use of computers as important for instruction.

Apart from the individual role of the educator, it is also important to consider the environment in which learning takes place. Barriers and sup-ports for the use of technology have been identified across the past several decades of research.

What are the barriers and supports?

The rapid advances in computer technology and the resulting changes within schools make it challenging to evaluate the impact of some of the barriers identified in the past; they also make it difficult to identify poten-tial barriers that may affect educators in the future. For example, given the high prevalence of technology in most Western schools today, access issues that were highlighted in the early 1990s may no longer be relevant. Indeed, short term longitudinal studies have found significant changes in computer use and technical issues over periods as brief as two years (Conlon & Simp-son, 2003).

As educators progress through the different phases of integration, the barriers become more technical. At first, even simple interventions such as providing educators with information and practice using computer tech-nology reduces the common obstacle—familiarity with technology (Hadley & Sheingold, 1993; Wood, Willoughby, Specht, Stern-Cavalcante, & Child, 2002). Previous research has suggested that although educators may see the potential of computer technology, they need sufficient resources in terms of computer equipment, curriculum-compatible software, technical support, and human resources (Wood et al., 2002; Wood et al., 2005).

The means for identifying barriers in past research typically involved surveying educators and administrators (Becker, 1994). There are several concerns when reviewing the conclusions from these studies. First, there is the concern of generalizing from more dated research to present times. Second, and perhaps more important, there is also the concern that even if these barriers still exist, they may not represent the issues perceived by educators as most critical. When educators respond to closed survey items rather than open-ended questions, only the issues questioned can be evalu-ated. There may be other more pertinent issues that have not been identified. In addition, some previously identified barriers may still be important, but the nature of these barriers may have changed. Such questions can only be assessed through direct and extensive communication with the frontline practitioners—educators.

Clearly, changes are occurring with respect to the integration of technology in the classroom (Windschitl & Sahl, 2002). In many cases, there is a reported shift in the educator's role, with educators assuming the role of facilitator (e.g., Schofield, 1997), interacting with students more, and conducting fewer whole-group lessons. Long term changes, however, are slow (e.g., Sandholtz et al., 1997) and mechanisms that support these changes, like the barriers that inhibit them, are not wholly understood. Previously identified supports, such as in-house specialists, technical support, administrative support, and opportunities for training (Hadley & Sheingold, 1993; Sandholtz et al., 1997) have face value validity. Educators' instructional aims and purposes (Dexter, Anderson, & Becker, 1999), their beliefs about instruction (Ravitz, Becker, & Wong, 2000), the degree of professional involvement and collaboration (Becker & Riel, 2000; Ronnkvist, Dexter, & Anderson, 2000), and the school principal's leadership for technology use (Anderson & Dexter, 2001) have been identified as having an impact. However, the relative importance of these supports and others is best understood when educators identify their own concerns.

Hearing the educator's voice

In a study of Canadian educators that combined traditional survey methodology with focus group methodology (Wood et al., 2005), educators identified the most critical barriers and supports to computer integration in their classrooms. Educators were asked to provide their perceptions of computer implementation in elementary and secondary classrooms, describe what computers are used for, where they are used, what integration means to individual educators, what supports their use of technology, and what, if anything, still stands in the way of successful implementation.

When educators responded to closed survey questions, consistent with previous research, educators had experience with computers both at home and at school (Becker, 2000; Collis et al., 1996; Conlon & Simpson, 2003). In addition, use of technology predicted greater comfort with technology, and comfort with technology was the only significant predictor of integration of technology in the curriculum (Becker, 1994; Hadley & Sheingold, 1993). Together, this pattern of outcomes suggests that one of the most critical features for the integration of technology is the individual educator's level of experience and comfort with technology.

When educators had an opportunity to express their thoughts in an open environment (i.e., focus groups), two things became very salient. First, the integration of technology is an emotionally charged issue, and second, educators can clearly identify barriers and supports to computer integration. However, with respect to emotion, the majority of responses were neither simply negative nor positive. Instead the greatest portion of discussion was accounted for by a "complex category" which was comprised of both positive and negative affect statements.

The complex category spoke to the barriers in the integration process.

Educators were excited about using computers and stated that computers are a useful tool, but the lack of money and time for training, equipment breakdowns, and lack of time to develop lessons and incorporate computers in the curriculum, were all discussed as obstacles to successful integration.

Positive affect was most prevalent when educators told success stories of using computers to explore databases, create legible reports, do simulations, support peer tutors, and research current information. They were enthusiastic about sharing accomplishments and acknowledging the support from their students and colleagues. Educators saw computers as a functioning part of their environment when resources were adequate and available. However, when hardware, software, and personnel to manage computers were limited, educators were frustrated and searching for help. In these portions of the discussion, participants indicated resentment about support that had been taken away, including technical personnel, release time for educator experts, and librarians.

Some differences were noted across levels of instruction. Elementary educators were quite positive about human resources and educator characteristics but there were definite individual differences. Some of the educators were struggling with the rapid pace of change and novelty of computer technology. They made note of their own weaknesses and the lack of time to become an "expert" before the next innovation was introduced. Others embraced the knowledge and computer skills of students, and the resources available to them. Secondary educators focused on access difficulties, such as the inability to book a computer lab, and computers that did not have the capabilities to run current software. Their negative comments were often directed at a mismatch between content-heavy curriculum requirements and the knowledge construction possible using technology.

The specific supports and barriers were captured through six major themes. See Table 11.1 for themes and subthemes.

Overall, time was identified as a persistent barrier by educators in terms of fitting in curriculum, planning lessons, troubleshooting computer glitches, and educator training and development. This may be a reflection of the constantly changing face of technology, where educators find themselves in the role of a perpetual novice (Wood et al., 2005). The rapidity of change and the flexibility needed to plan around such a dynamic system increases workload, vigilance, and frustration to a level not experienced in other lesson preparations. For example, educators described situations where they created lesson plans only to find out that they were unable to deliver them due to malfunctions or the unavailability of websites.

It is clear, however, that the level of external support offered to educators plays a critical role (e.g., Becker, 1994; Sandholtz et al., 1997). In fact, external support might be the necessary prerequisite to having all educators,

Table 11.1. Content themes extracted from focus group transcriptions.

Theme and Subtheme	Definition and Example
I. Support Issues	Discussion surrounding the presence or absence of support for computer integration.
a. Material resources	Discussion of material resources referred to the presence or absence of material resources including equipment, software, programs, and systems. Educators also made frequent reference to the allocation and distribution of equipment and financial support. Internet resources were included as a material resource.
	E.g., "I think our school is pretty computer-rich, but even with you know 600 kids sharing basically 40 computers around the school, that sounds like a lot, it's more than a lot of schools have, but it is not enough to teach adequately . . ."
b. Human resources	Human resources referred to the presence or absence of people or their positions, including technicians, computer contacts or administrators, computer experts, and librarians. Also, general references were sometimes made about a need for supervision of students during computer instruction and the need for smaller classes.
	E.g., ". . . and the librarian was supporting little mini enrichment groups across the grades and so now, as you say, what's going to happen . . . The library is closed for half the day. It does, and then you can't go in there without supervision to these computers."
c. Training and professional development	This category referred to the presence or absence of training programs or opportunities, evaluation of those programs, and/or discussion of a need for training as a support for implementation and use of computers.
	E.g., "I think, I mean, I think the school board over the years has done a great job at offering courses on software, learning software packages, and stuff, um. I know I've, over the last, you know, 5–10 years, I've taken probably 20 or 30 courses on software just to learn it and I mean when new stuff came out, you learn it and you kind of get a starting point that you can then go from to kind of discover on your own and you know that stuff. I think the school board's done a good job from that area."

d. Admin-istrative and parental support	This category referred to the presence or absence of support for computer implementation in general or specific ways from government, administration, or parents. Communication among administration, departments, and educators regarding computers was also a topic of discussion included in this category.

E.g., "Ha, but the major frustration being though that although the curriculum and the government are asking us to do all these wonderful programs and I believe in the validity of that, but they're not keeping up with their end of the bargain and providing us with things that are workable with the classes that you have." |
| **II. Educator Issues** | Issues that were related to individual educators and their philosophy, skills, or specific curriculum concerns. |
| *a. Philosophy/ pedagogy* | This category referred to beliefs about if, when, and how computers fit within teaching and learning. References to the computer as a tool were part of this subcategory. Teaching methods, strategies, and examples of computer-related activities were also included.

E.g., "Yeah. Get bio's, get any specs on the movie that they can get. So it's a really useful tool in terms of accessibility of information for me because of course I teach English so I don't use it in the same way that you would use computers but, um . . ." |
| *b. Skills and characteristics* | This category included references to the skills, knowledge, comfort, and experience level of educators who do or do not use computers. Statements that referred to the time or interest an individual educator spends with computers were included here.

E.g., "I find myself, um, anxious to use a computer, but at the same time I'm very much a . . . user . . . I'm not as familiar with computer technology, with the background." |
| *c. Curriculum* | This category refers to curriculum guidelines and expectations. Discussions surrounding "too much stuff to fit into the curriculum" are also included here.

E.g., "And I would say that's a general problem, just as a teacher-librarian and seeing all different subject areas, one of the major complaints is, again we'll talk here about the government and curriculum, is that it is so content-driven, . . . as a result a lot of things that were extremely worthwhile to do, including giving your classes time to say go work in a lab or go work in the library on an assignment, the teachers aren't doing it anymore . . ." |

d. Digital divide	Specific references were made to a division in terms of computer experience and/or expertise between educators or between educator and student.
	E.g., "But an awful lot of the kids at the grade level that I am teaching have way more expertise than the teachers."

III. Context and Access	Discussion topics that were coded into this category referred to issues surrounding the location in which computers were placed in the school. There also were issues surrounding the access to the computers in these locations.
a. Access	Discussion in this category revolved around the ability or lack of ability to book labs, find time in the schedule for computer use, and generally gain access to computers and software.
	E.g., "The thing is it's difficult to book in times for your class to use the computer lab because there are so many classes and ah, there will be times in the year when for example the grade 3's are all doing that learning how to type thing."
b. Context	This category included references to the set-up and consequences of where computers are used (i.e. in a lab, classroom, pod, or library).
	E.g., "Now nobody's facing you, everybody's spinning around and I mean, the classes next year, our classes are going to balloon again, and uh, I mean this year it was great, I had small classes, you were able to do a lot with them. Next year, again, and when you want, if you get computers in your classroom, now the students are shut off from the teacher unless you've got such small classes that they can work in one part of your room and then you can move them to doing something else in the other half of your room. But some schools have really teeny rooms."

IV. Student Issues	Direct reference to students and computers were also made but to a lesser extent than the support and educator issues.
a. Motivation, skills, and characteristics	This category included discussion about the knowledge and skills that students have or need, as well as their motivation, opinions, and feelings surrounding computer use. Educators also made comments about differences and difficulties related to the developmental stages and characteristics of students.
	E.g., "They all have videogames, mind you, and so they view a computer as an extension. It's just a videogame and, um, as far as knowing anything that they're doing, they don't. It's just random play . . ."

b. Digital divide	Specific references were made to a distinction among students according to computer access and/or computer skill. Differences also were identified between the computer systems students used at home and those available at school in terms of quality and Internet speed.
	E.g., "And they're always complaining about how outmoded our computers are at the school compared to the ones they have at home."
c. Sabotage	Some discussion included problems related to vandalism or sabotage of computers by students. Reference to hackers or students interrupting the operating system was included here as well.
	E.g., "That would become dangerous in my school because I have kids who could hack into it and change it."
V. Hardware and Software Problems	Issues discussed at this level concerned not the presence or absence of resources but problems using those resources in terms of malfunctions, compatibility, and change.
a. Mal-functions	Educators reported a number of problems and frustrations with equipment breakdowns or "glitches" in the operating systems or Internet functioning.
	E.g., "We have computers in all the shops and other rooms but we have as you're experiencing, once a week the server goes down and takes out three or four classrooms at the same time . . . that is if the power doesn't go down completely!"
b. Compati-bility	Specific references were made to problems arising from incompatibility of equipment and/or software. Educators reported problems with computers that were not all the same.
	E.g., "I bought a book by mistake at —— on keyboard shortcuts which was really dumb. I'll never use it because the keyboard shortcuts for Corel and the keyboard shortcuts for PageMaker, they're not the same, and Adobe isn't the same, in Adobe PageMaker and Illustrator. That's another frustration too but that's programming."
c. Pace of change and outdated equipment	Some problems were identified as being related to the pace of change in technology and the presence or use of outdated equipment or software.
	E.g., "And then as soon as you've taken that course that software is outdated. I've taken several and gotten pretty happy about what I'm doing with this particular software, and the next thing you know that won't load on this computer any more."

VI. External Issues and Other Priorities	External issues and other priorities accounted for less than 3% of the discussion for both elementary and secondary educators. The issues raised included references to the use of computers in the wider community (beyond the school), technical assistance available from corporate programs, and the priority of textbooks beyond computers.
a. Corporate programs	E.g., "I guess the other thing I guess we didn't mention is that there is a program called, ah, Libraries to Schools or something along that, where you can get free computers, old computers from businesses . . . they get refurbished and then the school board sends them out if you request them and there's no cost but there's no service once you get them."
b. Community resources	E.g., "Well at my husband's work everything is done on the computer. If he is signing up for anything to do with human resources, anything to do with a benefit plan, anything to with anything, they do not use paper and it's all, it's all on computer and I don't know if our kids could . . . could do it."
c. Textbooks	E.g., "You won't know until the year starts which textbook your educator chose." "Exactly, we haven't decided yet." "You won't know in terms of planning so I'm wondering what kind of impact that may have. Are they going to put some things online? I feel they have to address this issue because really, the money is not there for the textbooks. What's going to happen to these students that can't take home a textbook? Where are they going to get the material from?"

regardless of individual differences, integrate technology in the curriculum. Indeed, the focal point for the majority of discussions in the focus groups centerd on support. Educators highlighted the need for personnel and material resources to support their integration of technology. There was also indication that the support needed to be near at hand and consistent with the needs of the moment—suggesting that just-in-time instruction would be deemed most effective. (Wood et al., 2005)

Educators have many demands on their time and their skills, from curriculum issues to student management and accountability. The integration of technology is not only an innovation but may also require changes in the actual role of the educator (Becker, 1994; Hadley & Sheingold, 1993; Reil & Becker, 2000; Schofield, 1995).

Van den Berg (2002) suggests that educators' reactions to externally imposed expectations (in this case, computer integration) and changing internal conditions (the role of educator and, possibly, changes in ped-

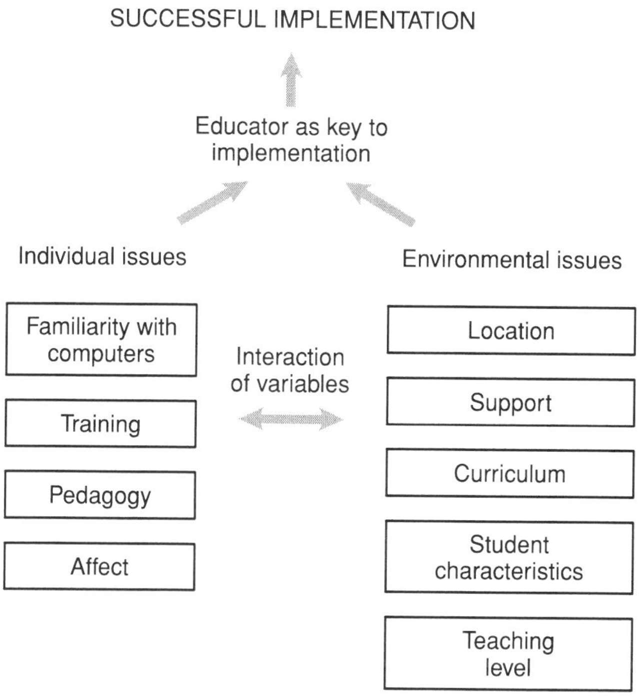

SUCCESSFUL IMPLEMENTATION

Educator as key to
implementation

Individual issues   Environmental issues

| Familiarity with computers |
| Interaction of variables |

| Location |

| Support |

| Training |

| Pedagogy |

| Curriculum |

| Affect |

| Student characteristics |

| Teaching level |

Figure 11.1. Framework for examining the implementation of computer technology.

agogy) are often "ambiguous, filled with emotion, and even contradictory" (p. 580). These more subjective components must also be recognized and considered in any form of program development or support.

Although many of the barriers identified by these educators (knowledge, time, comfort level, support, and technical issues) were also identified in past research (e.g., Anderson, 1996; Conlon & Simpson, 2003; Cuban et al., 2001; Schofield, 1995), some barriers were less prevalent (limited number of computers, technical difficulties, and computer anxiety), suggesting that the focus of computer integration has shifted from hardware/software/technical concerns to individual and wider environment-based influences. A visual summary of the barriers and supports that limit and facilitate the integration of computer technology is presented in Figure 11.1. The two key variables are the individual educator and the environment in which the educator works.

The framework outlined in Figure 11.1 depicts the global issues that educators perceive to be important, and hence sets the groundwork for further investigation of factors that predict integration of technology in different environments and across different groups of individuals. In this framework, the educator is the key to our understanding of what is currently happening within the schools. What is needed now, however, is to consider how these variables interact and what interventions can mediate the barriers to computer integration.

Part II The Special Case: Early Childhood Education (ECE) Environments

It is no surprise that computer technology has started to become a prevalent feature in ECE environments where our youngest learners could potentially reap the benefits from early exposure to it (e.g., Ko, 2002; Schofield, 1997; Shade & Watson, 1990; Wood, 2001). Along with the promise of increased learning opportunities for these students, however, the presence of computer technology brings additional burdens and responsibilities for educators of small children (e.g., Becker & Ravitz, 2001; Rosen & Weil, 1995; Specht, Wood, & Willoughby, 2002).

What is different about the ECE context?

As noted earlier in this chapter, the research with elementary and secondary school educators points to a number of potential variables that can affect the integration of computers in these higher grades. Intuitively, it would appear that many of these barriers and supports also would apply in an ECE setting. This environment, however, has features that make it unique from higher-grade contexts. Specifically, the learners are younger, less skilled verbally and physically, less independent in their ability to work alone, and less knowledgeable. In addition, there are management issues facing early childhood educators that differ from educators in the higher grades. In early childhood education contexts, formal learning situations are shorter (for example, circle time) and less frequent; there are more transitions between activities; there is less seatwork, more active hands-on exploration, and more supervision. These unique elements may require supports and produce barriers to the integration of technology that are not found in higher-grade environments.

In addition, the infrastructure of early childcare environments (daycares, preschools, nurseries, etc.) differs markedly from elementary or secondary school systems. Elementary and secondary grades typically have a specified curriculum that is prescribed and monitored by external agencies (e.g., school boards, governments, etc.). Most early childcare environments, on the other hand, are independent facilities. Many are privately owned and operated, and the curriculum is developed within the center. As a function of being an independent organization, opportunities for in-service instruction, technical support, and funding for technology requires that the center solicit external support—typically from the private sector on an ad hoc basis. Together these specific features of early childhood education make it important to investigate early integration separately from elementary and secondary environments.

What are the perceptions toward introducing computer technology in the ECE setting?

The introduction of computer technology for very young learners has met with both support (e.g., Shade & Watson, 1990) and concern (e.g., Barnes & Hill, 1983; Elkind, 1996). Initially, there were fears that using computers with preschoolers would result in poorer social skills, less active learning opportunities, and fewer age-appropriate play activities (e.g., Barnes & Hill, 1983; Kaden, 1990; Zajonc, 1984). Subsequent research revealed, however, that computers could facilitate social, cognitive, and play development among very young learners when handled appropriately (e.g., Kelly & Schorger, 2001; Ko, 2002; Muller & Perlmutter, 1985; Narrol, 1997; Podmore, 1991; Sandberg, 2002; Schofield, 1995). However, debates regarding the value and desirability of computers for young learners continue (e.g., Plowman & Stephen, 2003). Given the debates within the literature, it is important to investigate the perceptions of the early childhood educators who experience the effects of computers directly.

How do early childhood educators feel about integrating computer technology?

Research indicates that educators in ECE contexts support the integration of computer technology in their classrooms (Specht et al., 2002; Wood, Willoughby, & Specht, 1998); but, similar to the elementary and secondary educators, they may require more exposure to computers, and more training, in order to provide greater confidence in their ability to use it effectively and comfortably (Wood et al., 2002).

In a recent study (Wood, Specht, Willoughby, & Mueller, 2006), the majority of early childhood educators concurred with early childhood educators sampled in previous studies in their support of computers as potentially positive additions to the ECE environment (Specht et al., 2002; Tsitouridou & Vryzas, 2003). In particular, computers were perceived to be a highly motivating alternative means for providing instructional opportunities that satisfied the general constraints of a child-centered approach. Computers were generally depicted as providing an additional or alternative activity for children, or as an independent learning tool. None of the educators identified the computer as a central means of instruction.

This characterization of computers as an ancillary rather than a central feature of instruction echoes one of the ongoing debates in the elementary and secondary school literatures. Specifically, current discussion suggests that there are two ways of incorporating computers into the classroom: one views computers as an additional add-on activity, and the other involves more extensive integration where the computer is used as a medium for instruction (e.g., Conlon & Simpson, 2003; Goos, Galbraith, Renshaw, & Geiger, 2003). This latter form of integration may not be possible given the present limitations in resources in the ECE environment. For example, educators would not have enough computers to engage groups of children interactively on the computers since, on average, only one computer was available in each center. In such settings, perhaps limited computer resources are driving the instructional use of computers rather than pedagogy.

Alternatively, it may be that early childhood educators do not perceive the full integration of computers as appropriate for their young learners. Indeed, some educators voiced concern that computers should be limited to specific programming goals or contexts and identified potential risks to social development from the integration of technology, similar to the concerns that were identified in the early literature in this area (e.g., Barnes & Hill, 1983; Kaden, 1990; Zajonc, 1984). These concerns were seen as especially salient for the youngest children at their centers. First, children were perceived to have less time to interact with peers, observe peer models, and engage in social problem solving during these critical early years. Second, there was a concern that young children would be engaged with an inanimate object rather than with their peers. Clearly, concern about the potential social impact of computers is an ongoing issue in the literature and an important one for these educators, with both positive and negative outcomes being identified (Attewell, Suazo-Garcia, & Battle, 2003; Healy, 1998).

Interestingly, educators only targeted social concerns for the younger children at the centers (children under 3). Among the older children (4- and 5-year-olds), computers were perceived as promoting cooperative activity and also providing an outlet for individual quiet time. The educators highlighted modifications to the classroom setting that could maximize social interaction when using computers, such as providing multiple chairs around the computer and providing access for more than one child on the computer at any given time. Modifications such as these could be used to encourage peer interaction while using the computer and reduce educators' concerns about isolation (Willoughby, Wood, Leacy, & Wells, 2001).

Early exposure to computer technology was perceived as providing the fundamental skills that would prepare the children for school and for future use of computers. In addition, having computers available in the centers was perceived as "[leveling] out the playing field for those who don't have computers at home," and hence as remedying some of the potential effects of the digital divide. Early childhood education centers, then, may be in the unique position to offer children fundamental learning opportunities that are not available at home.

For younger children, computers were perceived as physically challenging because of immature motor skills. Existing literature also highlights the motoric, cognitive, and spatial challenges for novice computer users inherent in different input devices (Scaife & Bond, 1991; Thomas & Milan, 1987; Wood, Willoughby, Schmidt, Porter, Specht, & Gilbert, 2004). In some cases the physical requirements involved with more demanding devices such as the mouse can be reduced by using alternative less demanding devices (e.g., Thomas & Milan, 1987; Wood et al., 2004). These alternative devices, however, entail additional expenses which may strain or exceed available resources.

With respect to achieving educational goals, computers were seen as offering "variety to the curriculum" as well as being an available resource for information. Specific advantages for children included the motivational appeal of the computer; its speed, color, and dynamic presentation; opportunity for individualized instruction and independent learning; and the ability to do something and see an immediate effect. Together, these qualities indicate the richness of computer technology and its unique potential to enhance the instructional environment.

A number of limitations and barriers to the integration of computer technology in the classroom were identified. Concerns included problems with managing children's access to the computers as well as training and technical/financial issues. Specifically, educators highlighted challenges in moving and supervising children in order to access computers which were restricted to one location within the center, thus making their use impractical. In addition, children argued over their time on the computers; some children seemed consumed by them. Thus there were definite concerns about maintaining a balance or setting limits on computer time. There also were worries about the computer becoming a babysitter, like the television. Anticipating management issues related to access, turn-taking, and supervision requirements would be an essential requirement to the successful integration of computer technology.

Limited resources, both in the structure of the center (i.e., electrical outlets) and in the number of computers available, yielded additional concerns. Consistent with previous research (Wood, Willoughby, & Specht, 1998), access to hardware, software, and funding to support ongoing renewal was felt to be a distinct disadvantage for integrating computers in the classroom.

Supporting computer technology in the ECE environment may be a particular challenge because these programs are not government funded, networked, or organized through a central administration unit. Hence each center is isolated, increasing the pressures on individual early childhood educators. Consistent with previous research (e.g., Specht et al., 2002), these educators perceived that lack of training and comfort with technology, coupled with limited technological support resources, may have important implications for the selection of appropriate hardware and software for the children they supervise. Specifically, there was limited support (either external or internal to the center) to assist in the selection of appropriate software, or to facilitate the selection, maintenance, and trouble-shooting of computers; nor were there resources for consultation regarding the integration of technology in their classrooms. The absence of external resources necessitates that ECE educators themselves select, acquire, and implement technology. ECE educators must be familiar with the technology to the extent that they can facilitate its implementation with their young students, as well as manage basic issues related to selection and use of appropriate hardware and software (e.g., Clements, 1995; Samaras, 1996).

In summary, early childhood educators have the motivation, the interest, and the desire to introduce and use computer technology in their centers. They perceive support for the integration of computers from the parents of the children they supervise. The caveats, however, are that the computer technology must be age-appropriate to the learner, reflect the skills promoted through ECE environments, allow for ease of use without compromising safety and supervision of children, and be accompanied by sufficient training and support for the educator.

There is limited research that examines the impact of integrating computer technology from the perspective of early childhood educators (Specht et al., 2002; Tsitouridou & Vryzas, 2003; Wood et al., 2002). Because these educators may serve a pivotal role in introducing children to computer technology, it is critical that we understand their perspective, concerns, and needs. Further, it is important that researchers in the area of early childhood education continue to investigate the integration of computers in order to provide answers to the concerns and provide explicit examples of the opportunities that computer integration can offer for very young learners.

In summary, educators at all levels experience challenges and supports in the integration of computer technology in their classrooms. The onus is on researchers, educators, and schools to find ways to make technology available, accessible, and effective so that students have the best opportunity for learning in this digital world.

Acknowledgments

Support for this research was provided by a grant to Eileen Wood and Teena Willoughby from the Canadian Language and Literacy Research Network.

References

Abbey, B. (2003). *Instructional and cognitive impacts of web-based education.* Hershey, PA: Idea Group Publishing.

Abrami, P. C. (2001). Understanding and promoting complex learning using technology. *Educational Research and Evaluation, 7*, 113–136.

Anderson, A. A. (1996). Predictors of computer anxiety and performance in information systems. *Computers in Human Behavior, 12*, 61–77.

Anderson, R. E., & Dexter, S. (2001). *School technology leadership: Incidence and impact. Report #6 from the Teaching, Learning, and Computing 1998 Survey.* Irvine, CA: Center for Research on Information, Technology, and Organizations at University of California, Irvine. Retrieved from http://www.crito.uci.edu/tlc/html/finding.html

Attewell, P., Suazo-Garcia, & Battle, J. (2003). Computers and young children: Social benefit or social problem? *Social Force, 82*, 277–296.

Barnes, B., & Hill, S. (1983, May). Should young children work with microcomputers—Logo before Lego? *The Computing Teacher*, 11–14.

Becker, H. J. (1994). How exemplary computer-using teachers differ from other teachers: Implications for realizing the potential of computers in schools. *Journal of Research on Computing in Education, 31*(4), 356–385.

Becker, H. J. (2000). Who's wired and who's not: Children's access to and use of computer technology. *The Future of Children, 10*, 44–75.

Becker, H. J., & Ravitz, J. L. (2001). *Computer use by teachers: Are Cuban's predictions correct?* Paper presented at the 2001 Annual meeting of the American Educational Researchers Association, Seattle.

Becker, H. J., & Riel, M. M. (2000). *Teacher professional engagement and constructivist-compatible computer use.* Report no. 7 for Centre for Research on Information, Technologies and Organizations, University of California, Irvine and University of Minnesota.

Brophy, J. E., & Good, T. L. (1986). Teacher behavior and student achievement. In M. C. Wittrock (Ed.), *Handbook of research on teaching* (3rd ed., pp. 328–375). New York: Macmillan.

Chambers, B., Abrami, P., McWhaw, K., & Therrien, M. C. (2001). Developing a computer-assisted tutoring program to help children at risk to learn to read. *Educational Research & Evaluation, 7*, 223–239.

Clements, D. H. (1995). Teaching creativity with computers. *Educational Psychology Review, 7*, 141–161.

Collis, B. A., Knezek, G. A., Lai, K., Miyashita, K. T., Pelgrum, W. J., Plomp, T., et al. (1996). *Children and computers in school.* Mahwah, NJ: Lawrence Erlbaum.

Conlon, T., & Simpson, M. (2003). Silicon Valley versus Silicon Glen: The impact of computers upon teaching and learning: A comparative study. *British Journal of Educational Technology, 34*, 137–150.

Cuban, L. (2001). *Oversold and underused: Computers in the classroom.* Cambridge, MA: Harvard University Press.

Cuban, L., Kirkpatrick, H., & Peck, C. (2001). High access and low use of technologies in high school classrooms: Explaining an apparent paradox. *American Educational Research Journal, 38,* 813–834.

Demetriadis, S., Barbas, A., Molohides, A., Palaigeorgiou, G., Psillos, D., Vlahavas, I., et al. (2003). "Cultures in negotiation": Teachers' acceptance/resistance attitudes considering the infusion of technology into schools. *Computers and Education, 41,* 19–37.

Dexter, S. L., Anderson, R. E., & Becker, H. J. (1999). Teachers' views of computers as catalysts for changes in their teaching practice. *Journal of Research on Computing in Education, 31,* 221–239.

Elkind, D. (1996). Young children and technology: A cautionary note. *Young Children, 51*(6), 22–23.

Ertl, H., & Plante, J. (2004). *Connectivity and learning in Canada's schools.* Research paper no. 56F0004MIE—no. 011, Science, Innovation and Electronic Information Division. Ottawa, Ontario: Statistics Canada.

Evers, W. J. G., Brouwers, A., & Tomic, W. (2002). Burnout and self-efficacy: A study on teachers' beliefs when implementing an innovative educational system in the Netherlands. *British Journal of Educational Psychology, 72,* 227–243.

Flowerday, T., & Schraw, G. (2000). Teacher beliefs about instructional choice: A phenomenological study. *Journal of Educational Psychology, 92,* 634–645.

Fuchs, L. S., Fuchs, D., & Bishop, N. (1992). Instructional adaptation for students at risk. *Journal of Educational Research, 86,* 70–84.

Goos, M., Galbraith, P., Renshaw, P., & Geiger, V. (2003). Perspectives on technology mediated learning in secondary school mathematics classrooms. *Journal of Mathematical Behaviour, 22,* 73–89.

Greene, B. (2000). *Teachers' tools for the 21st century: A report on teachers' use of technology.* Washington, DC: US Department of Education, Office of Educational Research and Development.

Hadley, M., & Sheingold, K. (1993). How exemplary computer-using teachers differ from other teachers: Implications for realizing the potential of computers in school. *Journal of Research on Computing in Education, 26,* 291–321.

Healy, J. (1998). *Failure to connect.* New York: Simon & Schuster.

Hokanson, B., & Hooper, S. (2000). Computer as cognitive media: Examining the potential of computers in education. *Computers in Human Behavior, 16,* 537–552.

Kaden, M. (1990). Issues on computers and early childhood education. In C. Seefeldt (Ed.), *Continuing Issues in Early Childhood Education* (pp. 261–275). New York: Teachers College Press.

Kelly, K., & Schorger, J. (2001). "Let's play puters": Expressive language use at the computer centre. *Information Technology in Childhood Education Annual, 12,* 125–138.

Ko, S. (2002). An empirical analysis of children's thinking and learning in a computer game context. *Educational Psychology, 22*(2), 219–233.

Lian Chua, S., Chen, D., & Wong, A. F. L. (1999). Computer anxiety and its correlates: A meta-analysis. *Computers in Human Behavior, 15,* 609–623.

Mayer, R. E., & Moreno, R. (2002). Aids to computer-based multimedia learning. *Learning & Instruction, 12*, 107–119.

Mercer, N., & Fisher, E. (1992). How do teachers help children learn? An analysis of teachers' interventions in computer-based activities. *Learning and Instruction, 2*, 339–355.

Moreno, R., & Mayer, R. E. (2002). Learning science in virtual reality multimedia environments: Role of methods and media. *Journal of Educational Psychology, 94*, 598–610.

Mueller, J., & Wood, E. (2006, May). *Predicting computer integration in elementary and secondary classrooms: Individual characteristics of teachers.* Paper presented at the Canadian Society for Studies in Education Annual Conference, Toronto, Ontario.

Muir-Herzig, R. G. (2004). Technology and its impact in the classroom. *Computers & Education, 42*, 111–131.

Muller, A., & Perlmutter, M. (1985). Preschool children's problem-solving interactions at computers and jigsaw puzzles. *Journal of Applied Developmental Psychology, 6*, 173–186.

Narroll, H. (1997). Computers, thinking, and education. In M. Luther & E. Cole (Eds.), *Dynamic assessment for instruction: From theory to application* (pp. 221–224). North York, Ontario, Canada: Captus Press.

Pelgrum, W. J. (1992). International research on computers in education. *Prospects, 22*, 341–349.

Pelgrum, W. J. (2001). Obstacles to the integration of ICT in education: Results from a worldwide educational assessment. *Computers & Education, 37*, 163–178.

Plowman, J., & Stephen, C. (2003). A "benign addition"? Research on ICT and pre-school children. *Journal of Computer Assisted Learning, 19*(2), 149–164.

Podmore, V. N. (1991). 4-year-olds, 6-year-olds, and microcomputers: A study of perceptions and social behaviors. *Journal of Applied Developmental Psychology, 12*, 87–101.

Poynton, T. A. (2005). Computer literacy across the lifespan: A review with implications for educators. *Computers in Human Behavior, 21*, 861–872.

Ravitz, J. L., Becker, H. J., & Wong, Y. (2000). *Constructivist-compatible beliefs and practices among U. S. Teachers.* Report #4 from the Teaching, Learning, and Computing 1998 Survey. Irvine, CA: Center for Research on Information, Technology, and Organizations at University of California, Irvine. Retrieved from http://www.crito.uci.edu/tlc/html/finding.html

Richardson, V. (2003). Constructivist pedagogy. *Teachers College Record, 105*, 1623–1640.

Riel, M., & Becker, H. (2000, April 26). *The beliefs, practices, and computer use of teachers.* Paper presented at the American Educational Research Association, New Orleans.

Ronnkvist, A., Dexter, S. L., & Anderson, R. E. (2000). *Technology support: Its depth, breadth and impact in America's school.* Report no. 5 for Center for Research on Information, Technologies and Organizations, University of California, Irvine and University of Minnesota.

Rosen, L. D., & Maguire, P. D. (1990). Myths and realities of computerphobia: A meta-analysis. *Anxiety Research, 3,* 175–191.

Rosen, L. D., & Weil, M. M. (1995). Computer availability, computer experience and technophobia among public school teachers. *Computers in Human Behavior, 11,* 9–31.

Saettler, P. (1990). *The evolution of American educational technology.* Englewood, CO: Libraries Unlimited.

Samaras, A. P. (1996). Children's computers. *Childhood Education, 72,* 133–136.

Sandberg, A. (2002). Preschool teachers' conceptions of computers and play. *Information Technology in Childhood Education Annual, 14,* 245–262.

Sanders, W. L., & Horn, S. P. (1994). The Tennessee Value-Added Assessment System (TVAAS): Mixed-model methodology in educational assessment. *Journal of Personnel Evaluation in Education, 8,* 299–311.

Sandholtz, J. H., Ringstaff, C., & Dwyer, D. C. (1997). *Teaching with technology. Creating student-centred classrooms.* New York: Teachers College Press.

Scaife, M., & Bond, R. (1991). Developmental changes in children's use of input devices. *Early Childhood Development and Care, 69,* 19–38.

Scansoft, Inc., Peabody, MA (2007). http://www.dragonsys.com

Schofield, J. (1995). *Computers and classroom culture.* Cambridge, UK: Cambridge University Press.

Schofield, J. (1997). Computers and classroom social processes—a review of the literature. *Social Science Computer Review, 15,* 27–39.

Scott, T., Cole, M., & Engel, M. (1992). Computers and education: A cultural constructivist perspective. *Review of Research in Education, 18,* 191–251.

Shade, D. D., & Watson, J. A. (1990). Computers in early education: Issues put to rest, theoretical links to sound practice, and the potential contribution of microworlds. *Journal of Educational Computing Research, 6,* 375–392.

Specht, J., Wood, E., & Willoughby, T. (2002). What early childhood educators want to know about computers. *Canadian Journal of Learning and Technology, 28,* 31–40.

Staub, F. C., & Stern, E. (2002). The nature of teachers' pedagogical content beliefs matter for students' achievement gains: Quasi-experimental evidence from elementary mathematics. *Journal of Educational Psychology, 94,* 344–355.

Steinberg, E. R. (1991). *Computer-assisted instruction. A synthesis of theory, practice, and technology.* Hillsdale, NJ: Lawrence Erlbaum.

Sutherland, R., Armstrong, V., Barnes, S., Brawn, R., Breeze, N., Gall, M., et al. (2004). Transforming teaching and learning: Embedding ICT into everyday classroom practices. *Journal of Computer Assisted Learning, 20,* 413–425.

Thomas, C., & Milan, S. (1987). Which input device should be used with interactive video? In H. Bullinger & B. Schackel (Eds.), *Human Computer Interaction-Interact '87.* Amsterdam: Elsevier.

Tsitouridou, M., & Vryzas, K. (2003). Early childhood teachers' attitudes towards computer and information technology: The case of Greece. *Information Technology in Childhood Education Annual, 15,* 187–207.

Valdez, G., McNabb, M., Foertsch, M., Anderson, M., Hawkes, M., & Raack, L.

(2005). Computer-based technology and learning: Evolving uses and expectations. North Central Regional Educational Laboratory. Retrieved from http://www.ncrel.org/tplan/cbtl/toc.htm

Van den Berg, R. (2002). Teachers' meanings regarding educational practice. *Review of Educational Research, 72,* 577–625.

Vygotsky, L. (1978). *Mind in society: The development of higher psychological processes.* Cambridge, MA: Harvard University Press.

Willoughby, T., Wood, E., Leacy, K., & Wells, J. (2001, April). *Gender and social interaction as a function of availability of computers with preschoolers and elementary school children.* Paper presented at the Annual Convention of the American Educational Research Association, Seattle, Washington.

Wilson, J. D., Notar, C. C., & Yunker, B. (2003). Elementary in-service teacher's use of computers in the elementary classroom. *Journal of Instructional Psychology, 30*(4), 256.

Windschitl, M., & Sahl, K. (2002). Tracing teachers' use of technology in a laptop computer school: The interplay of teacher beliefs, social dynamics, and institutional culture. *American Educational Research Journal, 39,* 165–205.

Wood, E., Mueller, J., Willoughby, T., Specht, J., & DeYoung, T. (2005). Teachers' perceptions: Barriers and supports to using technology in the classroom. *Education, Communication, & Information, 5,* 183–206.

Wood, E., Specht, J., Willoughby, T., & Mueller, J. (2006). *Integrating computers in early childhood education environments: Issues raised by early childhood educators.* Paper presented at Canadian Language and Literacy Research Network Annual Conference, June, Charlottetown, Prince Edward Island, Canada.

Wood, E., Willoughby, T., Schmidt, A., Porter, L., Specht, J., & Gilbert, J. (2004). Assessing the use of input devices for teachers and children in early childhood education programs. *Information Technology in Childhood Education Annual, 1,* 261–280.

Wood, E., Willoughby, T., & Specht, J. (1998). What's happening with computer technology in early childhood education settings? *Journal of Educational Computing Research, 18,* 235–241.

Wood, E., Willoughby, T., Specht, J., Stern-Cavalcante, W., & Child, C. (2002). Developing a computer workshop to facilitate computer skills and minimize anxiety for early childhood teachers. *Journal of Educational Psychology, 94,* 164–170.

Wood, J. (2001). Can software support children's vocabulary development? *Language Learning & Technology, 5*(1), 166–201.

Wooley, G. (1998). Connecting technology and learning. *Educational Leadership, 55,* 62–65.

Zajonc, A. G. (1984). Computer pedagogy? Questions concerning the new educational technology. *Teachers College Record, 85,* 569–577.

Summary and Looking Ahead

Children's Learning in a Digital World

Eileen Wood and Teena Willoughby

The array of possibilities and challenges presented throughout this text points to the diversity in use, resources, and insights with respect to understanding and applying technologies in formal and informal learning contexts. The various authors have presented a vision of what can be achieved, what has been achieved, and what promotes or detracts from our ability to understand and employ technologies effectively. One obvious issue that needs to be considered in any of these discussions is the impact of the "digital divide."

What Is the Digital Divide?

The term "digital divide" is likely a very familiar one to all of us. Within the research literature, however, consensus in precisely defining what constitutes "the divide," as well as how to define its structure, continues to be debated (e.g., Jung, Qiu, & Kim, 2001; Rodino-Colocino, 2006). When the construct of a digital divide was initially introduced, it provided a means to identify those who had access to digital technologies from those who did not (Rodino-Colocino). The term *access* typically coincided with a quantification of the number of computers available, or number of connections (for the Internet). Hence, there is much available evidence to quantify who has a computer and is connected and who doesn't or isn't. Contrasts have been made at numerous levels ranging from individuals to groups (gender, race) to societies, in order to reveal the gap between the haves and the have nots. Initially, the importance of identifying a divide was measured primarily in economic terms, with those who had access being the ones who had the potential to reap economic gains (e.g., job opportunities, greater skills, higher incomes, etc.). Those without the technology were perceived to be at a disadvantage or at risk economically (Crews & Feinberg, 2002).

Over time, the impact of the divide expanded to include disadvantages or risks related to social, cultural, and educational issues in addition to traditional economic impacts. The continuous advancements of computer technology and, most notably, the introduction of the Internet, have changed the nature of children's communication and social interaction (Wilson, Wallin, & Reiser, 2003). The second wave of research (Rodino-Colocino, 2006) examining the digital divide is charged with exploring its specific opportunities and challenges in the broader social, educational, and cultural contexts (e.g., Ching, Basham, & Jang, 2005; Dutta-Bergman, 2005).

The digital divide can be described in terms of three structures which form a chasm or gap: the width, slope, and depth (e.g., Riel, Schwarz, & Hitt, 2002). In this model, the width refers to the traditional notion of access. That is, what does one individual, group, or society have that another individual, group, or society does not have access to? The greater the difference in access, the wider the gap, or digital divide.

The slope of the divide refers to the culture or beliefs surrounding the use of technology. For example, among educators, there are those who see technology as an integrated part of the curriculum, important for allowing students to experience events and initiate contacts with people that would otherwise be unavailable to them. On the other hand, there are educators who see little value in using technology at all and see it as a limiting agent because it might prevent students from experiencing other more relevant life or educational events. Similarly, some educators feel that there is limited support for their efforts to use technology in the classroom. These two dichotomous cultures regarding the use of technologies provide examples of flat and steep slopes. Flat slopes occur when the culture of thinking about technologies allows for its inclusion, steep slopes occur when the culture is prohibitive to the inclusion or integration of technologies.

Finally, the depth of the digital divide is best understood as how the technology is being used, or whether youth and educators are familiar enough with it to take advantage of the technology and its multitude of available uses. In other words, the centrality of technology in a child's life defines the depth. The deepest divide occurs between children for whom integration of technology is an important part of their interaction with society and culture, and those for whom technology is not. While the width of the divide has received a lot of attention, awareness of the slope and depth of the digital divide is just now becoming prominent (e.g., Akhter, 2003; Driori & Jang, 2003; Jung, Qui, &Kim, 2001).

As the authors in this book make clear, we need to pay more attention to how youth use technologies, both in formal and informal settings, particularly through well-designed research studies that cross the many available technologies. This includes computers, games, and the Internet, as discussed in this text, as well as other technologies such as iPods, digital television, and digital cameras. It is also clear that media literacy principles need to be taught explicitly to ensure that there is no divide. Children cannot be left to discover these principles themselves. And that task involves more than schools and educators. As Henry Jenkins argues in chapter 1, these media principles should be part of every educational context, from schools, daycare centers, libraries, museums, churches, community organizations, to the media itself.

References

Akhter, S. (2003). Digital divide and purchase intention: Why demographic psychology matters. *Journal of Economic Psychology, 24,* 231–327.

Ching, C., Basham, J., & Jang, E. (2005). The legacy of the digital divide: Gender, socioeconomic status, and early exposure as predictors of full-spectrum technology use among young adults. *Urban Education, 40*(4), 393–411.

Crews, M., & Feinberg, M. (2002). Perceptions of university students regarding the digital divide. *Social Science Computer Review, 20*(2), 116–123.

Drori, G., & Jang, Y. S. (2003). The global digital divide: A sociological assessment of trends and causes. *Social Sciences Computer Review, 21*(2), 144–161.

Dutta-Bergman, M. (2005). Access to the Internet in the context of community participation and community satisfaction. *New Media and Society, 17*(1), 89–109.

Jung, J. Y., Qui, J. L., & Kim, Y. C. (2001). Internet connectedness and inequality: Beyond the "divide." *Communication Research, 28*(4), 507–535.

Riel, M., Schwarz, J., & Hitt, A. (2002). School change with technology: Crossing the digital divide. *Information Technology in Childhood Education Annual,* 147–179.

Rodino-Colocino, M. (2006). Laboring under the digital divide. *New Media and Society, 8*(3), 487–511.

Wilson, K., Wallin, J., & Reiser, C. (2003). Social stratification and the digital divide. *Social Science Computer Review, 21*(2), 133–143.

Index

Printed in the USA/Agawam, MA
December 10, 2012

571099.088